Barretts Solicitors' Guide to Property in Notting Hill and Holland Park

by Michael Barrett and John Adler

Rowallen Limited

Barretts Solicitors' Guide to Property in Notting Hill and Holland Park

Published by Rowallen Limited,
107 Gray's Inn Road, London WC1X 8TZ, UK

Copyright © 2011. Michael David Barrett. All rights reserved. Michael David Barrett has asserted his right under the Copyright, Designs and Patents Act 1988 to be identified as the author of this work.

Except as permitted by that Act, no part of this publication may be reproduced by any means electronic, mechanical, photocopying or otherwise, now known or to be devised, without the written permission of the author.

Disclaimer of warranty and limit of liability.

The author, the publishers, the partners of Barretts Solicitors, and anyone else involved in preparing this work ('the parties') make no representations or warranties with respect to the accuracy or completeness of the contents of this work and each specifically disclaim all warranties, including without limitation warranties of fitness for a particular purpose. You cannot rely on statements made in this book as giving you advice on specific situations. The advice and strategies contained in this book may not be suitable for every situation. Laws change and this book may be out of date when you read it. In any case, this book is a simplification of complicated laws and issues. You should always consult relevant authorities or a competent professional person before making specific personal arrangements or contracts. This work is sold on the understanding that the publisher is not engaged in legal or other professional services. None of the parties accepts responsibility for misstatements made in this work or misunderstandings arising from it. None of the parties shall be liable for damages arising from this work. No responsibility for loss occasioned to any person acting or refraining from action as a result of the material included in this work can be accepted by any of the parties.

Design by CJ Field Design

Cover photograph by: Michael Barrett

Printed and bound in Great Britain by
CPI Antony Rowe, Chippenham and Eastbourne

ISBN: 978-0-9568084-1-7

Contents

The short story	5
Holland Park south	11
Holland Park north	33
Notting Hill: West of Ladbroke Grove	49
Notting Hill: Ladbroke Grove to Portobello Road	85
Notting Hill: Portobello Road to Chepstow Place	109
Notting Hill: The North East frontier	129
Campden Hill Square area	149
Hillgate Village	157
Flats and houses	165
How to buy well	185
How to sell well	211
How to extend your flat's lease term	233
Estate agents	241
Index	245

About us

We have been helping our clients buy and sell properties in Notting Hill and Holland Park for over 30 years, and we would like to share with you some of the knowledge and experience we have gained.

Our firm, Barretts Solicitors, specialises in central London property, and we would be delighted to act for you if you are buying or selling a house or a flat, or looking to extend your lease.

We have had a lot of help from Niall McMahon with our research for this book. Niall McMahon has been the pre-eminent estate agent in Notting Hill for at least the last forty years, and he has been involved in the sale of a considerable number of significant properties in the area at one time or another. We have worked with him on local property transactions for many years. As The Times once wrote 'Niall McMahon of McMahon & Co is still selling more houses on communal gardens in W11 than anyone else; his close friendships and long residence in the area making him a natural.' Remarkably this success was achieved from the front room of his house in Lansdowne Road, without the need for a shop front or a website. Niall has recently retired from practice, but is still regularly consulted by buyers and potential sellers. While he has helped us considerably with research, Niall isn't responsible for the use we have put it to, and any mistakes in the text are our own.

A considerable amount of research has gone into this book, but we should particularly acknowledge the invaluable Survey of London.

MICHAEL BARRETT
JOHN ADLER

Barretts Solicitors, 107 Gray's Inn Road, London WC1X 8TZ
T: 020 7404 0702 | E: mail@barrettssolicitors.co.uk
Our website: www.BarrettsSolicitors.co.uk

The short story

Notting Hill Gate was originally a Roman road through the countryside, later known just as the road to Uxbridge. Roads attracted settlers. In Anglo Saxon times a village gradually formed at Notting Hill Gate, and it became a centre for gravel mining. Another village formed at the junction of Kensington High Street and Kensington Church Street, where the parish church stood, and this became the village of Kensington. 'Ing' meant a group or settlement in Saxon times, and 'Nott' and was once assumed to relate to King Canute, but now it is thought the name referred to a Saxon princeling in the area called Cnotta.

By Norman times there was a Manor of Kensington. By the 16th century Kensington had been split into several manors. Modern-day Notting Hill was the Manor of Notting Barns. By the mid-18th century the Notting Hill area was used as gravel pits and pasture land, and only a handful of people lived in the hamlet of Notting Hill (or 'Knotting Hill' as it was also written).

When Queen Victoria came to the throne in 1837, Buckingham Palace was almost the edge of London. But her reign saw an extraordinary increase in the residential population of London, and by the time she died in 1901, London had extended west far beyond Notting Hill. In fact, the population of London expanded 20-fold in the 19th century.

The first tentative steps in development in this area took place in the late 18th century, when William Phillimore had a terrace of houses built along Kensington High Street. But living this far out of London didn't catch on and it was over half a century before his successors, as owners of the Phillimore Eastate, tried their luck again. Charles Richardson, the purchaser of the Norland estate, also found he was too far ahead of his time when he built Royal Crescent in the 1840s; he went bankrupt in the 1850s.

The Notting Hill area was originally intended to be called Kensington Park, which is why streets have names such as Kensington

Park Road and Kensington Park Gardens. The area part of the telephone number – 727 – is the numerical version of the old telephone exchange name of PARk.

The main period of building in the Notting Hill area was between 1841 and 1871. The first surge of building took place in the 1820s when the Third Earl of Holland and J W Ladbroke began to develop their estates. It was not until the early 1840s that genuine enthusiasm began for buying houses in Notting Hill. During the 1840s, Richard Roy (p. 53), Charles Blake (p. 98)and Dr. Walker (p. 71) carried out considerable development. The market crashed in 1853 when interest rates went up dramatically, but the market picked up again in 1859 and demand for houses continued until 1868. In fact, most of the house-building in Kensington as a whole was concentrated in the Notting Hill area over this period. The market collapsed again in 1868, and there was not much building in the 1870s.

The heart of Notting Hill is the former Ladbroke Estate. In the mid-18th century, Richard Ladbroke of Tadworth Court Surrey bought 170 acres of land, just north of the ancient road to Uxbridge (now Holland Park Avenue) between Portland Road on the West and Portobello Road on the east. This became known as the Ladbroke Estate. James Weller Ladbroke inherited the estate in 1819 and by 1821 he had plans under way to develop his land for housing, even though Notting Hill was then still a fair distance out of London. Ladbroke didn't take much personal interest in the development of the estate and generally gave a free hand to his estate surveyor, Thomas Allason, while he concerned himself with country pursuits in West Sussex.

Allason devised a lay-out plan with a huge circle a mile across, cut into two equal halves by a straight road (the future Ladbroke Grove) running up from Holland Park Avenue. Other roads would run across it and divide the circle into further segments. So far, this was vaguely derivative of Nash's Regent's Park. But Allason's major innovation was to propose only to build on the inside of the circle and the road, so that the houses would back onto 'secret gardens' accessed from the backs of the houses. This turned the traditional Georgian square of the period inside out. The standard London square had a central garden with the fronts of the houses facing onto it with a road in between. In terms of enjoyment for the houses owners, there is an obvious advantage in Allason's plan; they could get straight into the garden from the back of their houses, and not be overlooked by passers-by. His scheme was not built, but the basic idea survived and fifteen hidden gardens were ultimately built on the estate.

In 1836, with development plans on hold due to lack of interest in Notting Hill as a residential area, Ladbroke agreed to let 140 acres of land to an entrepreneur named John Whyte for a racecourse called 'The Hippodrome'. This opened in 1837 and was used for steeplechases and flat racing. But it quickly ran into difficulties. The locals objected because it cut off a public footpath and the racecourse had to be altered to avoid it. Racing began again in 1839 but the ground was heavy clay and was just not suitable for horseracing. In 1840 Whyte gave up, and sold his lease to his solicitor, John Duncan.

John Duncan was a partner in the firm of Roy, Blunt Duncan & Johnstone, with offices in Westminster and the City. Duncan and a partner negotiated with Ladbroke to take over the racecourse land for house development. The property market was getting going again and they thought this was their opportunity. Unfortunately, they quickly found themselves in financial difficulties and couldn't raise the money to pay their builders. Everyone wanted to get into property and by the time Duncan went bankrupt he had dragged the partners in his solicitors practice and several of their clients into the mess. Fortunately, one of his partners, Richard Roy, had experience of doing a successful development in Cheltenham with his partner Pearson Thompson. So rather than just walk away and accept a loss, Roy took over management of the project for everyone's benefit and together with Thompson turned a potential disaster into a resounding success. Roy and Thompson appointed James Thomson as their architect. It was he who put Thomas Allason's plans for secret gardens into practice and introduced the idea of concentric crescents around the north-west part of the hill, centred on Lansdowne Crescent and Stanley Crescent.

Two new major players arrived on the scene. Charles Blake was an indigo planter in Bengal - in fact, he was born and lived in India and came to England for the first time in the 1820s when he was already in his 50s. He then started a new career as a property developer in Notting Hill. He turned out to be the most successful of all the people involved in the Ladbroke Estate. At the same time, another of the clients of Roy's law firm was persuaded to try his hand at property development. This was Dr Samuel Walker, a church of England Minister. Walker was already a very wealthy man. In 1851 he had just inherited a fortune from his father. He was also the rector of a parish in Cornwall which provided the richest living in England. His great ambition was to have a town in Cornwall elevated to a cathedral town, and he was even prepared to build the Bishops Palace from his own pocket if the church would agree to appoint a bishop there. He probably thought he could make even more money for his scheme by dabbling in property in Notting Hill. But instead he lost almost all his money within a couple of years. Ministers of the church are not Nature's businessmen. He set about buying 56 acres of land in the Notting Hill area, nearly always paying way over the odds. In fact, there were several developers, including Blake, who narrowly escaped bankruptcy themselves in the early 1850s, when the market unexpectedly collapsed, by selling their land on to Walker in the nick of time. Eventually Walker had to sell his holding at a considerable loss, and it was Blake who then snapped up most of it. Cornwall never got its bishop's palace.

In 1844 Ladbroke entered into a building agreement with William Henry Jenkins for the development of 28 acres in the north east of the Notting Hill area. Jenkins was a civil engineer working in a Lincolns Inn Fields. After only a few months, Jenkins assigned his interest to a relative, William Kinnaird Jenkins who was already a successful building speculator in the Paddington area. He proceeded to develop the land very successfully, despite the economic downturn in the mid-1840s.

The main new road which Jenkins constructed was Pembridge Villas. Westbourne Grove, which started in Paddington, was extended through the land to join in Portobello Lane. Chepstow Villas and

Chepstow Crescent were also built partly on this land. In 1846 Jenkins leased a further 10 acres to the west from Robert Hall, another landowner, so he could extend Chepstow Villas to Portobello Lane and build Denbigh Road and Pembridge Crescent.

Robert Hall owned most of the land which encircled the Ladbrokes'. In 1848 he turned to Francis and William Radford to develop the southern part of his land. The Radfords were originally from Devonshire, but had moved to Kensington. They were responsible for building Pembridge Square and Pembridge Gardens and most of the other land down to Notting Hill Gate itself.

Henry Edward Fox, the Fourth Baron Holland, had inherited the Holland Estate in 1845. He embarked on ambitious development plans for the construction of over 800 houses between Addison Road and the railway lines to the west. This plan included houses in Addison Crescent, Addison Gardens and Holland Villas Road. Houses there were built by various builders over about a 25 year period. He died in 1859 shortly after entering into a contract with William and Francis Radford to construct the streets called Holland Park. They developed their skills in the Pembridge Gardens and Square area, before moving on to the construction of Holland Park along the same very distinctive design lines. Over a period of about 30 years, from 1848 to 1880, they built more than 200 houses in Holland Park, Pembridge Square and Pembridge Gardens, and these were mainly extravagant detached villas.

These were the grandest areas. At the other end of the scale Pottery Lane is a very fashionable place to live nowadays, but in the 19th century it was the centre of a particularly awful slum called 'The Potteries and the Piggeries'. While most of the land in the area was being bought to construct houses, Ralph Adams, a bricklayer from Gray's Inn Road, bought this area from Ladbroke to create an industrial site for in the manufacture of bricks and tiles to service all the building going on in Notting Hill. At the same time pig keepers forced out of Marble Arch and Tottenham Court Road moved west into this area. As clay was dug to create bricks, the holes got filled with pig slurry and sewerage pouring down from higher residential streets. One notorious lake was ironically called 'the Ocean'.

The large family houses ceased to work for families in the 20th century, when families no longer had cohorts of servants, so houses generally came to be divided up into flats or bedsits. After the Second World War, the area really went downhill and the northern part is famous for being the area where Peter Rachman was a notoriously bad landlord. Notting Hill became an area popular with Afro-Caribbean immigrants. The Notting Hill race riots occurred in September 1958 as a racially motivated clash between white "teddy boys" and the Afro-Caribbean population. The area began to improve throughout the 60s and 70s. By the 1980s, people began to rediscover the attractions of living in large family houses with access to private, safe gardens, and many of the houses have been restored to single occupation houses again. This process was helped by the film 'Notting Hill'.

Notting Hill is famous for the Notting Hill Carnival, organised by the Afro-Caribbean community, which takes place every year over the August bank holiday. It is one of the largest street festivals in Europe with up to 1.5 million people attending.

It is a little difficult to pin down exactly what Notting Hill comprises. Most of the postcode 'W11' is certainly Notting Hill, but there are parts of 'W10' south of Westway, which are nowadays regarded as Notting Hill.

Notting Hill as we know it today is an area of contrasts. It contains some of the most expensive and exclusive housing in the country, right next door to areas which could still be described as 'edgy'.

Holland Park south

QUICK REFERENCE					
STREET	PAGE	STREET	PAGE	STREET	PAGE
Abbotsbury Close	15	Holland Park Road	20	Napier Road	22
Abbotsbury Road	15	Holland Villas Road	30	Oakwood Court	17
Addison Crescent	29	Ilchester Place	16	St Mary Abbots Terrace	21
Addison Road	23	Lower Addison Gardens	28	Strangways Terrace	20
Holland Park	11	Melbury Road	18	Upper Addison Gardens	27
Holland Park Gardens	28	Napier Close	22	Woodsford Square	26
Holland Park Mews	14	Napier Place	23		

The roads known as **Holland Park** actually consist of three linked roads (with Holland Park Mews in between) and a connection to Holland Park Avenue at each end. The houses on Holland Park are considered to be among the most exclusive in London. Many of the houses are now converted into very high-class luxury flats, but there are still many family houses left. There are also a number of embassies and other diplomatic missions. The streets are wide and they have rows of mature trees. At the Holland Park end the houses back onto the park and have deeper gardens and better views, and consequently are more expensive. The first residential building, No. 80 Holland Park Avenue, is a rather faded brick-built block of flats on six storeys, containing 28 flats.

Typical Holland Park houses start further along. The house numbers on the southern side run from Nos. 2-16 at the Abbotsbury Road end, then back up the northern side from No. 17-35 (with Nos. 36 and 36A on the other side of Holland Park Mews). The houses in the section of Holland Park nearest Holland Park Avenue run from Nos. 37-57 on the south side and No. 58 back to No. 75 on the north side. Nos. 81-89 are a separate row of houses on the east side of the short section of Holland Park between Abbotsbury Road and Holland Park Avenue.

Finally, No. 90 stands on its own between Holland Park and Holland Park Mews.

The Third Baron Holland and his wife

Richard Fox, the Third Baron Holland, had an affair with Elizabeth, the daughter of a plantation owner in Jamaica. Her husband divorced her, so they were able to marry in 1797. As a divorcee she was not welcome at court. She was clearly a charismatic character because, while the real court of George III operated at Kensington Palace up the road, Lady Holland operated her own salon at Holland House, which became a magnet for leading figures who were out of sympathy with the establishment of the day. Lord and Lady Holland were Napoleon sympathisers. Lady Holland sent Napoleon plum jam and a refrigerator to make his life more pleasant in Elba.

The buildings were constructed between 1860 and 1880. Each house has a frontage of about 45 feet. The houses are all almost identical in their basic design. They are large, beautifully proportioned, detached houses on five storeys, made up of a lower ground floor, an imposing raised ground floor, an equally imposing first floor, a second floor, and rooms in an elaborate attic storey. In most houses the raised ground floor has a central double door, a porch supported by Roman Doric columns and wide stairs leading up to the entrance. The stairs are covered by an elaborately decorated cast-iron and glass entrance canopy – one of the most defining features of this estate. Canted bays rise up to the first storey on either side of the entrance. (There are similar bays at the back.) The second storey windows open onto small balconies on the top of these bays. Above the second storey is an imposing cornice and above that the gables contain more rooms. The facades of the houses are also quite elaborately decorated, with a row of plaster rings below the first floor windows, quoins at the corners of the houses and round the central windows, balustrades around the second floor balconies and between the exuberant gables. The houses seem relatively unchanged externally, except that No. 33 has a completely new extension where the gables once were, and several have been altered to turn one side of the lower ground floor into garages – a really unfortunate modification which ruins the symmetry. There is no exact colour plan for the houses: they vary from white Christmas cake confections, to Mediterranean greens and yellows, with features picked out in white.

Most of the properties are still privately owned although there are some embassies. Many of the buildings have been converted into flats, which have particularly large rooms, ideal for entertaining on an ambassadorial scale.

There were apparently no freehold house sales in Holland Park in 2010, but a number of flats changed hands. The most expensive were two flats at No. 68, which sold for £3,450,000 and £2,150,000. A flat at No. 17 changed hands for £1,800,000 and another at No. 46 for £1,750,000. Smaller flat sales included a flat at No. 85 for £830,000 and one at No. 38 for £750,000.

William and Francis Radford

William and Francis Radford were builders who originally came from Devon. They concentrated their building operations in the Notting Hill and Holland Park area. During the 30 odd years from 1848 to 1880 they built more than 200 houses. These were mainly extravagant detached villas. At their height, they were employing 60 workers. They died rich men and it is recorded that there were ten mourning-coaches at Francis Radford's funeral in 1900. The Radfords developed their skills in the Pembridge Gardens and Pembridge Square area, before moving on to the construction of Holland Park along the same design lines.

Holland Park Mews which runs between the two sections of Holland Park, and was also built by William and Francis Radford, has a stone entrance like a triumphal arch. The mews itself is very charming. It is a cobbled mews running uphill with terraces of dainty two-storey houses on either side. By the 1950s a lot these properties were being used as car showrooms and commercial garages but they have all been converted into family homes now (or, in some cases, are integrated into the main houses of the Holland Park roads as staff accommodation and garaging.) These houses were built with coach - now garage - double doors on the ground floor, and a steep flight of steps with nice metal railings up to front doors on the first floor. The first floor is set back slightly to allow for the steps, so there is room for a few chairs on the balcony outside the front door. The nicest mews houses have been renovated with a light touch. Inevitably, some owners have allowed their builders to run riot with their cement trowels, but for the most part the charm has been retained. At the west end of the mews, the houses start with No. 1A on the south side and run to No. 34. Then on the north side they run back in the other direction from No. 35 to No. 67.

There were two house sales in Holland Park Mews in 2010. No. 3 was sold for £1,525,000 and No. 37 for £1,300,000.

The Fourth Baron Holland

Henry Edward Fox, the Fourth Baron Holland, inherited the Holland Estate in 1845. He embarked on ambitious development plans for the construction of over 800 houses between Addison Road and the railway lines to the west, including Addison Crescent, Addison Gardens and Holland Villas Road. Baron Holland died in 1859, shortly after entering into a contract with William and Francis Radford to construct the Holland Park streets.

Abbotsbury Road takes its name from one of the Dorset estates of the Earl of Ilchester (p. 16). It runs between Melbury Road and Holland Park. It is a wide tree-lined street and most of the houses have off-street parking – some with their own garages. The road has humps in it to slow down the traffic. Work began on houses along this street in the early years of the 20th century, but only Nos. 3-9 (odd), and Nos. 8-10 and Nos. 24-28 (even) were built before the Second World War. They are fairly uniform terraced and semi-detached brick houses, many with small front gardens or yards, and decent-sized rear gardens. Some of the houses overlook the large garden at the rear of the Peacock House in Addison Road and many at the front have a good view of Holland Park on the other side of the road. During the 1960s, houses and blocks were built on the west side of Abbotsbury Road. These include Abbotsbury House at No. 139, a 10-storey block containing 37 flats, which has a sunken garage area. Although most of the houses on the west side of Abbotsbury Road are modest, many of the houses on the east side are lavish two-storey, detached villas, wide enough to have three windows on each side of the central front doors. They were probably built in the early part of the 20th century.

There was one house sale in Abbotsbury Road in 2010, with No. 123 selling for £2,800,000. A flat in Abbotsbury House sold for £965,000.

Abbotsbury Close is a series of small linked crescents with houses and landscaped gardens, designed by Stone Toms & Partners and built by Wates Builders. They are nice houses, on three storeys, including an attic storey. Some of the houses have little balconies. There are planted 'islands' in the road, and the road winds round between the terraces of houses. The corner houses have, what looks at first glance like large picture windows but are, in fact, large apertures, so you can see cars coming round the corner.

In 2010, No. 7 Abbotsbury Close was sold for £2,350,000 and No. 22 was sold for £1,150,000.

The Fifth Earl of Ilchester

Lady Holland, the widow of the Fourth Baron, had an expensive social life, and she needed to sell off bits of the estate to raise funds. So she turned to a distant relative, Henry Edward Fox-Strangways, the Fifth Earl of Ilchester, for help. (The First Earl of Ilchester, his ancestor, had been the elder brother of Henry Fox, the First Baron Holland.) He agreed to take over the estate along with the mortgages on it and, in return, to pay Lady Holland an income for life. The estate changed hands in 1874. The Fifth Earl initiated much of the residential development on the estate. Ilchester Estates still owns a number of freeholds in the area.

Ilchester Place runs between Abbotsbury Road and Melbury Road. It takes its name from Edward Fox-Strangways, the Fifth Earl of Ilchester, who bought the estate from Lady Holland in 1874 (p. 16). The houses were designed by the architect, L Martin, and built in 1929 as a series of grand semi-detached mansions, stacked one against the other as they process uphill. Even in 1929 people wanted antique houses, and these look distinctly Georgian with their orderly sash windows and restrained door cases. The houses are extremely wide, with two-window widths on either side of the main door, and they contain three storeys, including attic rooms in the hipped roofs. The houses have attractive small front gardens, with neatly trimmed hedges and well-cut lawns. Some of the houses are attractively covered in creeper. The houses run up to No. 23 on the south side, which is a lavish single house as big as a pair of semis combined, and with more lavish stone dressings. They are popular houses because they are relatively modern and large - 6,000 square feet and upwards - and close to Holland Park itself. When properties come on the market they are usually snapped up immediately.

Just before Ilchester Place joins Melbury Road, there is Park Close, which contains 54 flats in two blocks, nine storeys high, set in gardens.

The views from the upper flats, especially those facing the park, must be good, but the buildings themselves are work-like concrete frames with brick facings.

There was only one sale in Ilchester Place in 2010: No. 15 changed hands for £13,000,000 .

The Scheme of Management

There is still an Ilchester Estate owned by the successors of the 19th century Hollands and Ilchesters. The estate still owns the land on which many of the houses and blocks of flats in Holland Park stand. Someone who owns a long lease of their house usually has the right to buy the freehold from the estate. Flat owners can also club together to buy the freehold of their building. To prevent well-run estates deteriorating, the law gives an opportunity for traditional estates to get court approval of a 'scheme of management' which allows the estate to continue to control what freehold owners can do, just as it controls the activities of its own leaseholders. There is such as scheme of management for much of the south Holland Park area. Residents have to get the estate's permission for alterations, and they have to pay a service charge to cover estate-wide expenses. There are detailed regulations. For instance, you can't have poultry or ferrets but you are allowed to keep gerbils and hamsters, and *small* fish – I quite like the idea of surveyors knocking on residents' doors to measure their fish.

Oakwood Court runs between Abbotsbury Road and Addison Road. It is a complex of Victorian mansion blocks, which have the same name as the street. In about 1900, some speculative builders, William Henry and Edward James Jones, of Victoria Street, Westminster, bought Oak Lodge, which was a mansion and grounds near St Barnabas Church. They knocked down the house and filled in the medieval ponds which had survived to form an ornamental lake. On the site, they began the construction of Oakwood Court as a series of 7-storey mansion blocks in red brick. The original designs were by William Hunt, an architect from Kensington. It took several decades for all the blocks to be built. The block comprising Nos. 31-62 Oakwood Court was built later than the rest, in about 1928-30, to designs by Richardson and Gill. They were built as three sides round a central courtyard, using a darker brick than the previous blocks. The blocks are surrounded by lawns and there is a small garden of trees and shrubs in the middle of the street at the Abbotsbury Road end.

The blocks have bays extending at either end with terraces for the flats between them up to fifth floor level. The flats themselves have as many as 4 bedrooms and can be very large indeed. They make ideal family flats. A major refurbishment of the blocks and the flats has recently been carried out. There is a more modern development of flats and houses on the corner of the street, called Manderley.

The largest flat sale in Oakwood Court in 2010 was the sale of a flat at No. 98 for £3,250,000. No. 112 sold for £2,150,003, and there were several smaller flat sales at prices between £560,000 and £691,000.

Melbury Road is named after the original home of the Earls of Ilchester (p. 16) in Dorset. It runs between Addison Road and Kensington High Street, and it mingles Victorian individually designed houses with 20th century blocks. Farley Court stands at the corner with Addison Road. The blocks are at right angles and the inner faces look onto St Barnabas Church and a nice garden area. There are 37 flats in all (including the caretaker's flat), and there are lock-up garages at the back.

Continuing on the northern side of the road, there are a series of plush late-Victorian houses and grounds, especially Nos. 9-11 Melbury Road, with large bay windows with terracotta panels beneath, the mother of all hipped roofs, and beautiful gables. Nos. 19-27 are lavish versions of the traditional townhouse, with grand processional steps up to very high raised ground floors, with two storeys above. No. 31 is a very large Edwardian detached house and garden.

On the other side of the road at No. 6, Kingfisher House is a block containing 19 flats, built in 1965. Stavordale Lodge at Nos. 10-12 Melbury Road, has ten flats on five storeys, and looks like it was designed in Sweden, with very severe modern lines and a mixture of white and metallic tiles and nice wide hardwood windows. No. 14, called Woodsford, is another 1960s block of flats. Nos. 16-18 is a really delightful late-Victorian folly built in 1877 by William Turner, a speculative builder from Chelsea, with dramatically carved terracotta decoration, beautiful red brick, and very ornate windows.

Melbury Road has very large single houses at the Kensington High Street end. Some have been converted into flats, such as No. 47 which contains nine flats. No. 47 (originally No. 13) was designed by Robert Dudley Oliver for Walford Graham Robertson, a playwright, and was built in 1892 by W J Adcock, a Dover builder. In 1912 Basil Procter designed an extra storey and an extra north wing. The house was converted into flats in 1948.

At the end of Melbury Road is Melbury Court, a gigantic 1930s mansion block with 71 flats, many facing onto Kensington High Street. It still looks quite sumptuous, with stone dressings on the window and stone balustrading above the ground floor shops.

The only sale in Melbury Road in 2010 was in Farley Court, where No. 16 changed hands for £990,000.

The Holland Park Conservation Area

The Holland Park Conservation Area runs from Holland Park Avenue in the north to Kensington High Street in the south, and extends roughly from Holland Walk in the east to a route close to Holland R1oad on the west side. This is only a rough description and if you are interested in a particular property, you need to check specifically – some streets are excluded. Being located in a conservation area can have a significant effect on property values. The area was formed in 1981 by combining two smaller conservation areas. The council has increased powers in a conservation area to require approval for works, and can also issue directions suspending automatic approvals for some kinds of works.

Strangways Terrace is a development of flats and town houses on a private road between Melbury Road and Kensington High Street, along the back of Addison Road. It takes its name from Edward Fox-Strangways, the Fifth Earl of Ilchester (p. 16), who bought the estate from Lady Holland in 1874. The main feature is Monckton Court which contains 40 flats on ten storeys, and there are also two terraces of 11 townhouses, and underground garages. All the buildings use a mixture of yellow and brown brick, with balconies in small white tiles. An interesting feature is that the balconies are set at different angles to each other. The little estate is built round a circular pond with a waterfall trickling through stacked pieces of metal, overhung by a couple of willows; it has a rather Japanese feel to it (spoilt only by the floating plastic ducks).

Strangways Terrace saw one flat sale in 2010, with a flat at Monkton Court selling for £700,000. The most recent price achieved for a house was £1,550,000, paid for No. 5 in 2008.

Holland Park Road runs between Addison Road and Melbury Road. At the junction with Melbury Road, Nos. 2-8 are Queen Anne-style buildings in red brick, with large bow and canted bay windows. These are all now flats. The buildings merge into Melbury House round the corner. No. 14 has been converted into 13 flats. All the buildings on the north side of the road appear to use a really gorgeous red brick. Nos. 20-30 (even) Holland Park Road (originally called 'The Studios') were built in about 1877 as a group of studios round a courtyard, entered through an arch. This is a very attractive enclave; even the courtyard is laid out in matching red tile. No. 24A Holland Park Road, designed by A M Cawthorne, was an extra house slotted in around 1929, and originally called Court House. Nos. 32 and 34 are houses designed by Albert Cockerel and built in 1900. Nos. 54-64 Holland Park Road are 3-storey houses which are part of the Strangways Terrace development.

There were two house sales in Holland Park Road in 2010. No. 60 was sold for £2,400,000 and No. 7 for £1,375,000.

The Artists' Quarter

In the 19th century Holland Park Road was an artists' quarter with many artists' studios. Two artists, Frederic Leighton and Val Prinsep, who were close friends, started the fashion. In the 1860s Lady Holland needed to sell off bits of the estate to raise funds to maintain her expensive social life, In 1866 she sold land to Frederick Leighton, the eminent Victorian artist, so he could build a house at number 12 Holland Park Road. Lord Leighton used George Aitchinson as his architect to build 'Leighton House'. Val Prinsep bought adjoining land at No. 14 and constructed a house there too in about 1866, using Philip Webb as his architect. (Leighton House was purchased by Kensington Borough Council in 1925 and is now open to the public.)

In contrast with the north side of Holland Park Road, which specialises in impressive red-brick period mansions, the south side consists of **St Mary Abbots Terrace**, a 1960s development of neo-Georgian townhouses with gardens, built as a series of cul-de-sacs off Holland Park Road. The architects were Stone Toms and Partners. It was built by Wates. The first thing you see is Abbots House, which is a nine-storey block overlooking Addison Road, and which looks like it was flung up hastily. The metal windows are now showing the strain, but the entrances appear to have been renovated. But most of St Mary Abbots Terrace is houses: 59 in all. They are terraces of town houses, so popular with 20th century developers in this area. The houses have garages on the ground floor, and two residential storeys above. In the case of the long terrace parallel with Holland Park Road, the second storey is part of the main structure, and the roofs are hardly visible. The shorter terraces, at right angles running to Holland Park Road, have prominent pitched roofs and the second storey is in the form of mansard windows in the roof. The houses generally have small attractive front and rear gardens. Tucked in between St Mary Abbots Terrace and Kensington High Street is Kenbrook House, a not-very-exciting block, which has shops on the Kensington High Street side and 30 flats facing Kensington High Street in the six storeys above.

The most recent significant sales in St Mary Abbot's Terrace were in 2009 when No. 18 was sold for £2,250,000 and No. 6 for £2,150,000.

Napier Road is a rather nice little road between busy roads. It runs from Russell Road across Holland Road to Addison Road. There are Victorian terraces on either side of the road but those on the south side have shops on the ground floor. Originally the Earl of Holland had entered into a building agreement with John Parkinson, the builder responsible for Nos. 50-59 Addison Road, to construct these houses, but the work was carried out by other builders. It is known that James Randell Thursby, a builder from Poplar, definitely built Nos. 1-9 and John Palmer, a builder from Pimlico, built Nos. 7-13. No. 14 was added in 1875.

Holland Road and Russell Road Gardens

There is a communal garden between the backs of the houses in Holland Road and Russell Road, running from Holland Gardens to Napier Road. It is maintained by the council under the terms of the Kensington Improvement Act 1851.

Through an arch under the end of the terrace on the north side, you enter **Napier Close,** which contains a little clutch of modern townhouses on two storeys, quite small, and also a series of garages.

In 2010, 5 Napier Close was sold for £1,105,000 and a flat at No. 1

was sold for £585,000.

Napier Place, off the south side of Napier Road, is quite quaint, with a long terrace of what look like original two-storey townhouses of the sort you would find in a village street, interspersed with the odd new or very refurbished one. One has been refurbished, with very jazzy blue tiles round the door and windows. The houses are only on the western side of the street; the eastern side contains the garden walls and back entrances of houses in Addison Road. Then Napier Place turns the corner to become a cobbled courtyard surrounded on three sides by more townhouses. The houses are still on two storeys but there are a lot of later attic conversions in addition. Napier Place ends with Hungerford Court, which is a fairly modern block of flats containing 24 flats on six storeys, some overlooking Holland Road, and incorporating a communal garage on the ground floor.

No flat sales were recorded in Napier Place in 2010, and the most recent was a flat in The Garden House, which sold in 2009 for £560,000.

Addison Road is a long road stretching from Kensington High Street to Holland Park Avenue. It takes its name from Joseph Addison (p. 41). The southern part consists of a busy southbound one-way traffic system. Addison Road was the first street to be constructed for house development on the Holland Estate, to connect Holland Park Avenue and Kensington High Street. The road was constructed by William Woods, a builder, who began work in about 1824. There is a curve in the road where it goes round St Barnabas Church. This was not out of respect for the church but because the builders had to work round some extensive ponds called 'the Moats', which weren't finally filled in until about 1900. The best properties have mainly been restored to single family houses.

On the west side of Addison Road, almost opposite Holland Park Road, Nos. 36-39 Addison Road are houses built by James Mugford Macey of Drury Lane in about 1845, and originally called Vassall Cottages. These are brick-faced houses, built as pairs, on basement ground and one upper storey. Each pair of houses share a pediment above stuccoed cornices. Between those houses and the Napier Road junction, Nos. 40-47 form a delightful terrace of houses, distinctly Gothic in appearance, with little alcoves in the walls (which in a church would contain saints), carved rosettes in the stonework, and battlements for railings on the balconies above the church-like porches, and arrow-slit windows suitable for pouring oil on Vikings. The terrace was originally called Warwick Villas and it was built in about 1850 by Thomas Moore, who was also the builder of some of the houses in Holland Place. The end houses, Nos. 40 and 47, are double-fronted, and the six inner houses are built as matching pairs. Above the Napier Road junction, Nos. 50-59, opposite St Barnabas Church, is a series of late Victorian houses in yellow brick, with distinctively curved first-floor windows. These were built between 1852-5 by John Parkinson, a builder from Hammersmith, and they were originally called Abbotsford Villas. These houses are terraced, but with paired entrances on the side which are set back to make them look like a row of semi-detached houses. They contain three main storeys (basement, ground and first floor) and some have converted attic rooms. They are brick-faced, but they have painted stucco decoration round doors and windows. Nos. 48, 49 and 60-61 Addison Road are detached houses, built in 1856-7 by Nicholson and Son of Wandsworth.

Further north, particularly above the southern leg of Addison Crescent, ranks of fabulous detached houses march in single file up the street to Holland Park Avenue. These are huge cream-painted stucco-faced villas set back from the road behind front gardens, mostly now paved or tarmacked for cars. These houses have wide frontages and the accommodation consists of a basement, a raised ground floor, and a first floor, with some attic rooms behind the balustrade which tops off the facade. The houses have a central main entrance with imposing porticos and windows on either side, topped with a triangular pediment on brackets. Overall the decoration is classy but quite restrained (with the exception perhaps of No. 81, which has two life-sized naked men having a "you looking at me?" moment on top of the porch). This procession of grand villas is broken by Redlynch Court, an attractive red-brick block of flats on the corner of Addison Road and Addison Crescent, which contains 12 flats on six storeys (with an additional basement storey in the Addison Crescent wing). Most of these houses on the west side of Addison Road were built by the builder, James Hall (p. 29), who built about 120 houses in the estate in the 1850s. By 1860 Hall had constructed Nos. 64-69 between the two ends of Addison Crescent. (No. 69 was later demolished). Hall's project continued on the other side of Addison Crescent where he built Nos. 70-84 at the same time as Nos. 64-69 and to a similar pattern. (No. 70, the corner property, was later demolished.) His most northern houses were Nos. 85-88, which are larger brick-faced houses. (No. 88 no longer exists).

The eastern side of the road also contains many attractive detached and semi-detached houses behind mature front gardens. It contains the largest of them all, an ornate blue and green glazed-brick and tiled mansion known as 'The Peacock House', at No. 8 Addison Road. This Grade I listed mansion was built in 1906 for Ernest Debenham of the supermarket store of the same name. The other houses were built by William Woods, from 1839, when he built Nos. 11-17. They are all stucco-faced houses, with basements, but with different numbers of upper storeys. Nos. 11, 14 and 15 have two upper storeys; Nos. 12, 13, 16 and 17 have three. They are all semi-detached except for No. 11, which was built as a double-fronted house. Nos. 12 and 13 have porches and balconies at ground floor level. Nos. 14 and 15 have an elaborately decorated frieze at the top of the façade. Somerset Square is a big development of townhouses with its own private roads and gardens, just like Woodsford Square, dating from the late 70s or early 80s, and built, I believe, by Trafalgar House. The houses have garages at ground level and two residential storeys above. The estate is built in a brick which is somehow reminiscent of The Inns of Court, and the houses have a profusion of attractive flower beds and bushes. Apart from the townhouses, there is Serlby Court, which is a rather sumptuous looking 1970s block containing 33 flats (plus a porter's flat) on nine storeys.

At No. 1 Addison Road (on the east side of the road) is the

entrance to the popular Holland Park Lawn Tennis Club, which has been a tennis club since the 1930s.

There were quite a few house and flat sales in Addison Road in 2010. The headline sale was No. 68, which changed hands for £12,000,000. Smaller house sales included: No. 24 for £185,000, No. 51 for £520,000, No. 7 for £435,000 and No. 6 for £495,000. The largest sale was a penthouse at Park Court, which sold for £3,500,000, while another flat in that block went for £705,000. There were several flat sales in the 90s: one at No. 94-95 for £725,000, a flat at No. 97 for £550,000, a basement flat at No. 91 for £820,000 and a flat at No. 99 for £535,000.

The bastard's house

Addisland Court and Holland Park Gardens were built on the land formerly occupied by No. 1 Addison Road, one of several large villas built by William Woods. It became available for development in 1873 on the death of Charles Richard Fox, the owner. Fox was the eldest son of Lord and Lady Holland. But since he was born before they were actually married, he could not succeed to the title. His father gave him No. 1 Addison Road. Apart from inheritance issues, being a bastard was not a problem in Georgian England. Fox married the daughter of the future King William IV and became a general. After he died in 1873 his house was demolished.

Woodsford Square is a series of interconnecting squares hidden behind the eastern side of Addison Road and containing 133 townhouses in terraces. The estate was built by Wates Builders between 1967 and 1974 and designed by the architects, Drew & Partners, and a fine achievement it is. At first glance, the houses are just very straightforward rectangular shapes, but there's a real feel that a lot architectural sweat went into creating a real sense of style and balance.

The houses are mainly on four-storeys, with some of the corner houses having interesting first floor extensions (painted white) on stilts. The ground floors are taken up by garages which have beautiful garage doors faced with vertical strips of wood. (There are hundreds of townhouses with hundreds of ugly metal garage doors in Holland Park, and only here did anyone think to make them a positive feature.) Another attractive detail: entrance doors of pairs of houses are side by side, and the architects inserted a striking cobalt-blue tiled dividing wall between them. There is a lot of pleasant greenery and brick-lined flowerbeds at the front, and plenty of room for car parking. Woodford Square has climbed the ladder of respectability over the last 20 years. A lot of the houses were bought as rental investments when they were first built, but they are now mainly family-owned homes. They are usually in demand.

There were several house sales in Woodford Square in 2010. No. 25 and No. 123 each went for 2,010,000. No. 15 sold for £3,020,150 and No. 114 for £1,600,000.

Upper Addison Gardens runs between Holland Road and Holland Villas Road, and is lined on both sides with terraces of brick-faced houses. They were built using yellow brick with stucco dressings, and the houses are crowned with an elaborate cornice. The houses have a 25-foot frontage and contain basement, raised ground, and two upper floors. Some later attic conversions have taken place. Nos. 2-13 and Nos. 30-43 Upper Addison Gardens were built by James Hall (p. 29) over several years from 1857. Most of these houses were converted into flats in the mid-20th century but many have now been re-converted as family houses. The houses do not have large gardens. Those on the north side are overlooked by commercial buildings.

Two flats were sold at No. 3 Upper Addison Gardens in 2010, with the top floor flat going for £1,300,000 and a first-floor flat selling for £587,500. In addition, a lower-ground and ground-floor maisonette at No. 17 sold for £1,000,000 and a second-floor flat at No. 25 for £750,000.

Addison Communal Gardens

There is a communal garden between the backs of the houses in Upper Addison Gardens and Lower Addison Gardens, running from Holland Road to Holland Villas Road. It is maintained by the council under the terms of the Kensington Improvement Act 1851.

Holland Park Gardens is a short road between Holland Park Avenue and Addison Road – really it's the true extension of Addison Road, rather than the bit which actually carries the name. The street was built on land formerly belonging to Charles Fox (p. 26). The first houses on Fox's land were Nos. 94-100, built in about 1880 on the west side of the street, just below Holland Park Avenue. (No. 96 no longer exists.) It is fairly commercial, with some bed-and-breakfasts and bedsits, as well as normal residential properties. It backs onto the top end of Addison Road. It has a small communal garden. On the east side of Holland Park Gardens is a semi-detached red-brick mansion block, built in around 1900. The first half at No. 13 is called Holland Park Court and has 12 flats. The other half at No. 15 is called Carlton Mansions and has 13 flats. The building is on five storeys, with the traditional balconies on the upper floors running between the canted bays at either end. Next door at No. 16 is another late Victorian or Edwardian red-brick mansion block, called Holland Park Mansions, with 11 flats.

Several flats, but no houses, changed hands in Holland Park Gardens in 2010. A flat at No. 24 sold for £1,865,000; a flat in Holland Park Mansion went for £1,480,000, while a flat at No. 26 sold for £725,000.

Lower Addison Gardens runs between Holland Road and Holland Villas Road. On both sides, the road is lined by terraces of virtually identical houses on basement, raised ground and two upper storeys, in brick with white painted window and door surrounds. Most of the houses were built by James Hall (p. 29) over several years from 1857. Some have extra floors at roof level, created from later loft conversions.

Lower Addison Gardens saw a number of flat sales in 2010: £555,000 at No. 29, £260,000 at No. 28, £250,000 at No. 17, £625,000 at No. 24 and – the largest sale – a flat at No. 26 for £1,516,000.

James Hall

James Hall was a builder from St Pancras. His first large-scale excursion into development was the building of 60 houses in the Chepstow Villas and Pembridge Place areas in the 1840s. That was a success. But then in the 1850s he took on a commitment to build about 120 houses in the Holland Estate. His ambition outran his ability to finance it and in 1864 he was declared bankrupt. His career was typical of many Victorian builders who lacked business sense, effectively gambled on the market, and ultimately got burnt.

Addison Crescent is a smaller version of Addison Road. It consists of north and south sections. The south section runs from Holland Road to Addison Road and it is an extremely busy traffic route. The north section between Holland Villas Road and Addison Road is a more charming proposition. It contains large and very attractive detached houses behind mature front gardens. Nos. 1-13 Addison Crescent were built by James Hall (p. 29) over a period of several years from 1857. The plots in Addison Crescent have 60-foot wide frontages and the houses are mainly detached and semi-detached villas, two or three main storeys high, with basements. Most of the house have painted facades at ground floor level and exposed brick at upper floor levels. The houses have central main doors with canted bays on either side, and attractive front gardens. The street was named after Joseph Addison (p. 41).

There was one house sale in Addison Crescent in 2010, with No. 6 changing hands for £10,250,000. A flat at No. 4 was sold for £1,143,500.

Holland Villas Road is a wide tree-lined avenue which runs between Upper Addison Gardens and the junction of Addison Crescent and Holland Road. This is considered one of the most desirable addresses in Holland Park, and could lay claim to the 'Billionaire's Row' title. The street still has some of its Victorian street lamps - but converted from gas to electricity these days. Some of the houses on the west side of the street are very large indeed. The houses in Holland Villas Road are generally large detached houses of two or three storeys with basements, many with their own swimming pools. (The two storey houses are mainly at the southern end; the houses get bigger as they proceed north.) These are very grand houses of 6,000 square feet or more, with large gardens to match. Some are used as ambassadorial residences. It could almost be a separate gated community. One problem is that it is a long way to anywhere, so you need a car and a chauffeur, which is probably not a problem for the residents. The builder was James Hall (p. 29) who built the houses over several years from 1857. They are similar in size to his houses in Addison Road, but of a more modern design. The houses are brick-faced, and the brick is a rather pleasant yellowy-brown colour. Many of the houses are stuccoed at basement level and have attractive cream-painted stuccoed dressings round the door frames and windows. Some houses have mansard windows for rooms in the tiled roofs above. Most of the houses have front gardens with small driveways and high security gates. No. 20 has a full-size statue of a naked man sitting outside the first-floor window – it must be a surprise to guests when they open the curtains in the morning. There is a 1960s-style little block of flats containing five flats at No. 7 - presumably an infill where a house was bombed in the War. At the north end of the street, there is a modern block of flats called Fitzclarence House. Almost at the top of Holland Villas Road, on the east side, there stands Addisland Court, a substantial 8-storey block of flats, which is an imposing red-brick construction in 1930s-style, containing 40 flats.

The outstanding sale in Holland Villas Road in 2010 was the sale of No. 10 for £16,200,000. No. 46 sold for £1,062,000. A flat at Addisland Court changed hands for £1,360,000.

Holland Park South

Holland Park north

QUICK REFERENCE						
STREET	PAGE	STREET	PAGE	STREET	PAGE
Addison Avenue	41	Princedale Road	46	Royal Crescent	34
Addison Place	41	Princes Place	43	Royal Crescent Mews	35
Norland Place	44	Queensdale Place	40		
Norland Square	44	Queensdale Road	39	St Ann's Villas	33
Penzance Place	38	Queensdale Walk	43	St James's Gardens	36

St Ann's Villas leads into Royal Crescent. It is a busy road, but it is pleasantly tree-lined. In the section between Royal Crescent and Queensdale Road, Charles Stewart put up terraces on either side of the street in 1843: Nos. 2-10 (even) on the east side and Nos. 1-9 (odd) on the west side. Each terrace contained five houses. The houses are four storeys high and were built in the same style as Royal Crescent, but they seem to be slightly compacted versions, and the canted bays (which extend up to all floors) extend further forward than the porticoed entrances. They are painted in a slightly creamier colour than the Royal Crescent houses.

In 1845 Stewart began work on the next section, between Queensdale Road and St James's Gardens. Each side contained six semi-detached pairs of houses: Nos. 11-33 on the west and Nos. 12-32 on the east side of the road. (No. 32 is now a school.) The style is called Tudor-Gothic. Red and blue bricks were used to create interesting patterns, and the quoins and windows are in Bath stone. They have a definite castle-like feel to them and distinctly Gothic entrances, but the exaggerated gables are more like Aztec ziggurats.

There was a mixture of flat and house sales in St Ann's Villas in 2010. No. 1 changed hands for £2,865,000, No. 9 sold for £2,600,000 and No. 33 sold for £2,751,610. A ground-floor flat at No. 6 was bought for £410,000 and a basement flat at No. 8 for £370,000.

The Norland Estate

The Norland Estate comprises 52 acres just above Holland Park Avenue, from the present West Cross Route in the west to Portland Road and Pottery Lane in the east. When a Westminster brewer named Thomas Greene bought the land in the early 18th century, it already had a large house called 'Norlands' near today's Norland Square. In 1740 Greene died and his grandson, Edward Burnaby Greene, inherited it. Greene died in 1788 and in 1792 Benjamin Vulliamy, a Pall Mall watchmaker, bought the house and the surrounding land and moved into it. The original Norland House burnt down in 1825, but the family continued to own the estate until 1839. The development of the Norland Estate was carried out by Charles Richardson (p. 40)

Royal Crescent is on the north side of Holland Park Avenue and it consists of two curving terraces of white-painted 5-storey houses, bisected by St Ann's Road. This layout was due more to sewerage than artistic requirements. St Ann's Road was the route of the new sewer and had to be beside a road where it could be dug up. It is a busy thoroughfare and bus route. A lot of the houses are in multiple occupancy, as in bedsits or very small flats. Nos. 1-22 Royal Crescent comprises the eastern segment up to St Ann's Villas. The western segment contains Nos. 23-44. Nos. 22 and 23 are facing corner houses, and they have circular corners which add an interesting dimension to the architecture of the crescent. In the centre of the crescent is a mainly grassed communal garden with some mature trees and a gazebo. The houses are all very much the same. There are street steps down to a basement storey, and steps up to a porticoed entrance with rounded columns. At raised ground floor level, each house has a single window next to the main door. There are two main storeys above ground floor level, then a cornice, topped by a third storey not much smaller than the second. Finally, there are attic rooms set back within the sloping roof. Most of the houses have been divided into four flats. A unifying balcony with black metal railings runs along each terrace at first floor level and the houses have French windows which open onto it. The houses are all painted in a mushroom colour, with white round the windows and doors, but the paint on the columns of many of the porches is peeling, and the terraces could do with a bit of care and attention.

Royal Crescent Gardens

In contrast to the secret gardens in much of Notting Hill, this is a traditional garden across the road in front of the houses. The main feature is two huge plane trees planted when the crescent was first laid out in the 1840s. The original railings were restored in 2008. A gazebo was specially designed and installed in 2007 and much of the original garden has been replanted. The garden regularly wins awards. Access is via a double gate opposite No. 5 on the east side of the Crescent. (See p. 180 for more information on communal gardens.)

If you have a property in Royal Crescent you may have rights of access to Royal Crescent Gardens (p. 35). But to find out if your property does have any such rights, you need to check with the garden committee. (See p. 180 for more information on communal gardens.)

In 2010, a basement flat at No. 16 Royal Crescent was purchased for £1,750,000 and another at No. 14 (presumably much smaller) for £483,000. A flat at No. 44 sold for £780,000 and one at No. 21 for £485,000.

Royal Crescent Mews is entered off the corner of Queensdale Road and Norland Road, and it runs behind the west segment of Royal Crescent. It is a long curving terrace of little townhouses with ground floor garages and first floor living areas with French windows leading onto tiny individual balconies. One or two people have managed to get dormer windows into the slope of the pitched roof, but not many. They are quite nice looking houses, painted at ground floor level and bare brick at first-floor level. The properties are popular with rental investors.

No. 25A Royal Crescent Mews was sold for £525,000 in 2009, and there have been no subsequent sales in 2010.

Robert Cantwell

Robert Cantwell was an architect. He became the Norland Estate (p. 34) surveyor and designed Royal Crescent. He was also a speculative developer. In 1823 he took over from Robert Hanson the development of land in Ladbroke Grove, Ladbroke Terrace and Holland Park Avenue, where he built many of the houses.

A plaque on No. 1 declares that the first stone of **St James's Gardens** was laid on 1 November 1847. The square has the interesting distinction of containing a synagogue, Islamic centre, an Anglican church and a Roman Catholic church, each on a corner of the square. The houses start at the Addison Avenue end with a terrace containing Nos. 1-8 on the west section of the south side of the square, which were built in 1847. It was called St James's Square at the time. John Barnett designed most of the houses in the square. The houses are big semi-detached houses on four storeys (including basement) with a slightly recessed section between them containing both entrance doors. Most of the houses are part brick- and part stucco- faced. The main doors themselves are large church-style doors with curved heads, such as you would find on the side of a Norman cathedral, and perhaps they were deliberately intended to complement the nearby church. This is repeated in the two ground floor windows, all of which are also curved, but the windows above are square headed. The houses are stuccoed and pastel-painted to just below first-floor level and brick-faced above. A common motif of the houses is an elaborate cornice along the top of each house, which is echoed in the cornice above the top of the first floor.

St James's Gardens

This is quite a small communal garden which lies on either side of the church of St James Norlands. The church was designed by the architect, Lewis Vulliamy, and was built between 1844 and 1855. But it was based on subscriptions from local residents and they never managed to collect enough money to build the spire. (The spire was finally constructed a few years ago.) The gardens are laid out to look like traditional English woods, and they contain a number of trees planted when the estate was first developed. The entrance to the gardens is on the south side of St James Gardens. (See p. 180 for more information on communal gardens.)

Nos. 9-13 make up the short west side of the square. These houses were built in 1848 and continue the same design of houses. The long north side of St James's Gardens starts with Nos. 14-24, in exactly the same style. These houses were built in 1849 so clearly work was carried out very systematically round the square up to this point. But then there is a complete change in style for the adjoining terraces running east, which are Nos. 25-41. These are actually three separate terraces, as you can see from looking at the cornice line at the top, but they are all joined together and they share a near identical style. These houses were built about 15 years after completion of the rest of the square. Each house has a basement, ground and two upper main storeys. The two end terraces have a little third-floor on top of the façade, and the middle terrace has mansard rooms in the roofs instead. There is a similar style of balcony running along the first-floor of all three, but too shallow to really form a balcony anyone could put chairs out on. The rooms up to and including first-floor are quite high. Each house has a canted bay running up to first-floor level, and horizontal lines to mimic stonework have been incised into the plaster between the bays. The east side of St James's Gardens contains Nos. 42-46, which return to the original design, and these were built in 1851. Then the other eastern section of the south side takes the houses back to Addison Avenue. These houses, Nos. 47-54, were completed in 1850. David Nicholson and Son, builders from Wandsworth, were the principal contractors. They built Nos. 47-54, Nos. 14-24, and Nos. 42-46, and they also completed some of the houses started by Robert Adkin, a local builder, who began work on Nos. 9-13 and then went bust. Nos. 55 and 56 were built by George Drew in 1865.

Darnley Terrace is an extension of the northern side of St James's Gardens, running west to St Ann's Road. It contains a single northern terrace of restrained but charming, brick-built late Victorian houses on basement, ground and two upper floors. The houses have rather unusually wide and square ground floor windows, which are actually completely out of kilter with the first and second floor windows, which are more traditionally positioned.

If you have a property in St James's Gardens you may have rights of access to St James's Gardens (p. 37). But to find out if your property does have any such rights, you need to check with the garden committee. (See p. 180 for more information on communal gardens.)

St James's Gardens saw one house sale in 2010, with No. 18 selling for £3,149,160.

Opposite the primary school in **Penzance Place,** Hayne House is a 1930s style mansion block on four storeys with 19 flats. Penzance Place then crosses Princedale Road. Nos. 2-12, on the north side of Penzance Place, are brick and stucco Victorian terraces of houses containing basement, ground and two upper storeys. Nos. 6-10 have a cornice at the top of the façade supported by rather ornate little brackets. Most of these houses are gaily painted. Nos. 3-9 on the south side are similar. They are perhaps rather small to be called family houses, but most of them are now in single occupation.

There was one flat sale in Penzance Place in 2010; a flat at No. 9 sold for £467,000.

Queensdale Road is a long road, running east to west, broken up into small sections by other roads crossing it. Consequently, it is a collection of isolated Victorian terraces. They are part of the Norland Conservation Area and so are generally well maintained. The best part of the road runs east of St Ann's Villas. Starting at Princedale Road, Nos. 11A-11D on the south side make up a quirky block of brick-faced townhouses with garages on the ground floor and two upper storeys with extending bays. On the north side of the road, between Norland Square and Princes Place, Nos. 18-28 form a terrace of identical four storey houses. (Nos. 18 and 20 have an extra storey, matching the height of the Norland Square houses which they link to.) The outstanding feature is the first-floor windows, which are floor-to-ceiling, but are still sash windows, not French doors. These houses are more impressive than elsewhere in Queensdale Road, particularly because of the height of the windows and the nice sashes, and also the bracketed pediments on top. The second-floor windows are very plain in contrast. These houses are stuccoed at basement and ground floor level, bare brick above, and with a balcony running along the frontage at first floor level.

On the south side of the road, between Addison Avenue and Addison Place, Nos. 15-27 are ornate, fully stuccoed, four storey houses, with particularly tall ground floor windows. On the north side of the road, from Addison Avenue to St Ann's Villas, Nos. 32-38 are individually built stucco-faced houses on 4 storeys including basements.

Crossing St Ann's Villas, Nos. 31-37, on the south side, make up a rather charming little terrace in restrained style, on ground and two upper storeys. In the stretch to Norland Road, Nos. 39-57 are a terrace of little Victorian houses, with basements (quite close to the street), very slightly raised ground floors and two upper floors. In style they look quite basic and unadorned. Next to the Gurdwara Centre opposite, on the northern side, nos. 54-60 are larger, but more run-of-the-mill properties on four storeys (including basements). The windows look modern, compared with the terrace opposite.

In 2010, No. 4 Queensdale Road was bought for £2,217,500, No. 23 for £2,150,000 and No. 11B for £1,490,000.

Charles Richardson

Charles Richardson was a rich solicitor who bought a large part of the Norland Estate (p. 34), and began development there in 1839. Initially he had trouble persuading investors or speculators to take plots in this far away part of London. To give the false appearance of commercial interest in the development so as to encourage other takers the impression of actively, his brother, Walter Richardson leased the northern section above Queensdale Road. Charles Richardson was so desperate to get investors and builders on board that he gave contracts to people like James Emmins, a builder from Bayswater who was well known for periodically going bankrupt, leaving his creditors with nothing. (Richardson got the same treatment.) Development in this area was highly speculative in the 1840s. In 1854 Richardson went bankrupt. He is next heard of in 1855 as a dealer in patent medicines on the Glasgow Stock Exchange.

Queensdale Place is a turning north off Queensdale Road and it is a cul-de-sac. It contains terraces of similar brick-faced houses on either side. Most, but not all, have basements; some entered through railings off the street, and some from inside the property. There are ground and first floors above. It looks like some houses have been altered, especially the doorways, but overall they have an identical feel to them. At the end, Nos. 21-25 have been substantially converted. It's a pleasant little backwater.

No. 8 Queensdale Place changed hands for £1,815,000 in 2010, and there was also a sale for £1,305,000 at No. 3 Waterden Court.

Addison Place is quite a wide side street, winding off the south of Queensdale Road and then joining Addison Avenue. The street was named after Joseph Addison (p. 41). On the north east side, Nos. 14-22 are very charming two-storey Victorian cottages with delicate sash windows, almost hidden away behind the climbing plants and overgrown front gardens. The original houses in the street were probably built by James Hall (p. 29) around 1857 as part of this development in the area. On the south west side, Nos. 7-23 are strange wood and brick two-storey houses, all painted in white or pastel colours, and with wide windows. There is a sort of temporary structure look about them, as if thrown up for a film project - for the crew, not the backdrop – which would be Nos. 14-22 on the other side. Further along the northern side there are some more typical townhouses on two storeys. Finally you pass traditional mews properties with authentic black-painted stable doors as you come out onto Addison Avenue.

There was just one house sale in Addison Place in 2010; No. 12 was sold for £1,030,000.

Joseph Addison

Joseph Addison, an essayist and poet of the late 17th Century, married the Third Earl of Holland's widow and then lived in Holland House until his death in 1719. He is mainly remembered now as the founder of the Spectator Magazine.

Addison Avenue is a charming and very wide tree-lined road, wide enough, in fact, to have cars parking nose to pavement on either side all the way up, and still leave room for two lines of traffic. The street was named after Joseph Addison (p. 41). With its quaint houses and with St James's Church Norlands at the end, you could be 100 years back in a country town. You almost expect to hear the clip clop of horses. The properties here tend to be popular with buyers and are usually in demand.

From Holland Park Avenue upwards, the street is lined on either side with two- and three-storey properties. Nos. 1-11 (odd) were built in 1850-2 by John Parkinson, a plumber. Nos. 2-10 (even) were built by George Langford, a builder, much later in the 1860s. The buildings are generally painted cream, and have shops on the ground floor and, presumably, flats above.

From roughly Addison Place up to Queendale Road, the houses are generally two-storey houses with stuccoed façades, built in semi-detached pairs. These consist of Nos. 18-36 (even) on the east side (overlooking Queensdale Walk at the back) and Nos. 17-35 (odd) on the west side. The houses are all on three storeys - basement, ground and first floor - and they have pitched roofs. The houses are not identical because individual plots were taken by many different builders. Generally speaking, houses on the west side have basements and raised grounds floors; on the east side most of the houses do not have basements, and the ground storeys are not raised. Otherwise, they all look very similar in style. The builders included: James Wood, a bricklayer from Hampstead (Nos. 18 and 20); Thomas and Christopher Gabriel, timber merchants from Lambeth (Nos. 22-28); James Livesey, a plumber from Lisson Grove (Nos. 30-36); Charles Patch, a builder (Nos. 17 and 19); George Pratt (Nos. 21 and 23); John Cole Bennett (Nos. 25 and 27); Walter Hawkins and William Strong, plasterers from Rochester Row (Nos. 29 and 31); and Thomas Warwick and Christopher Garwood, builders from Oxford Street (Nos. 33 and 35).

North of Queensdale Road, Addison Avenue continues with semi-detached houses on either side, but now they have become larger. All the houses follow a standard design, unlike the houses to the south of Queensdale Road. There are two main storeys with basements and attic rooms. The houses are joined by paired entrances which were built as recessed side units between the houses, so there is much more living space inside. In place of the single window next to the ground floor entrance which the houses further south have, these houses have two large ornate windows in the ground floor. The ground-floor windows are all quite heavily constructed with triangular pediments above; the first-floor windows have curved heads. Generally the first-floor windows open as French windows, but onto balconettes rather than full-scale balconies. John Brewer (aptly named since he was a wine merchant) took the plots for Nos. 37-55 on the west side of the street. But he went bankrupt in 1843 before he could build all the houses. So Michael Goodall, a carpenter, and John Parkinson, a glazier, then built Nos. 53-55, and John Arrowsmith, a house decorator from New Bond Street, built Nos. 49-51 in 1847. On the east side of the street, John Parkes, an ironmonger, built Nos. 38-40 in 1841, and John and Samuel Peirson, ironmongers from Bishopsgate, built Nos. 42 and 44 in 1844. In 1847, the plots for Nos. 54-56 were granted to John Buckmaster, described as a gentleman of Hungerford Market, but it is not known who actually built them for him. The remaining houses - Nos. 46-52 - were built by W G May, a Bayswater builder in about 1850.

Taverners Close is a turning off Addison Avenue opposite Addison Place. It is a little gated development of two-storey townhouses, but with rather weird attic extensions in some cases, looking as if garden sheds were dropped on top of the houses.

There was a single house sale in Addison Avenue in 2010, with No. 1 changing hands at £2,000,000.

Princes Place is a small road leading from Queensdale Road to Princedale Road, and it mainly contains back gates and garages from houses of the main street on either side. No. 2 is a modern house with a garage on the ground floor, goggle windows above and a whole brotherhood of windows in the mansard roof. Nos. 3 and 4 are rather garishly coloured, two-storey, late-Victorian workers cottages, with mansard rooms let into the steep sloped roofs. Princes Place then turns the corner into Carson Terrace, which has a long post-war terrace of houses or flats in bare brick with incongruous fake gas lamps attached at intervals along the front of the building.

There were no sales in Princes Place in 2010. The highest price previously obtained was £1,025,000 in 2007 for No. 2 Carson Terrace, No. 4 also sold for £725,000 in 2007.

Queensdale Walk starts with some strangely Arabian looking houses with mosque-style doors and harem windows (the kind with fretwork patterns that veiled ladies peer through in movies). Then from No. 5 onwards, there are more traditional-looking little cottages on two storeys. It's quite a nice little street. The houses are only on the east side, because the west side contains the back garden walls of the Addison Avenue properties. There are a number of large trees overhanging the street from some neighbouring back gardens.

There were no sales in Queensdale Walk in 2010. The last sale was of No. 9 in 2006 at £1,150,000.

Norland Place runs between Princedale Road and Norland Square. Norland Place has a rather stylish new property at No. 13. But for the most part, this is a quaint cobbled road of village-style period houses. They are on two storeys with bow windows and garage doors, and are painted in pastel colours. This leads through to Norland Square. In 2010, No. 5 Norland Place was sold for £2,215,000 and No. 7 for £2,300,000. No. 14 was sold for £1,710,000.

Norland Square is an attractive garden square (although strictly speaking three-sided), with a central garden, lawns and a private tennis court. The railings were replaced several years ago, and this was financed by selling rights to use the gardens at £25,000 a house to nearby home owners who wouldn't otherwise be entitled to use it. Many of the houses in the square were converted into flats and bedsits in the mid-20th century but many have now been restored to their original one family use. The south side of the square is Holland Park Avenue, but the other three sides contain terraces of attractive houses. They all have gardens. The houses are mainly on 4-storeys (with basements) and are stucco-faced. The houses are built quite close to the street, so there is an unusually abrupt set of steps up to the ground floor with a shallow porch for the entrance door. Next to the entrance door is a bow window, not the usual canted bay. Above this runs a long balcony right along the terrace with a rather dainty metal railing with attractive designs. French doors open onto it at first floor level, two for each house. The windows are quite tall, with an extra pane above the opening French doors. There's a second floor and third floor above, separated by a prominent cornice. The buildings are the same all round the square. There's no sign of mansard or attic extensions. Although the houses look as if built by a single developer, in fact most of the builders took one plot only. Work began in 1844 but the square was not finished until 1852.

Norland Square Garden

This communal garden lies in the centre of Norland Square (p. 44), and it was designed by Robert Cantwell (p. 36) in the 1840s as part of the development of this part of the Norland Estate (p. 34). The railings round Norland Square were melted for armaments during the Second World War. The Norland Square Garden Committee arranged for them to be replaced in 2007 with the new railings created by The Cast Iron Company. They have also recreated the original path layout. The garden contains tennis courts. (See p. 180 for more information on communal gardens.)

The eastern terrace contains Nos. 2-18. The northern section contains Nos. 19-33, interrupting Queensdale Road which continues on either side. The western section contains Nos. 36-52. At the Holland Park Avenue end, stands Norland Square Mansions, a pre-War mansion block on five storeys, containing 25 flats. It is stuccoed on the ground and the top floor with the three middle floors being brick-faced. The first to fourth floors have little balconies looking over Norland Square.

If you have a property in Norland Square you may have rights of access to Norland Square Garden (p. 45). But to find out if your property does have any such rights, you need to check with the garden committee. (See p. 180 for more information on communal gardens.)

In 2010, a basement flat in Norland Square Mansions was sold for £320,000 and flats at No. 45 and No. 51 for £517,000 and £626,555 respectively.

Norland Conservation Area and Society

The Norland Conservation Area was created in 1967. The council has increased powers in a conservation area to require approval for works, and can also issue directions suspending automatic approvals for some kinds of works. The Norland Conservation Society (also called the Norland Society) was founded in 1969 to represent the interests of local residents. The conservation area covers most of the area from the West Cross Route in the west to Clarendon Road in the east and goes up to St James's Gardens and Princedale Road. This is only a rough description and if you are interested in a particular property, you need to check specifically – some streets are excluded. It can have a significant effect on property values. You can find more details at norlandconservationsociety.org.uk.

Princedale Road is a road of two halves: the southern part contains small but sought-after Victorian houses, and the northern part contains mainly council properties. The road runs north from Holland Park Avenue and is generally considered to be on the border between the Holland Park and Notting Hill areas. On the west side of the road, there is a terrace running up to Queensdale Road and ending at No. 33, which consists of traditional late-Victorian houses. The houses are on four storeys, including basements. One unusual feature of these houses is that the first floors seem to be unusually high, going by the very high floor-to-ceiling first-floor windows behind a rather dainty metal balcony running right along the terrace; in contrast, the ground floor window next to the main entrance is unusually small. On the east side there is a long range of houses from No. 2 up to No. 82, which are on three main storeys, brick built, usually very heavily altered at ground floor level, with some changes in style all the way along, showing that they were built by many different builders. At the top, near Kenley

Walk, there are two similar terraces on either side. There is a pub and some small speciality shops at the north end of the street.

Prince's Yard, which is off Princedale Road just north of Norland Place, is a 1980s (I guess) development of little houses on three storeys, rather crammed into the available space, built in brick, with big wooden box balconies. The end is dominated by one enormous tree; it must virtually obscure the windows of the end houses.

In 2010 No. 21 Princedale Road was sold for £2,970,000 and No. 52 for £1,505,000. There was a sale at No. 28 for £1,325,600.

Holland Park North

Notting Hill: West of Ladbroke Grove

QUICK REFERENCE						
STREET	PAGE	STREET	PAGE	STREET	PAGE
Blenheim Crescent	58	Hippodrome Mews	53	Lansdowne Road	65
		Ladbroke Crescent	58	Lansdowne Walk	76
Boyne Terrace Mews	70	Ladbroke Grove	81	Portland Road	50
		Ladbroke Mews	81	Pottery Lane	49
Clarendon Road	54	Ladbroke Road	78	St John's Gardens	75
Codrington Mews	61	Lansdowne Crescent	72	St Mark's Place	60
Cornwall Crescent	58	Lansdowne Mews	71		
Elgin Crescent	62	Lansdowne Rise	74		

Pottery Lane starts as a fork off Portland Road. On the east side, it is mainly the backs of the Portland Road houses, but on the west side there is a whole series of little cottages which are basically two storey properties; some still have garage doors - albeit mainly new ones - but some garages have been converted into normal living rooms. They were obviously all built by different builders, and this is reflected in the completely different decorative styles all the way down the road. Most of the properties are Victorian but there are one or two modern in-fills, such as No. 17. Halfway down the road, similar houses start on the east side. No. 24 Pottery Lane, is a modern office building taking up a lot of this side of the road. Nos. 37-45 opposite on the west side also seems to be offices, built in the 1980s or 90s with big windows. There's a little group of larger houses on the east side before you reach Penzance Place. Nos. 36-44 are quite attractive but unadorned late-Victorian houses on four storeys, including basements. There are some original two-storey houses mixed in with converted office buildings facing onto St Francis of Assisi Catholic Church. There are no trees, but it is a friendly little road.

In 1823 James Ladbroke (p. 61) granted this area to Ralph Adams, a bricklayer from Gray's Inn Road, for development. Instead of putting up houses, he set up a pottery manufacturing business, and that is where the name comes from.

There were no sales in Pottery Lane in 2010. The most recent sales were in 2009, when No. 35 and No. 47 changed hands for £500,000 and £405,000 respectively.

Ladbroke Conservation Area and Association

The Ladbroke Conservation Area was created in 1969. The conservation area includes most of the area east of Clarendon Road and as far as the Portobello Road, and up to Westbourne Park Road and it goes down as far as Holland Park Avenue. This is only a rough description and if you are interested in a particular property, you need to check specifically – some streets are excluded. It can have a significant effect on property values.

The council has increased powers in a conservation area to require approval for works, and can also issue directions suspending automatic approvals for some kinds of works. Local residents set up the Ladbroke Association at the same time, to protect their area, and they achieved a quick success by beating a proposal by the council to cut down trees in Ladbroke Grove. The Association aims to promote good architecture, not to preserve all buildings forever. You can find out more on their website ladbrokeassociation.org.

Portland Road was named after Lord Portland, a prominent member of the House of Lords when the Ladbroke Estate was being developed.

On the east side of Portland Road, close to Holland Park Avenue, there's a smattering of flats in converted buildings above shops. On the west side, there is a substantial terrace from Nos. 1 to 31 with a smaller terrace tacked on - Nos. 33 to 41A. The houses in the first terrace have good-sized areas for the basements, and the basement windows are almost at street level. They are typical Victorian houses on four storeys (including basement), stuccoed up to ground floor level, with bare brick above. A rather unusual decorative feature is that the first floor windows have the heads of monkeys in the stuccoed window surrounds. A more alarming feature is that the columns supporting the heavy porch structures on the central houses appear to be falling out into the street, but I think that is just a visual impression. One house has a rather turgid little fountain, which would annoy me if I lived there. The second terrace from No. 33, are similar in height, but they have canted bays at basement and ground floor level, and they are much closer to the street.

Beyond Pottery Lane, Nos. 18-80, on the east side of Portland Road, are a long range of houses designed to look like semi-detached houses - they have recessed side entrances and separate overhanging eaves for each pair, but strictly it is a terrace. The houses are on four storeys (basement, ground and two upper storeys). The houses are relatively narrow, with a single canted bay at basement and ground floor level for each house with a short balustrade round the top to form a rather dangerous-looking balcony outside the first-floor window. A particular architectural feature of the terrace is the triple windows with semi-circular heads surmounted by prominent overhanging eaves. The style changes slightly from No. 58 onwards. The first-floor windows become wider and are constructed in three parts, like the second floor windows; and the second floor windows become slightly taller. At the front, a curved wall beside the steps to the main entrance is a feature. Where the road opens out and meets Penzance Place, a different builder can be discerned.

On the west side, there are terraces from No. 43 (on the corner with Pottery Lane) to No. 117. The houses are all built to the same basic plan but each one is slightly different; clearly many different builders were involved. The houses are also on four storeys (including basements), but they are closer to the streets than the houses on the east, so they generally have steps straight from the street. The houses are flat fronted with very little decoration; some are fully stuccoed, but mostly they're stuccoed up to ground floor with bare brick above, painted in pastel shades. From No. 67 the houses have bulky porches on columns. On both sides of the street an identical balcony structure appears, in the form of curved metal railings. A distinctive railing design is used all along the curved west side from Nos. 121 to 139. There are shops on the ground floor, but there may be flats above in the first and second floors. Opposite on the east side, from No. 94, there is a terrace presumably by the same builder, and these houses have four storeys (including basements), and with tall floor-to-ceiling sash windows at first floor level.

Over Clarendon Cross, there is a final segment of Portland Road. The long terrace on the west side, from Nos. 143 to 177, was constructed as a single visual unit, and the two middle houses, Nos. 159 and 161, extend forward from the terrace with quoins on the edges. The houses are on four storeys (including basements which are very close to the street). The main entrance doors are at ground level (not raised) and have circular heads (except for the central ones, which are square). The first floor windows are much taller than the second floor windows. On the east side, Nos. 102-110 are houses with small front doors and ground floor windows, but with massive triple windows for the first-floors and smaller triple windows with curved heads for the second floors. There is a different style from Nos. 112 to 124 onwards, where the houses are also on four storeys (including basements) but the first and second floor windows are separate single windows, although they continue to have curved heads. Nos. 126-134 are back to having large triple windows at first-floor level and second-floor levels again.

Portland Road takes a right turn at the top before joining Clarendon Road. On the south side is a fairly modern block of eight flats at No. 140, which was probably built in the 1980s or 90s using council-yellow brick.

In 2010, a number of houses changed hands in Portland Road. These were: No. 155 for £2,275,000, No. 82 for £3,500,000, No. 188 for £2,750,000, No. 145 for £2,375,000, No. 115 for £2,600,000 and No. 123 for £1,650,000. A flat at No. 107 was sold for £355,000 and another at No. 105 for £405,000.

Richard Roy

Richard Roy was a solicitor, not a builder, but he became, almost by accident, the pivotal developer on the Ladbroke Estate (p. 61). Roy was a partner in the firm of Roy Blunt Duncan & Johnstone, with offices in Westminster and the City. They and some of their clients had lent money to the promoters of the doomed racecourse venture called the Hippodrome (p. 54), a venture which went badly wrong. One of these promoters was their partner, John Duncan. Richard Roy and his partner, Pearson Thompson, had already jointly developed property in Cheltenham, so they took the site on as a building project in an attemp to recover all the lost money. Roy had day-to-day control. He even moved to the Ladbroke Estate in 1847 to be closer to the project. He carried out the development with great efficiency. This gave him a taste for development. He then took on three acres between Pottery Lane and Portland Road, which he successfully developed, mainly using William Reynolds (p. 57), an experienced builder. He made a lot of money out of it, and he died in 1873, aged 76, still living at No. 42 Clarendon Road.

Hippodrome Mews, round the back of the top of Portland Road, contains 29 fairly modern brick town-houses (from the late 1970s, I guess). They have garages and little front doors at ground floor level, protruding first floors with canted bay windows above, and a recessed second storey, with the area in front forming a balcony. It is a cobbled street, and the cobbles are original, so I assume the original houses were all knocked down to make way for these new houses. Hippodrome Place is nearby. Hippodrome Mews was built on the site of the old Potteries and the dining room of No. 22 is in fact a converted kiln.

Two houses changed hands in Hippodrome Mews in 2010: No. 10 for £975,000 and No. 2 for £1,015,000.

The Hippodrome

In 1836, property development in Notting Hill had stalled. So James Ladbroke (p. 61) agreed to let 140 acres of his land to John Whyte for a racecourse called The Hippodrome. This opened in 1837 and was used for steeplechases and flat racing. It quickly ran into difficulties. The locals objected because it cut off a public footpath and the racecourse had to be altered to avoid it. Racing began again in 1839 but the ground was heavy clay and was just not suitable for horseracing. In 1840 Whyte gave up, and sold his lease to his solicitor, John Duncan (p. 53)

Various landowners owned bits of **Clarendon Road** before its development. (The road itself was named after Lord Clarendon, a prominent member of the House of Lords at the time.) At the Holland Park Avenue end, James Ladbroke (p. 61) was the freeholder and he allocated the land to William Drew (p. 101) for the construction of houses. In 1845, Drew arranged for William Liddard (described as a 'gentleman' in the agreements) to build Nos. 2-10 on the east side, and for Thomas Allason (p. 78), Ladbroke's architect, to build Nos. 12 and 14. These are now shops with flats on the upper floors. On the west side, Nos. 1-11 were allocated to the same builders, but were later demolished. These have been replaced by some attractive modern houses on four storeys, from No. 1A-11, built in brick cladding and concrete.

From Ladbroke Road to Clarendon Cross there are a series of terraces on the west side of Clarendon Road. Nos. 13 and 15 are two halves of a very stately white-painted mansion on four storeys, built by Drew in 1840. Nos. 17-21 are a terrace of four-storey flat-fronted houses with little architectural decoration, but painted in pleasant pastel colours. These were constructed by Liddard in 1845. Nos. 23-29, designed by Allason (p. 78), are slightly more ambitious, with bow windows running up the entire four storeys. Most of the houses have private parking at the front of the houses.

Clarendon Road and Lansdowne Road Communal Garden

There are in fact two communal gardens, on either side of St John's Gardens (p. 75) – each about one acre in size – and lying between the houses on the east side of Clarendon Road (p. 54) and the houses on the west side of Lansdowne Road (p. 65). There is an entrance from St John's Gardens. These gardens were laid out in around 1860. They slope slightly towards Clarendon Road. The original design of the northern garden was for a central bed of shrubs surrounded by lawns, and with paths like spokes from the shrub area to a perimeter path. But the shrubs have been replaced by a copse of birch trees and only the perimeter path remains. The southern garden has a large lawn area fringed with trees and shrubs, including large plane trees and hawthorns, and an area of shrubs in the middle. There is an original path which runs west to east across the middle of the garden. There used to be a corresponding path running north to south, which no longer exists. (See p. 180 for more information on communal gardens.)

The next part of Clarendon Road was built on land controlled by Richard Roy (p. 53) and the houses were built by his building partner, William Reynolds. Nos. 16-26, on the east side, form a terrace of four-storey flat-faced houses with large shared porches. Nos. 31-39 on the west side is a terrace of houses which are mainly flat-faced, but with the first-floor windows of the end houses protruding as canted bays supported on brackets, and with lobbies instead of open porches.

Between Lansdowne Walk and St John's Gardens, Nos. 28-42 are well-spaced semi-detached houses built by Reynolds. Between St

John's Gardens and Lansdowne Rise, still on the east side, a new style of house appears. Nos. 44-58, also built by Reynolds, are still large semi-detached houses on four storeys, but now mainly stuccoed and cream painted. The late Victorian buildings merge almost invisibly into Clare Court at No. 54, which is a modern infill containing seven flats. There are a further eight flats at No. 56 on the corner, which is a conversion of one of the original houses. Between 1844-5 Reynolds built Nos. 41-77, also on the west side of the road. Generally speaking, these houses are set well back behind brick walls or railings, and they have basements, raised ground storeys (both painted white), and then two upper storeys in yellow brick with an attractive string course decoration. The entrances are generally in side extensions, providing increased living area. These houses are slightly more elaborate than those opposite, with white painted quoins and more decorative detail, including curved heads to the windows, more elaborate brackets, classical porches and Ionic heads for the columns.

North of Lansdowne Rise and Clarendon Cross, there are blocks of flats on the east side. No. 60 comprises two blocks of 1950s-style brick buildings on three and four storeys containing 22 flats. Opposite, Nos. 81-83 comprises an 80's block on five storeys containing 21 flats. On the west side, there is Garden Court at No. 66, and then houses again from Nos. 68-78, where the road turns right into Elgin Crescent. These are on four storeys, with lobby-style shared entrances. In 1851 Charles Blake (p. 98) who owned this part of the Clarendon Road site, leased the site for Nos. 68-76 to Thomas Holmes, a builder, and the remaining house, No. 78, to H W Smith, a builder. William Sim, the architect, may have designed them all.

Between Lansdowne Rise and Blenheim Crescent there are Victorian houses from Nos. 82 to 108. These are generally on four storeys (including basements), in different styles, and all converted into flats. Gradually the basements become actual ground floors as the houses accommodate the slight slope of the street, so in the later houses the steps to the front door are up to a genuine first-floor. This part of the Clarendon Road frontage was owned by Dr Samuel Walker (p. 71) and in 1853 he allocated the lots for Nos. 90-110 to William C Gazeley, a Camden Town builder.

Above Portland Road on the east, there are some well-designed Victorian semi-detached houses from Nos. 87 to 97 (No. 99 is a single house). These are four-storey houses (although some of the top storeys are quite low) and they are well set back from the road. From No. 101 onwards there are mainly fairly modern houses and conversions. Nos. 101-105 have steep driveways down to semi-basement garages with four storeys above. The land was owned by Stephen Phillips (p. 74) and in 1852 he allocated the land for Nos. 87 and 105 to William Reynolds. On the west side, there is a large estate called Nottingwood House which is a huge development on five storeys running right back to Walmer Road and then there is the Allom and Barlow Estate with post-war with buildings on four storeys.

If you have a property in Clarendon Road you may have rights of access to Clarendon Road and Lansdowne Road Communal Garden (p. 55) and/or Montpelier Garden (p. 75). But to find out if your property does have any such rights, you need to check with the relevant garden committee. (See p. 180 for more information on communal gardens.)

No. 29 was the only house sold in Clarendon Road in 2010; it went for £5,500,000. There were several flat sales: a flat at No. 87 for £547,259, a lower ground floor flat at No. 47 for £647,000, a flat at No. 96-98 for £530,000 and a flat at Allom House for £233,000.

William Reynolds

William Reynolds first appeared as a builder on the Ladbroke Estate (p. 61) in 1845 when he began construction of nearly 100 houses, but as was the case with so many Victorian would-be property magnates, he had taken on far more than he could afford and went bankrupt in 1847 before he could finish them. However, he was back in business again in 1849, putting up houses on Clarendon Road. He became a favourite builder of Richard Roy (p. 53).

In 1864 Charles Blake (p. 98) entered into a building agreement with G and T Goodwin under which they built Nos. 1-24 **Ladbroke Crescent**, of which some still remain. In 2010, the only sale in Ladbroke Crescent was of a flat at No. 10, which changed hands for £310,000.

The north side of **Cornwall Crescent** is mainly taken up with Camelford Court, which is two long blocks of the Lancaster West council estate. On the south side, nos. 1-29 are late-Victorian houses mainly on four storeys (including basements), with canted bays up to the second floor level and round-headed second-floor windows. The ground and basement walls and canted bays are painted and otherwise the houses are brick-faced above. Nos. 33-77, near the Clarendon Road end, comprises a long terrace of late-Victorian houses on four storeys (including garden flats with windows half above ground level). There are no railings or balconies above the bays and the porches, which is unusual. The properties are now mainly flats.

There was a flat sale at No. 29 Cornwall Crescent in 2010 for £520,000 and another at No. 7a for £330,000.

Blenheim Crescent is one of 47 streets in London named after the Duke of Marlborough's famous victory over the French on 13th August 1704, when the British army under Marlborough (John Churchill) defeated a larger French army near the village of Blenheim in Bavaria.

The south side, which has the communal gardens, is the most popular and more expensive side of the street. The houses are generally smaller than in Elgin Crescent (mainly a floor less and about 1,000 square feet less). Work on Blenheim Crescent began on the south side in 1861. (I am not including the stretch between Ladbroke Grove and Portobello Road.) The south side of Blenheim Crescent from Ladbroke Grove is a long curving terrace from No. 53 to No. 81. Blenheim

Crescent was mostly built on land belonging to Charles Blake (p. 98) and he entered into an agreement for its development with Charles Chambers, a timber merchant. Richard Crowley was the builder of No. 53. Thomas May, a surveyor, contracted with Chambers to build Nos. 55-77. He used his own contractors to build Nos. 55-73, but sold his rights in Nos. 75 and 77 to Alfred and George Secrett, who built those houses. Nos. 79 and 81 were built by John Scoley. This terrace has slightly different styles – the result of so many different builders being involved. Consistent features are that there are basement storeys (at least at the Ladbroke Road end) with wide steps up to porticoed front doors, with canted bays at lower ground and ground levels, and two storeys above. Another terrace from No. 83 to No. 135 extends to Clarendon Road. Chambers himself acquired the freehold of this area and granted leases direct to his chosen builders in 1863. Nos. 83 and 85 were taken personally by Chambers. Chambers assigned or subcontracted the building of many of the houses and arranged for Blake to issue leases direct to his chosen contractors. Henry Heard, a pub owner, built Nos. 87-91 (odd). Thomas Wesson, a builder, built Nos. 93-115 and Nos. 129-135 (odd). Benjamin Reynolds, a builder, took Nos. 117-127 (odd).

Blenheim and Elgin Crescents Garden

This communal garden lies behind the south side of Blenheim Crescent (p. 58), the north side of Elgin Crescent (p.62) and the east side of Clarendon Road (p. 54), in the section between Clarendon Road and Ladbroke Grove (p. 81). It is entered via Blenheim Passage which is between No. 81 and No. 83 Blenheim Crescent. This is a very uncluttered garden of two acres with large lawns, bordered by trees and shrubs. There is a gravel path round of the edge of the lawns. The garden was created in 1863; although the layout of the garden itself has kept to the original design, the previously more complicated paths have been simplified, probably during the Second World War. (See p. 180 for more information on communal gardens.)

The northern side of Blenheim Crescent mainly contains housing association buildings. On the north side, the terraces are interrupted by roads. One terrace, from No. 44-58, extends from St Mark's Place to St Mark's Road, and it is made up of a medley of house styles from five to four storey houses (including basements). There are generally no bay windows, unlike the south side, and the houses have more impressive entrance porches. The mixture of styles was due to the same arrangement as on the south side: Chambers acquired the building rights from Blake but allocated the plots among his chosen contractors. From St Mark's Road to Clarendon Road, on the north side, Nos. 64-82 form a terrace of four-storey houses with canted bays on lower ground and ground floor level, but unusually, without balconies at the top. Nos. 62-66 were built by J S C Small, a plasterer, and Nos. 68-78 were built by Thomas Wesson. Then there are some more modern houses probably post-war, and finally No. 96 which is a post-war block of flats on four storeys.

If you have a property in Blenheim Crescent you may have rights of access to Blenheim and Elgin Crescents Garden (p. 59). But to find out if your property does have any such rights, you need to check with the garden committee. (See p. 180 for more information on communal gardens.)

Several freehold houses changed hands in Blenheim Crescent in 2010. No. 111 was sold for £5,050,000, No. 123 for £4,175,000, No. 62 for £3,500,000 and No. 60 for £3,850,000. A basement flat at No. 38 was sold for £3,200,000 and an upper maisonette at No. 58 went for £1,370,000. There were other flat sales at prices ranging from £278,000 to £500,000.

The east side of **St Mark's Place** is mainly taken up by Hudson House, a post-war block on three storeys containing 12 flats. But Nos. 1-11, at the Blenheim Crescent end, are original houses on five storeys.

On the west section, Nos. 4-10 form a terrace on four storeys (including basement). They are stuccoed up to ground floor level and bare brick above, with half columns to decorate the doors.

In 2010, a property at 7 St Mark's Place was sold for £2,350,000.

The Ladbroke Estate

In the mid-18th century, Richard Ladbroke of Tadworth Court Surrey bought 170 acres of land, between what was to be Portland Road on the west and Portobello Road on the east, just north of the ancient road to Uxbridge (now Holland Park Avenue). This became known as the Ladbroke Estate. At the time the area was just used as gravel pits and pasture land. When Richard Ladbroke died, his son, also Richard Ladbroke, inherited the estate. He died childless in 1793 and he left the estate on trust to provide a life interest to various relatives in turn. The last of these was a nephew, James, who was required by his uncle's will to change his surname to Ladbroke before inheriting (which he did). James Ladbroke died in 1847 and was succeeded by a distant cousin, Felix Ladbroke, from Headley in Surrey. Felix was free of the restrictions in Richard Ladbroke's will, which had prevented James Ladbroke from selling the freehold of parts of the estate. Felix Ladbroke sold off the freehold of his Notting Hill estate to the various developers and builders who built the houses on it, and the Ladbroke Estate as an entity came to an end.

Codrington Mews is a mews off Blenheim Crescent. It has a tarmac surface rather than the traditional cobbles, and it contains 12 fairly plain brick-built mews houses on two storeys with garage doors, almost all painted white. It's a mixture of residential and commercial properties, including a little garden centre at the end which is probably the source of the profusion of bushes and shrubs outside many properties in the street. It's a rather friendly mews, without the over-manicured look which some mews have acquired.

There were no sales in Codrington News in 2010. The most recent sale was of No. 7 in 2009 for £1,750,000.

Elgin Crescent starts at Portobello Road, where there are a few flats above shops. Whole houses begin after it crosses Kensington Park Road. On the south side, from Nos. 17-61, there is a long and quite grand terrace of five-storey houses with shared three-columned porches, and plenty of stucco decoration. These were probably all built by Robert Russell, a builder, in 1852. The north side east of Ladbroke Grove was land owned by Dr Samuel Walker (p. 71), which he later sold to Charles Blake (p. 98). Dr Walker's property contained the range next to Ladbroke Road, and work began there slightly later than elsewhere in Elgin Crescent. Russell started work on Nos. 17-47 in 1852, and Nos. 49-61 presumably soon afterwards. On the north side, there are plainer four-storey houses from Nos. 16-36, some detached and some semi-detached. These have raised ground floors above a basement and a little front garden, with a canted bay and a porch which fits well into the design, and two storeys above, often with triple first-floor windows with flat or curved heads. (I don't know the names of the builders.) A few houses on either side of Elgin Crescent are still in single family occupation but most have been subdivided and sold off as flats. Finally, there's a post-war brick council block called Galsworthy House on four storeys with 16 flats.

Crossing Ladbroke Grove, Elgin Crescent has a sequence of very attractive houses on the north side starting at No. 50. There are various terraces all the way along, but they mainly conform to a similar style. They are generally on basement, ground and two upper storeys, and they are stuccoed-faced and painted in a pastel colour (although the door and window surrounds are generally white). Nos. 50-56 were built in 1862 by Edwin Ware, a builder from Paddington, on land owned by Charles Blake (p. 98), who bought this area from Dr Walker (p. 71). They have round-headed entrance doors and canted bays up to first-floor level. The rest of the land was retained by Dr Walker.

Arundel and Elgin Communal Garden

This communal garden is between the south side of Elgin Crescent and the north side of Arundel Gardens (p. 90) in the section from Ladbroke Grove (p. 81) to Kensington Park Road (p. 86). The entrances to the garden are in Ladbroke Grove and Kensington Park Road. The current layout of the garden is based on the original design when it was constructed in 1862 and it covers 1.3 acres. The garden is laid out to seem as natural as possible and there are plenty of mature trees and plants including a very large plane tree in the centre of the garden. (See p. 180 for more information on communal gardens.)

Nos. 58-76 are grander houses; they have an additional third storey above a cornice, grander porticoed entrances, and stuccoed balustrades for a first-floor balcony. The next terrace, Nos. 78-100, and the final terrace, Nos. 102-120, share a similar style: the houses have plain ground floor windows, not canted bays, and they have no balcony railings outside the first-floor windows. The first-floor windows for most of the terrace are usually triple windows, and the second floor windows alternate being square and round headed. Most of the houses have mansard rooms in the sloping roofs above the balustrade and cornice, but these are haphazard and were probably added later. These houses were all built by Henry Malcolm Ramsay (p. 65) with whom Dr Walker entered into a building agreement in 1852, and they were completed in 1858. Then there is Crescent Mansions, a pre-war mansion block of 14 flats in red brick, with canted bays, on four storeys, plus rooms in the gable ends and roof. Nos. 124 and 126 are brick-built houses on four storeys (including basements).

On the south side of Elgin Crescent, Nos. 69-103 were built by William Sim between 1852 and 1860, and they are very similar to Nos. 78 onwards on the north side of the road. All the houses on either side have quite substantial front areas, usually big enough for cars.

On the north side, again, No. 117 onwards are in an altogether different style. The houses are on basement, ground and two upper storeys with no attic or mansard rooms, and the areas are shallower. There are paired lobbies extending in front of the buildings for the entrance doors, but the windows next to them are flat to the facade and rectangular. The first-floor and second-floor windows are also rectangular and plain. The facades continue to be painted in many colours. That terrace runs to No. 153 where Elgin Crescent joins Clarendon Road. These houses were on land which Charles Blake (p. 98) had taken over from Dr Walker (p. 71) and work began in 1851. Nos. 117-145 (odd) were built by David Ramsay (p. 65), a nurseryman from Brompton. Nos. 149-153 (odd) were taken by H W Smith, a builder. For some reason, Blake allocated the single house at No. 147 to a different builder, Charles Preedy of Islington. It is believed that most of these houses were designed by William Sim, except for Nos. 149-153, which may have been designed by Thomas Allom (p. 96).

If you have a property in Elgin Crescent you may have rights of access to one or more of Arundel and Elgin Communal Garden (p. 63), Blenheim and Elgin Crescents Garden (p. 59), Lansdowne and Elgin Crescent Garden (p. 70) and/or Montpelier Garden (p. 75). But to find out if your property does have any such rights, you need to check with the relevant garden committee. (See p. 180 for more information on communal gardens.)

The only house sale in Elgin Crescent in 2010 was the sale of No. 106 for £6,050,709. A flat at Crescent Mansions was sold for £1,325,000, which was the largest flat sale price. Most of the other flat sales were confined to a single run of properties. Sales included: £699,950 for a first-floor flat at No. 21, £505,000 for a first-floor flat and £740,000 for a third-floor flat, both at No. 27, £735,000 for a third-floor flat at No. 33, £670,000 for a third-floor flat at No. 35, £590,000 for a second-floor flat at No. 45 and £755,000 for a flat at No. 61. The only sale on the other side of the street was of a flat at No. 28, which was sold for £510,000.

David Allan Ramsay

David Allan Ramsay started out as the owner of a nursery garden in South Kensington but he became one of the principal builders working in the Ladbroke Estate. Ramsay became Charles Blake's (p. 98) favoured builder. In 1851 Blake granted him building leases of plots in Elgin Crescent, followed in 1853 by 40 houses in the Stanley Crescent and Stanley Gardens. He worked with most of the big developers in the area. Between 1851 and 1853 Richard Roy (p. 53) granted him building leases of 80 plots in Portland Road and Heathfield Road. Ramsay also took a number of plots from Dr Walker (p. 71) on the north side of Elgin Crescent. But a doubling in interest rates pushed Ramsay into bankruptcy in 1853 and left Blake and Walker with a large quantity of half-finished houses. Blake survived; Walker was destroyed.

Lansdowne Road was named after Lord Lansdowne, for no discernible reason except that he was a prominent member of the House of Lords when the Ladbroke Estate was being developed. The first substantial building on the east side is Lansdowne House which was built in 1904 to designs by William Flockhart, originally as artists' studios. It looks like a Scottish castle and contains about 12 flats on seven storeys. Nos. 1-5 (odd) on the west side were built as three detached houses by W Liddard in 1845 on four storeys (with additional rooms in the mansard roof). They are rather ornately decorated with huge porch structures and canted bays rising up to the second storey. No. 1 is a large house in its own grounds. Nos. 3-5 were converted into a block of flats in the 1970s.

The main run of houses begins just north of Ladbroke Road, where William Drew (p. 101) was the overall developer under a building agreement with James Ladbroke (p. 61). Drew built Nos. 2-12 (even) on the east side in 1843. These are semi-detached houses, mainly with basements, ground floors, two upper storeys and then some mansard rooms in the roof. Drew used a fairly dark brick and there is a homely, almost cottagey, feel to the houses, perhaps because of their lavish and pleasantly overgrown front gardens. A particular architectural feature is that they each have pilasters (sunken columns) rising up the whole building and supporting the eaves, which is a sort of reference to classical design, otherwise they could be larger versions of houses in a Cathedral close.

The section from Lansdowne Walk to St John's Gardens was built on land where Richard Roy (p. 53), a property speculator, had the building agreement with James Ladbroke. Roy used Frederick Woods and William Wheeler to build Nos. 16-30 (even) on the east side in 1845. Behind these buildings are the communal gardens known as Hanover Gardens. A year later, Roy used his usual builder, William Reynolds (p. 57), for Nos. 9-27 (odd) on the west side. (The west side now ends with No. 25 at St John's Gardens.) These are all huge detached and semi-detached houses, built in dark brown brick. They have three main storeys with basements, and they are fully stuccoed up to ground floor level. They also have private parking. The houses on the west side have window heads shaped like scallop shells, while those on the east have white painted quoins at various protruding edges of the buildings.

Roy also had the contract to build houses on the land between St John's Gardens and Lansdowne Crescent, and he used Reynolds to build the houses there in 1846. These are Nos. 29-43 (odd) on the west, and Nos. 32-44 (even) on the east. (No. 43 is round the corner in Lansdowne Rise.) No. 34 follows the style of the odd numbers below St John's Gardens. Next to it is a 1960s low-rise block called Lawrence Court at Nos. 36-40 which contains flats. Most of the houses on the west side and, to a lesser extent, the two remaining houses on the east side are huge, fully-stuccoed, and classical-looking, semi-detached houses on three main storeys (plus basements) with a cornice on brackets at the top of the buildings, and triangular pediments above the first-floor windows. The only jarring feature is that the main doors, whether on the front or side, are square pillared lobbies with the side walls filled in, which is obviously not a classical feature.

Notting Hill Garden

This is a small communal garden, half an acre in size, between the east side of Lansdowne Road (p. 65), the south side of Lansdowne Rise (p. 74), the west side of Lansdowne Crescent (p. 72) and the north side of St John's Gardens (p. 75). It is between the backs of the houses of those streets except for sections of Lansdowne Crescent and St John's Gardens where it reaches to the road, but is concealed from view from Lansdowne Crescent by a hedge. The most prominent tree is a horse chestnut, which is at least as old as the houses, but sycamore and other trees have been planted in the last century. The paths are as originally laid out. (See p. 180 for more information on communal gardens.)

Roy (p. 53) had land for three remaining houses. In 1847, James Lamb, a builder from Hyde Park Square, built No. 46 for him on the east side of the road, and Reynolds built Nos. 45 and 47 opposite on the west side. Nos. 45 onwards continues the style used on the same side south of Lansdowne Crescent, in general terms. Most of the houses are stuccoed, but No. 51 is brick-faced. They come in terraces of three or more houses. Next to Roy's allocation of land, there were two plots owned by Charles Blake (p. 98) where Michael Longstaff, a builder, constructed Nos. 49 and 51 in 1851. North of that, the land was owned by Dr Samuel Walker (p. 71). He granted leases of all his building plots to builders in 1852. Up to Rosmead Road there were several takers of small amounts of land. David Ramsay (p. 65) built Nos. 53-59 (odd) which were finished by 1855; and Thomas Pocock built Nos. 61-75 (odd) which were finished by 1862. Thomas Allason (the architect son of the more famous Thomas Allason (p. 78)) took No. 77 over from Ramsay, half-built in 1856, and completed it. The main terrace from No. 61-77, on the corner with Rosmead Road, looks like a series of Christmas cakes by different chefs pressed together, and lacks the obvious symmetry you would expect from a classical terrace. This is probably because the street slopes steeply downhill at this point. The unifying theme all along is a signature style of decoration in the balcony wall above the ground floor, made up of a series of curves. The houses generally have three main storeys plus basements, and are topped with balustrades. Most of the first-floor windows are triple windows; the ground floor windows are all flush with the facade with no bays.

Lansdowne Road and Lansdowne Crescent Garden

This is also known as Lansdowne Gardens. This communal garden lies between the south side of Lansdowne Road (p. 65) and the north side of Lansdowne Crescent (p. 72), between Ladbroke Grove (p. 81) and Lansdowne Rise (p. 74). It is shaped like a curved dagger and because it is near the top of the hill, it slopes quite sharply down towards Lansdowne Road. It contains 1.2 acres of lawns and mature ash trees, along with more recently planted trees and shrubs. (See p. 180 for more information on communal gardens.)

The builder, Kenelm Chandler, undertook the whole range of houses on the west side of Lansdowne Road, beyond Rosmead Road, comprising Nos. 79-123 (odd). But he went bankrupt in about 1858-60 and various builders took over, including J D Cowland (Nos. 89 and 111) and William Reading (Nos. 113-117 (odd)). They were all completed by 1862. Nos. 105-111 and 121-123 were later demolished, and replaced mainly by blocks of flats, such as the post-war brick-built block of 12 flats at No. 121-123. The houses of Nos. 79-123 suddenly develop a very Dutch style. The houses are on basement, ground and two upper storeys. Facades are topped with an elaborate gable, and then there are some dormer windows in the sloping roof behind.

Going back again to the start of Dr Walker's (p. 71) land just north of Lansdowne Road, and beginning again on the east side of the road, Nos. 48 and 52 were built by James Emmins and completed in 1857. The longer terrace from Nos. 52-66 was constructed by Henry Wade Smith and completed in 1860. These houses were built in a very different style from those on the west. These are very symmetrical semi-detached houses, mainly painted cream. The central feature is a shared porch with recessed front doors. On either side are canted bays up to ground floor level. A conspicuous feature is that the windows above ground floor level all have curved heads on pillars like you might see on Romanesque churches. Nos. 68-102 (even) were started by another builder, Jacob Barry, who then went bust. In 1860 to 1862 Richard Roy (p. 53) (who had bought the land from Walker) allocated the plots to John Froud, a builder from Shepherd's Bush (Nos. 78-82) and Joseph Lane, a carpenter (Nos. 90-98). The houses of Nos. 68-102 have exactly the same Dutch style as Nos. 79-123 opposite.

If you have a property in Lansdowne Road you may have rights of access to one or more of the following gardens: Lansdowne Road and Lansdowne Crescent Garden (p. 68), Hanover Gardens (p. 77), Lansdowne and Elgin Crescent Garden (p. 70), Clarendon Road and Lansdowne Road Communal Garden (p. 55), Montpelier Garden (p. 75), and/or Notting Hill Garden (p. 67). But to find out if your property does have any such rights, you need to check with the relevant garden committee. (See p. 180 for more information on communal gardens.)

There were a number of decent house sales in Lansdowne Road in 2010: £6,100,000 for No. 58, £6,300,000 for No. 71, £5,950,000 for No. 65, £4,750,000 for No. 50 and £5,750,000 for No. 79. There were a few substantial flat sales as well, including: a flat at No. 3D for £2,950,000, a flat at No. 32 for £1,000,000 and a flat at No. 9 for £1,745,000. There was also an assortment of much lower flat prices, including three flats at No. 8 The Terraces, ranging in price from

£407,500 to £670,000, a flat at Aston Court for £325,000 and a flat at No. 39B for £190,000.

Rosmead Road is a short road joining Lansdowne Road and Elgin Crescent. It is mainly occupied by the sides of communal gardens but the end of terrace houses in those roads open onto it. There are two semi-detached houses actually in Rosmead Road. It is a Victorian building on basement ground and two upper storeys with joined enclosed porches.

If you have a property in Rosmead Road you may have rights of access to Lansdowne and Elgin Crescent Gardens (p. 70) and/or Montpelier Gardens. But to find out if your property does have any such rights, you need to check with the garden committee. (See p. 180 for more information on communal gardens.)

Lansdowne and Elgin Crescent Garden

This two acre communal garden lies behind the south side of Elgin Crescent (p. 62) and the north side of Lansdowne Road (p. 65), in the section between Rosmead Road (p. 70) and Ladbroke Grove (p. 81). It is slightly curved, following the contour of roads; and it is level, being near the foot of the hill. The entrance is through a gate in Rosmead Road and is then down a flight of steps and a short gravel slope. The garden is basically laid out as three large oval-shaped lawns, with thickets of shrubs and bushes at either end. Most of the paths are as originally designed. The railings along the Rosmead Road boundary are original. (See p. 180 for more information on communal gardens.)

Boyne Terrace Mews, which is off Lansdowne Road below Ladbroke Road, contains a series of modern townhouses, all individually designed, mainly on the south side, because the north side contains the backs of houses in Ladbroke Road. The houses are more substantial than normal mews or townhouses, and are mostly double-fronted, two-storey houses. There are 12 houses on the south side. There's also a little gated community in the centre of the mews with a terrace of houses on three main storeys and extra rooms in the mansard roof. It is right next to Holland Park tube station and properties here can be affected by rumble from the Central Line.

There were no sales in 2010 in Boyne Terrace Mews; the most recent sale was No. 11, which was purchased for £1,300,000 in 2009.

Lansdowne Mews runs between Clarendon Road and Lansdowne Road. This is mainly the backs of other streets' houses but Greens Court is a rather stylish low-rise development of 12 flats. Nos. 7-10 are little mock-Georgian houses on three storeys, flat faced, with curved front doors.

No. 5 Lansdowne Mews changed hands in 2010 for £1,037,500.

Dr Samuel Walker

Dr Samuel Walker was a doctor of divinity, and the rector of a rich parish in Cornwall. He inherited his father's estate in 1851 and so became a client of the solicitors, Roy Blunt Duncan & Johnstone. With their encouragement, he decided to increase his fortune by joining in the development of the Ladbroke Estate. His purpose was to raise money to establish a bishopric of Cornwall. Unfortunately, he was the worst businessman and property developer you could imagine. If any other developer found himself stuck with overpriced property in a slump, he would sell it at a profit to the ever eager Dr Walker. While Richard Roy (p. 53) and Charles Blake (p. 98) were buying land in the best parts of the estate at prudent prices, Walker was paying more for remote parts. He bought the land north of Lansdowne Road and Crescent from Blake. Then he started lending money to his builders on the security of the leases he was granting them, which meant he was lending on the security of his own land. So when the market fell and his builders, such as

David Alan Ramsay (p. 65) went bust, his fragile property empire suffered a double whammy. Cornwall never got its new bishopric.

Lansdowne Crescent starts opposite St John's Church of Notting Hill, and was named after Lord Lansdowne, a prominent member of the House of Lords when the Ladbroke Estate was being developed. St John's Church forms the highpoint and centrepiece of the Ladbroke Estate. Nos. 2-18 are the houses on the inner (east) side of the crescent. No. 2 on the corner with Ladbroke Road is a large Gothic castle-like house, converted into flats, built in stone rather than brick, on four main storeys (including basement) with attic rooms in the gables and roof, and with a church-like main entrance door. Nos. 3 and 4, also on four storeys, have a more sunny Italianate feel. They were all built by Joshua Higgs & Son of Davies Street, near Berkeley Square. Nos. 5-8 were built by William Reynolds. No. 5 has been extensively modernised; it has completely rectangular stuccoed bays up to the second floor level, and they demonstrate why bays with slanted (canted) sides are more attractive. Nos. 6-8 are semi-detached houses in a similar style, brick-faced but with stuccoed basement and ground storeys. An interesting feature is that the second storey on each side is like a turret with the roof in between containing mansard rooms. Nos. 9-12 were built by J W Bridger of Chigwell. These are a group of semi-detached mansions in a mixture of Gothic and Italianate style. The Gothic style can be seen in the chapel-like entrance porches and windows; the Italianate in the painted stucco. The houses are on four main storeys, with canted bays up to first-floor level. William Reynolds also built Nos. 13-18 as four-storey, semi-detached houses to the same design as he had used in Nos. 6-8, including the second-floor turrets on either side of the mansard roof. No. 18 has been replaced by a very minimalist concrete block with tall narrow (but actually rather stylish) windows, containing six flats on three upper floors, designed by John Poulsen.

Lansdowne Crescent Garden

This is the communal garden area behind the backs of the houses on the east side of Lansdowne Crescent (p. 72) and the properties on the west side of Ladbroke Grove (p. 81) at that point and it covers three quarters of an acre. The vicarage of St John's Church stands in the southern corner of the garden. There is an entrance from Ladbroke Grove. The original Victorian layout no longer exists. The garden is mainly laid out as lawns with flowering and climbing plants. (See p. 180 for more information on communal gardens.)

At the Ladbroke Grove end of Lansdowne Crescent, the house numbers go back the other way on the outer, western side of the road. The north part of this outer side of the crescent was owned by Stephen Phillips (p. 74), and he allocated it to Henry Wyatt, an architect from Munster Square, who built Nos. 19-38 in about 1860. These houses are long conjoined terraces of five-storey, stucco-faced houses. They are all built much closer to the street than on the inner side; they each have a basement access (usually straight off the street), a barely raised ground floor with a narrow (but deep) porch, with a balcony on top for the first-floor windows. The balcony railings run more or less all the way along the terraces. The houses do not have canted bays, but some of them have very attractive bow fronted features with the whole of the upper part above the first-floor balcony, comprising the second, third and sometimes fourth floors, in the form of a bow, although the windows within the bow walls are normal rectangular windows. (The bow fronted houses are Nos. 21-28 and Nos. 31-36.) At first and second floor levels, the windows have elaborate heads, with architraves, curved pediments, brackets, and plenty of swirling plasterwork. There are additional rooms in the sloping roofs, set back behind the balustrade at the top. There's a little post-war in-fill called '29 and a half'. Nos. 39 and 40 are a semi-detached pair on five storeys (including basements) with wide canted bays up to ground floor level. Nos. 41-41B is a terrace of three post-war townhouses on four storeys, with very low-ceilinged garages (which at No. 41 has been turned into part of the house) at the lowest level. The second floor is set back slightly behind railings to provide a terrace. On the other side of Lansdowne Rise is Lansdowne Court, a cream-faced mansion block in Art Deco style, which extends down Lansdowne Rise and contains 16 flats, including a more recent penthouse.

If you have a property in Lansdowne Crescent you may have rights of access to one or more of Lansdowne Crescent Garden (p. 73), Lansdowne Road and Lansdowne Crescent Garden (p. 68) and/or Notting Hill Garden (p. 67). But to find out if your property does have any such rights, you need to check with the relevant garden committee. (See p. 180 for more information on communal gardens.)

There were some large sales in Lansdowne Crescent in 2010. No. 43 was sold for £10,000,000, No. 31 for £8,000,000, No. 30 for £7,500,000 and, bringing up the rear, No. 41 for £3,900,000.

Stephen Phillips

In 1848 Stephen Phillips bought ten acres of land north of Lansdowne Crescent. Phillips employed William King, an Islington architect, to design most of his houses. Phillips was already an experienced builder with developments in Islington and Paddington under his belt. He granted leases to other builders at improved ground rents, which provided him with a significant profit.

Until 1937 **Lansdowne Rise** was called Montpelier Road, after a large mansion which stood nearby. Lansdowne Rise was developed by Richard Roy (p.) in 1846. In the section from Clarendon Road to Lansdowne Road, it is mainly taken up with the sides of communal gardens, but the end of terrace houses on Clarendon Road and

Lansdowne Road have entrances onto Lansdowne Rise. In the section between Lansdowne Road and Lansdowne Crescent, one of the two blocks on Lansdowne Court has an entrance onto Lansdowne Rise for flats 10-16. This is a pre-war mansion block, painted cream and with a glass structure at roof level.

If you have a property in Lansdowne Rise you may have rights of access to Montpelier Garden (p. 75) and/or Notting Hill Garden (p. 67) and/or Clarendon Road and Lansdowne Road Communal Garden (p. 55). But to find out if your property does have any such rights, you need to check with the relevant garden committee. (See p. 180 for more information on communal gardens.)

Montpelier Garden

This communal garden runs from Rosmead Road (p. 70) to Lansdowne Rise (p. 74) between the backs of the houses of Lansdowne Road (p. 65) and, first, Clarendon Road (p. 54) and then the first part of Elgin Crescent (p. 62). The garden slopes down towards Clarendon Road. Iron gates were installed to commemorate the Royal Jubilee in 1977. The garden itself is fairly open, with mature trees spread across 1.6 acres of lawn. There was originally a path through the middle of the garden which has been grassed over, and the only original path now surviving is the path round the edge of the garden. The garden apparently took its name from Montpelier House, a large mansion nearby which was bombed in the war. (See p. 180 for more information on communal gardens.)

St John's Gardens is the road between two gardens, running from Clarendon Road to Lansdowne Road, and then heading towards St John's Church. The end of terrace houses on the two main roads have entrances into St John's Gardens and they are quite grand. In the crescent section near the church there is a short terrace consisting of

Nos. 1 and 2 on the north side of St John's Gardens, linked to another property which becomes No. 44 Lansdowne Crescent. Nos. 1 and 2 St John's Gardens were built in 1846 by William Reynolds. They are very spacious houses with basement, ground and two upper storeys.

If you have a property in St John's Gardens you may have rights of access to Notting Hill Garden (p. 67) and/or Hanover Gardens (p. 77) and/or the two communal gardens between Lansdowne Road and Clarendon Road (p. 55). But to find out if your property does have any such rights, you need to check with the garden committee. (See p. 180 for more information on communal gardens.)

There were no sales in St John's Gardens in 2010.

James Ladbroke (p. 61) owned the land on which **Lansdowne Walk** was built. He entered into a building agreement with Richard Roy (p. 53) for the construction of the houses. Roy subleased building plots to other builders. For some reason, this and other local roads were named after Lord Lansdowne, a member of the House of Lords, with no obvious connection to the Estate. The houses are all on the south side; the north side is taken up with the gardens between the streets to the north. William Reynolds, who was Richard Roy's usual builder of choice, built Nos. 1-12 – the row from Ladbroke Grove to Lansdowne Road – in 1843 to 1845, and Nos. 16-19 – the houses west of Lansdowne Road – in 1845. Not all of the original houses still survive.

Nos. 1-5 Lansdowne Walk have rather massive porches and stone effect cladding at basement and ground floor level, and bare brick for the first and second floors. Nos. 7 and 8 are similar but without the second storey. Nos. 9, 10 and 11A are post-war in-fill buildings. No. 11a is a strange little infill with a small recessed ground floor entrance, a copper-plated first floor and nothing else above. Nos. 11-14, on the corner with Lansdowne Road, are back to the style of Nos. 1-5, but with bow windows for some of the houses. They seem to be deliberately laid out to be slightly asymmetrical. No. 14 was actually built in 1844 by Samuel Clothier, a marble mason, not by Reynolds. No. 15, on the other side, is similar to the earlier houses; the one glaring difference is a single hut-like structure on part of the roof. Nos.

16 and 16½ are pre-war and post-war respectively brick-faced rectangular houses. No. 16½ does look rather stylish on three storeys in a rather yellow brick with a rectangular side extension. Nos. 17-19 form a terrace with attractive porches. The central house has a bow window structure with a curving balcony on top; and the outer houses have flat windows and a bracketed balcony on top. Later houses continue along the street. They include some grand properties on basement, ground and two upper main storeys (plus attic rooms). Unusually, the entrance porch for No. 27 is at ground level but the canted bay windows are at raised ground level, so there must be stairs up inside.

Hanover Gardens

This communal garden of 1.9 acres lies between the east side of Lansdowne Road (p. 65) and the west side of Ladbroke Grove (p. 81) in the section between St John's Gardens (p. 75) and Lansdowne Walk (p. 76). It is quite a large garden square compared with some of the neighbouring gardens. It contains large lawns and woodland areas. The garden slopes slightly towards Lansdowne Walk. A meandering path runs through the centre of the garden, and there is also a path along the east side, both as originally designed. There is an entrance into the gardens opposite number 11 Lansdowne Walk. (See p. 180 for more information on communal gardens.)

If you have a property in Lansdowne Walk you may have rights of access to Hanover Gardens (p. 77) and/or the communal garden between Clarendon Road and Lansdowne Road (p. 55). But to find out if your property does have any such rights, you need to check with the garden committee. (See p. 180 for more information on communal gardens.)

Lansdowne Walk had one large house sale in 2010, with No. 16A selling for £4,250,000. A flat at No. 26 sold for £750,000 and two flats at Bartok House, No. 30, went for £540,000 and £660,000 respectively.

Secret gardens in Notting Hill

James Ladbroke (p. 61) didn't take much personal interest in the development of the Estate and generally gave a free hand to his estate surveyor, Thomas Allason (p. 78), while he concerned himself with country pursuits in West Sussex. Allason devised a lay-out plan consisting of a huge circle a mile across, cut into two equal halves by a straight road (the future Ladbroke Grove) running up from Holland Park Avenue. So far, this was vaguely derivative of Nash's Regent's Park. But Allason's major innovation was to propose only to build on the inside of the circle and the road, so that the houses would back onto 'secret gardens' accessed from the backs of the houses. The traditional Georgian squares of the period had their houses fronting onto a central garden across the road. Allason's scheme was not built, but the basic idea survived and 15 hidden gardens were ultimately built on the estate. (See p. 180 for more information on communal gardens.)

Ladbroke Road goes from Portland Road in the west to Kensington Park Road in the east. It is pierced by many other, more substantial, roads running across it, so it never gets a rhythm of its own. (The east section is east of Ladbroke Grove but is in this section to avoid splitting the road between sections.) The houses start on the south side near the junction with Kensington Park Road. Felix Ladbroke (p. 61) granted William Chadwick leases of Nos. 1-11 in 1847-8. Nos. 1-8 are now shops and other businesses with flats above in three-storey former houses. Nos. 2-10 form a single terrace as far as Horbury Crescent, with the houses on four storeys (including basements). Beyond Horbury

Crescent, Nos. 12-16 are detached or semi-detached houses.

Beyond Horbury Mews, No. 20 and 22 are semi-detached low-built houses on three main storeys. There is then a large pre-war mansion block called Bowden Court at No. 24 on five main storeys. This goes round the corner and a fair way back into Ladbroke Terrace.

Chadwick later bought the freehold of this area. In 1848, he granted leases of Nos. 13-19 to George Stephenson, a builder. From 1853 his son, W W Chadwick, leased Nos. 21-55 to William Wheeler. Nos. 9-25 (odd) are a variety of mainly three-storey semi-detached, or individual but connected, houses. Nos. 27-55 is a long terrace of three-storey terraced houses without basements which ends with No. 55 on the corner with Victoria Gardens. They have very decent front gardens, large enough to park a car in some cases. Beyond Ladbroke Terrace, Nos. 71-81 are terraced houses on basement, ground and two upper storeys, with additional rooms in the gable ends above the parapet. No. 83 was formerly a Victorian fire station with horse-drawn fire engines. It is now a ground floor flat and upper maisonette.

On the north side is the Ladbroke Arms Pub. This is a very attractive pub with seating outside at the front, which is south facing so it is a popular sun trap in the summer.

Between Ladbroke Grove and Lansdowne Road, there are nice houses on both sides, set back behind garden walls. On the south side, Bonham House, at No. 107, is a post-war brick-built block with a plastic fascia across most of the façade, which isn't too attractive, containing 18 flats. Nos. 109-119 are semi-detached houses in different styles but generally on four storeys and brick-faced. On the northern side of the road, there are some grander properties. No. 64 is a double-fronted stucco-faced detached house – now flats. Nos. 66-68 is called Weller Court and is a block of flats, on four main storeys (including basement) and additional rooms in the mansard roof. It is an attractive block of flats with off-road parking at the front and a private communal garden at the rear. Nos. 70-72 is similar, but without the mansard roof rooms. Nos. 66-72 were built by William Drew (p. 101), who was involved in much of the Ladbroke Road construction.

On the south side, Drew constructed the terrace from Nos. 109-119 in 1841. Cranleigh at No. 137 is a post-war block in dark brick on six storeys and containing 15 flats, with some pleasant front garden area. Mead House is a much bigger block on six storeys. On the north side of the road there is a little group of late-Victorian or early-Edwardian semi-detached houses at Nos. 80-86, with large front parking areas and high porched front doors. In 1845 William Drew arranged for James Ladbroke (p. 61) to allocate the land for Nos. 80-86 to Thomas Allason (p. 78), Ladbroke's surveyor, who then built the houses. The balustrades above the conjoined porches look like the sort of balconies on which South American dictators announce revolutions. Above the second-floor balustrades on Nos. 80 and 82, there are additional rooms in a steep roof.

Between Clarendon Road and Lansdowne Road there are small blocks of flats on the south side.

Three houses were sold in Ladbroke Road in 2010: No. 67 for £2,450,000, No. 19 for £2,925,000 and No. 55 for £1,942,000. A first-floor flat at No. 115 changed hands for £1,110,000. A flat at Cranleigh, Nos. 137-139, was sold for £690,000 and a flat at Weller Court, Nos. 66-68, for £775,000.

William Chadwick

William Chadwick built extensively in Southwark in the 1820s and in the City and Kensal Green in the 1830s. His first involvement in the Ladbroke Estate was to build stables for John Whyte's Hippodrome racecourse (p. 54). Whyte went bust in 1841 still owing Chadwick money, but Chadwick had taken the precaution of having the debt secured on the land and in 1843 he sold it to Charles Blake (p. 98). Chadwick also separately entered into a building agreement with James Ladbroke (p. 61) to develop 7 acres of land around the junction of Ladbroke Road and Kensington Park Road. By 1848 he had built and sold enough houses in Ladbroke Road, Kensington Park Road, and Pembridge Road to fulfil his financial commitment to Ladbroke, so he sold rights to the remaining land to other builders. Building in Notting Hill was speculative. Due to the frequent economic downturns, many builders went bankrupt. But Chadwick's experience and caution saw him through. Where other builders took on huge commitments which bankrupted them whenever the market slowed, Chadwick limited his commitments to what he could afford and prospered as a result.

Ladbroke Mews contains modern two-storey mews houses on the west side. Nos. 1-4 are painted white at ground floor level with bare brick for the first-floor above. No. 7 has an interesting curved front wall at first floor level extending over the garage. Nos. 7A and 7B at the end are new houses in white painted concrete and black window surrounds. No. 7B has particularly dramatic windows but not much of a view to take advantage of. The east side contains Nos. 8-13 which are mews houses with entrances up stairs along a narrow alley at the back, with barely bin room to pass, and they have a single upper storey with mainly garages on the side facing into the mews.

There were no sales in Ladbroke Mews in 2010 and the most recent sale was of No. 7A for £2,610,000 in 2009.

Building work in **Ladbroke Grove** began at the south end, near Holland Park Avenue, at a much earlier stage than most of the work on the Ladbroke Estate and then gradually progressed northwards. The first houses to be built were Nos. 11-19 (odd) on the west side, below Ladbroke Road. John Drew, a builder from Pimlico, took the lease from James Ladbroke (p. 61) in 1833. In 1838, Drew subleased Nos. 11-15 to William Drew (p. 101), to whom he was related, and R Charsley. These are traditional Victorian houses with long front gardens. Some of the houses have off-street parking.

The next bit to be built was Nos. 14-32 (even) on the east side, just above Ladbroke Road, which were built by J R Butler, a builder, in conjunction with George Buckle, a City architect. For Nos. 21-35, the terrace opposite, the building agreement in 1839 was between James Ladbroke and W J Drew, but Drew subleased the plots of Nos. 25-35 to Francis Read, a Pimlico builder, and Ladbroke granted the leases to him. The houses in this terrace are in pairs and the main part of the building is stucco-fronted and four windows wide (two for each house) separated by pilasters running from the ground floor to the roof line and apparently supporting heavy stonework above the first floor windows and a balustrade at the top of the house. The effect is dramatic but the plain flat pilasters are really little more than plaster strips, for decorative effect. The entrance doors are in separate low structures between the main buildings. The porticos of the houses were added later: Nos. 25-33 in 1857 and Nos. 31-35 in 1861. The terrace is painted in pastel shades, and in fact it was called 'Dulux Terrace' in the 1950s because it was sponsored by Dulux paints to show off their newly introduced range of paint colours. Further up Ladbroke Grove on the west side, Hillcrest, at Nos. 51 to 57, is a modern purpose-built block.

Ladbroke Grove Garden

This garden is a quarter of an acre of open area of grass with a few trees on the edge of Ladbroke Grove, where it joins with St John's Gardens (p. 81). (See p. 180 for more information on communal gardens.)

Nos. 36-40 were in part of the estate owned by Charles Blake (p. 98), and they were built in 1853, rather later than their neighbours, by David Ramsay (p. 65), to designs by Thomas Allom (p. 96). He went bankrupt before the houses were completed and they were finished by Philip Rainey, Blake's clerk of works. Nos. 42-58, in the centre of the crescents, were on Ladbroke land. The plot for Nos. 42-50 were let to Wiliam Parkin, a solicitor, in 1843, but he seems to have gone out of business and they were let them again in 1845, this time to John

Brown, a builder of St Marylebone. Ladbroke also leased Nos. 52-58 to him. Nos. 60-64 were built by Henry Malcolm Ramsay in 1854 and Nos. 66-68 were built by the Paddington builder, John Wicking Phillips, in 1858-61.

On the other side of Ladbroke Grove, No. 63 was built in 1844 by Joshua Higgs and Son, builders from Berkeley Square, on a large plot of land on the corner of Lansdowne Crescent. Ladbroke had agreed to let it to Richard Roy (p. 53) who subleased it to Higgs. Nos. 67-75 (odd) are right in the centre of the crescent, on the west side. They were built in 1841-2 on land then still owned by the solicitor, John Duncan. No. 83 was a single small plot on the corner with Arundel Gardens and a house was built there in 1852 by Kenelm Chandler, a builder. No. 87 is equally an isolated plot just above Elgin Crescent, and the house there was built by Edwin Ware, the Paddington builder, in 1862.

Nos. 91 and 93, just below Blenheim Crescent, were built by Richard Crowley in 1863 on land owned by Charles Chambers, a timber merchant. Nos. 78-94 were built opposite them, on the east side. They are believed to have been designed by the architect, Edward Habershon. There is then a relatively long range of houses between Blenheim Crescent and Westbourne Park Road, comprising Nos. 95-119. This was land owned by Charles Blake (p. 98) and it was George Drew, an architect, who agreed to build the houses in 1864. He seems to have built Nos. 95-109, but C A Daw, Builders, probably built Nos. 111-119 because Drew arranged for Blake to grant the lease of those houses direct to them.

There is a short range, Nos. 121-129, between Westbourne Park Road and Ladbroke Crescent which were built by G and T Goodwin in 1863. Nos. 98-104, between Westbourne Park Road and Ladbroke Crescent, were built by Edmund and Elias Cordery, builders from Bayswater, in 1860.

If you have a property in Ladbroke Grove, you may have rights of access to one or more of Ladbroke Grove Garden (p. 82), Hanover Gardens (p. 77) and/or Stanley Crescent Garden (p. 95) and/or Lansdowne Crescent Garden (p. 73). But to find out if your property does have any such rights, you need to check with the relevant garden committee. (See p. 180 for more information on communal gardens.)

No. 81 Ladbroke Grove was sold in 2010 for £5,300,000. A flat at No. 85 changed hands for £873,100 and another at No. 45 for £840,000. A second-floor flat at No. 86 was sold for £627,500 and a flat at No. 41 was sold for £605,000. A basement flat at No. 84 went for £519,000 and a flat at No. 70 was £540,000. There were two sales for £330,000 at No. 70 and at No. 112.

Notting Hill: Ladbroke Grove to Portobello Road

QUICK REFERENCE						
STREET	PAGE	STREET	PAGE	STREET	PAGE
Arundel Gardens	90	Ladbroke Gardens	91	Stanley Gardens	97
Horbury Crescent	106	Ladbroke Square	101	Victoria Gardens	105
Horbury Mews	105	Ladbroke Terrace	104	Westbourne Park Road	85
Kensington Park Gardens	99	Ladbroke Walk	104	Wilby Mews	103
		Portobello Road	107		
Kensington Park Road	86	Stanley Crescent	94		

Westbourne Park Road was constructed on land owned by Thomas Pocock (p. 85). He granted leases of Nos. 292-302 to Elias Cordery, a builder, in 1863. Cordery probably also built Nos. 304-314. Charles Blake (p. 98), who owned some of the land, granted leases for Nos. 316-352 to Cordery in 1860. On the south side, Nos. 305-317 (odd) were built by Paul Felthouse, a builder, in 1863. Nos. 319-351 were built by Cordery in 1863 under leases from Pocock. (Nos. 347-351 have been demolished.)

It is a long road and it is only residential in parts, so we are not attempting to describe the properties.

There were a large number of flat sales in Westbourne Park Road in 2010. Many of them were in the region of £500,000 or less. But a property at No. 72 sold for £2,410,000, a flat at No. 31A for £1,140,000 and a house at No. 340 for £1,365,000.

Thomas Pocock

Thomas Pocock was a lawyer in the City. But he turns up as a builder or developer in the Ladbroke Estate over almost the whole period of development there. He was often acting on behalf of wealthier clients, although he did take on some houses for his own account. His involvement started in 1846 when Felix Ladbroke agreed to sell him 30 acres. Either Pocock could not afford it, or he was always acting as an agent, but he immediately sold most of the land on to the Reverend Brooke Bridges, a parson in Bedfordshire, and kept only 4 acres for himself, most of which was between Kensington Park Road and Portobello Road. The land had already been leased by James Ladbroke to George Penson, a Newgate Street cheesemonger. It seems that Pocock represented Penson as well. He appeared at a hearing before the Commissioners for Sewers as his solicitor. From 1847 onwards Pocock took over the active management of the development on behalf of himself, Bridges and Penson. (By 1855, Bridges sold off most of his land to Dr Walker (p. 71), presumably at an attractive profit since Walker was no businessman.) In 1846 Pocock agreed to buy 33 acres north of Lansdowne Rise from Richard Roy (p. 53), but in the end bought five acres which he later sold on to Charles Blake (p. 98). Pocock also took leases from other land owners in the area. He leased 30 plots on Clarendon Road from Stephen Phillips (p. 74) and Nos. 61-75 (odd) Lansdowne Road from Walker. When Walker's business failed, he took over the half-finished houses in Lansdowne Road and Elgin Crescent from Walker's trustees and completed them. Pocock's main source of finance was Penson, who took mortgages on many of his properties. Pocock lived on the estate. His home was No. 30 Ladbroke Square for many years, before he moved to No. 24 Ladbroke Gardens, where he died in 1869. Penson died in 1879.

On the east side of **Kensington Park Road**, near the Pembridge Road junction, there is a long terrace from Nos. 8A-30 which were built by William Chadwick in 1848. These compact houses on four storeys (including raised ground floors and basements), are brick-faced with fairly square undecorated windows, and box-like balconies at first-floor level. Nos. 32-38 are two very large semi-detached, stucco-faced houses on four main storeys (including basements and gable rooms).

It was over a decade before construction began on the west side of the road. John Wicking Phillips, a Paddington builder, built Nos. 1-11 between the church and Horbury Crescent, in 1861. They are large and ornately decorated, stucco-faced houses on five storeys (including basements)

Returning to the east side, there is a series of mansion blocks. The buildings have a stone facing at ground and first floor level and are then red brick above. The signature style of these blocks is that they have bays all the way up, which are flat at the front, but have curved sides. No. 44 is a 1930s-style, red-brick block, containing 17 flats on five upper storeys. Matlock Court at No. 46 contains 57 flats, Buckingham Court at No. 48 has 57 flats, and Princes House at No. 52 has 56 flats. These blocks all go a long way back. Latimer House is a 1960s brick building with 16 flats, going through to Sarum House, with 8 flats. More traditional Victorian terraces begin again at No. 56 through to No. 70 on the corner with Chepstow Villas. The various houses have five main storeys. All the houses are set fairly well back from the main road, with unusually wide balconies running along the front at first-floor level; some of these balconies have canopies on top as well. This range of houses was built by Thomas Pocock, one of the several solicitors who embarked on property development in the Ladbroke Estate.

Ladbroke Square Garden

This communal garden lies behind the south side of Kensington Park Gardens (p. 99) and runs right to Ladbroke Square (p. 101). At seven acres this is the largest garden on the Ladbroke Estate (p. 61) and it is grade II listed. It was laid out between 1837 and

1849 to the designs of Thomas Allason (p. 78), the designer of this part of the Notting Hill area. This is not a hidden garden: it is open on three sides, but protected by railings. The entrance is through a gate opposite number No. 60 Kensington Park Road. The garden slopes downwards towards Ladbroke Square. There are mainly lawns in the centre, with paths winding round them. There is a circular flower bed (originally a fountain) surrounded by ornamental cast-iron urns on piers. One of a pair of wooden summerhouses survives, as well as a gardener's cottage in the north-east corner of the site. Many of the original trees remain; these include plane, lime, beech, oak, hawthorn and horse chestnut trees. (See p. 180 for more information on communal gardens.)

North of the junction with Chepstow Villas, there is a terrace from Nos. 74A-90. These houses are much closer to the street, with dramatically large and decorated tri-partite first-floor windows. These houses are on basement, ground and three upper storeys, although No. 88 has an additional fourth upper storey. Some of the terrace is occupied by an embassy. The land belonged to Charles Blake (p. 98). Nos. 76-90 were built in about 1859 by Philip Rainey, who had previously been Blake's clerk of works. The houses were designed by Edward Habershon. The houses opposite are part of Stanley Gardens. Past St Peter's Church on the east side, there is a big post-war block of flats in dark brick and white-painted concrete on four upper storeys, called Waterford House, which contains 40 flats. Before the corner with Westbourne Grove, Nos. 114-120 is a Victorian brick-faced terrace on four storeys, with shops on the ground floor and flats above.

North of Westbourne Grove, Thomas Pocock (p. 85) owned the land up to Elgin Crescent, and in about 1853 he constructed Nos. 126-184, on the east side of Kensington Park Road. Nos. 124-146 is a terrace of houses on four storeys (including the basement). They have got a slightly villagey feel to them with decent front areas, and they have three-part first floor windows with curved heads opening onto little balconies over paired entrances. Nos. 148-158 is a terrace which is so unified in appearance (with the central houses under a large triangular pediment headed 'Kensington Park Terrace North') that it almost looks like the front of a hospital. Further along, the houses are on basement, ground and two upper storeys. Unusually, the ground storeys have balconies outside the front windows, and then a continuous balcony outside the first-floor windows. A unique feature is that they all have a kind of wrought iron metal framing below the first-floor balcony in place of columns: it is rather charming, with a kind of swastika pattern with flowers, hopefully the Indian version rather than the Nazi one. A similar design appears in houses in Northumberland Place in Artesian Village. No. 16? starts again with an attractive terrace, very like the one previously described before, at Kensington Park Terrace North. These houses are all on four storeys and are stucco painted to give the appearance of stonework underneath, and painted in warm colours. The first-floor windows are curved and come in twos or threes. Up to No. 170 the first-floor windows have metal balconies and are grouped in threes. From No. 172 the first-floor windows are in pairs with balustrades. No. 100 is occupied by an embassy.

If you have a property in Kensington Park Road you may have rights of access to Stanley Garden South and/or Stanley Garden North (p. 97). But to find out if your property does have any such rights, you need to check with the garden committee. (See p. 180 for more information on communal gardens.)

Some houses changed hands in Kensington Park Road in 2010. No. 168 sold for £2,650,000, No. 146 for £1,950,000 and No. 184 for £2,225,000. There was also a sale at No. 176 for £2,750,000. The largest flat sales included two flats at Buckingham Court, No. 48, which went for £1,795,000 and £1,500,000 respectively, an upper maisonette at No. 212 for £1,385,000 and a flat at No. 7 for £1,600,000. There were also a few small flat sales, including three flats at No. 84, which went for prices between £400,000 and £580,000.

Bulmer Mews is a modern courtyard development of mews-style properties. Nos. 1-7 have recessed front doors and garages on ground floor, a first-floor above, and then a second storey in the mansard roof behind the top parapet wall. No. 8 is the basement of one of the houses in Ladbroke Road. It is a quiet little area, despite the heavy traffic on Kensington Park Road.

There were no sales in Bulmer Mews in 2010.

Arundel Gardens consists of two sets of facing terraces which were constructed in 1862 to 1863. The range of houses on the north side are Nos. 2-50. (Nos. 2-6 are physically in Kensington Park Road.) Edwin Ware was the builder of Nos. 2-14. Builders of other houses in the range included G W Simmonds and Leonard Cowling. These are four storey houses (including basements). The basement flats are set a decent distance back from the area wall, and then there are steps up to a porticoed front entrance, which has a canted bay for the ground floor windows next to it. Decorative iron railings run on top of the portico and the bay, and two sets of sash windows open onto them. The window surrounds are elaborately decorated with half sunken pillars and a profusion of entwined flowers in plasterwork. The second floor windows above have an almost violin-like shape to them. The third floor windows are normal square-headed windows but with just a hint of the violin shape at the bottom. There is a cornice running along the top of the facade but mansard rooms have been constructed in the sloping roof above that. The houses are all stuccoed and painted in various colours.

Arundel and Ladbroke Gardens

This communal garden of 1.2 acres is between the southern side of Arundel Gardens (p. 90) and the north side of Ladbroke Gardens (p. 91), in the section between Ladbroke Grove (p. 81) and Kensington Park Road (p. 86). The entrance is opposite No. 134 Kensington Park Road, and there are some steps down into the garden. It is quite a heavily wooded garden, with several very mature plane trees and a number of other well-established trees, with lawns and colourful flower beds and meandering gravel paths. The garden slopes quite steeply towards Kensington Park Road. (See p. 180 for more information on communal gardens.)

The houses on the south side are Nos. 1-47 (odd). The builder, William Wheeler, constructed most of them. These houses have the same number of storeys as those on the west side but are rather different in design. The porches are deeper, but the houses don't have bays. There is no continuous balcony along the front of the building, but there is a balcony above the porch, although it's inconveniently positioned for anyone to actually get out on to it. The houses are mainly stuccoed with horizontal lines suggesting stonework up to ground floor level, and then bare brick above, although the window surrounds are painted white. The windows were mainly traditional rectangles with architraves supported by brackets. The original Nos. 43-47 were later demolished and replaced by Arundel Court, a cream-painted, post-war building, which contains 21 flats.

If you have a property in Arundel Gardens you may have rights of access to Arundel and Elgin Communal Garden (p. 63) and/or Arundel and Ladbroke Gardens (p. 90). But to find out if your property does have any such rights, you need to check with the relevant garden committee. (See p. 180 for more information on communal gardens.)

There were quite a few flat sales in Arundel Gardens in 2010. The highest prices were £1,545,000 for a flat at No. 9 and £1,325,000 for a flat at No. 38. Slightly below that, £840,000 was paid for a flat at No. 10, £775,000 for a flat at No. 44A and £735,000 for a flat at No. 21. Various other flat sales were at prices from £283,000 up to £615,000.

Ladbroke Gardens is the continuation of Lansdowne Crescent across Ladbroke Grove. The house numbers run down the north side and back up the south side. When it was constructed, the land was owned by Richard Roy (p. 53), a solicitor. He employed Thomas Allom (p. 96) to design Nos. 1-23 Ladbroke Gardens Building started in 1858, with W Parratt and John Falconer as the builders, after the original builders, G Wilson and James Emmins, went bankrupt. They weren't too successful either and the houses were not finished till 1866 when the work was taken over by another builder, W Wheeler.

The north side starts with Nos. 1-14 (No. 1 is on the corner facing onto Ladbroke Grove.) The houses are on six storeys (including basements and attic rooms). Each house has a basement, and the steps go straight down from the street edge to a paved basement area. There are leisurely steps up to grand double entrance, with two ground floor windows next to it. Above, there is a balcony running right the way along the terrace, which the tall first-floor windows open onto. The windows in these houses are quite elaborate: the first-floor windows are in Greek style with flowery decorations and, unusually, the second floor windows are even more elaborately decorated with scallop designs. The houses are all stuccoed and painted cream or pastel colours. The houses at each end have bow window structures up to first-floor level, with balconies on top for the second floors. Nos. 12 and 13 have pillared porches with first-floor balconies on top, which unbalances the overall design of the terrace. Nos. 15-22 (No. 15 is entered round the corner in Kensington Park Road) is a terrace of similar design. But the ground floors are not so raised, and they all have walled-in porch entrances which provide little balconies at first-floor level. These houses also have six storeys, almost identical with the earlier terrace, but all a little bit smaller, so that the balustrade level at the top of the façade is a few feet lower. The ground slopes steeply down at the back of the terraces, so many of the houses were constructed with basement and sub-basement rooms at the front, but because of the slope, the sub-basements are garden level at the back.

Stanley Garden North

This communal garden lies behind the north side of Stanley Gardens (p. 97) and the houses on the south side of Ladbroke Gardens in the stretch between Stanley Crescent (p. 94) and

Kensington Park Road (p. 86). It slopes sharply downhill towards Kensington Park Road. A wide path runs along the south side of the garden. The garden, which covers nine-tenths of an acre, was designed with a central path, which has been grassed over. The original trees include hawthorn, lime and a central elm tree. Other trees, including a magnolia, were planted in the last century. (See p. 180 for more information on communal gardens.)

The south side of Ladbroke Gardens begins with No. 24 on the corner. Nos. 25-31 have entrances like normal houses, but the overall structure is more like that of a huge mansion block. They were laterally converted in the 1960s to provide decent-sized flats. The houses have shared porch structures on the street edge, which then have rooms above on the first, second and third storeys. The 'real' front of the building faces onto the gardens at the back where there is a basement, a ground floor with substantial canted bays, a first floor with stone balustrading, two further upper floors, with an elaborate cornice, and a fourth floor above that. Across Stanley Crescent, Nos. 34 and 35 comprise two large semi-detached houses with basements, very raised ground floors, and three upper storeys. The houses are built in mirror style, with entrance doors side-by-side in the middle and bow windows on the outer sides. The bow window structures rise to the first-floor level, providing balconies for the second floors. The original houses were built between 1858 and 1861 by John Wicking Phillips, a Paddington builder, but they were rebuilt in similar style in the 1970s.

If you have a property in Ladbroke Gardens you may have rights of access to Arundel and Ladbroke Gardens (p. 90) and/or Stanley Garden North (p. 92) and/or Stanley Crescent Garden (p. 95). But to find out if your property does have any such rights, you need to check with the relevant garden committee. (See p. 180 for more information on communal gardens.)

In 2010, No. 3 Ladbroke Gardens was sold for £6,400,000, and there were two flat sales at No. 10 for £810,000 and £443,000 respectively.

Unlike Lansdowne Crescent, where houses were built on both sides of the road, the houses in **Stanley Crescent** were only built on the west side (with their backs facing the gardens). The road was apparently named after Lord Stanley, a leading member of the House of Lords when the area was being developed. Charles Blake (p. 98) owned the land and he granted leases for the construction of Nos. 1-13 to David Ramsay (p. 65) in 1853. The houses were designed by Thomas Allom (p. 96). Ramsay went bankrupt in 1854 but his houses were completed by Philip Rainey, who was Blake's clerk of works. The story goes that the street was originally nicknamed 'The Sticks' because individual builders put up single narrow houses on their plots, and the houses were only gradually joined together as terraces by the gaps being filled in by other builders; the gap between No. 8 and No. 9 was filled with a lift shaft for the converted flats.

These are all large and elaborate buildings in two conjoined terraces. They all have ground, first and second storeys. Some of the houses nearer the middle of the terrace have a third storey. The houses have raised entrances beneath high pillared porches, with a stone balustraded balcony on top. The ground floor windows have curved heads, and the plasterwork has been carefully worked to give the appearance of stonework radiating round the windows. A unifying architectural feature is the carved coil design beneath the first-floor windows, but apart from that, different decorative features appear all the way along, from triangular pediments with scrolling brackets to Greek-style sunken pillars with flowering heads. As the numbers progress, the houses start to have canted bays up to first-floor level. Houses differ in size, as can be seen from the different number and size of ground floor windows. The first terrace appears to end at No. 9. Nos. 10 and 11 form a semi-detached building with entrances on either side, built in mirror style to look a bit like a Renaissance Italian castle, with turrets on either side providing a third floor, with the roof in between. Nos. 12 and 13 also form a semi-detached building which is similar in size, also with large canted bays side-by-side in the middle, and rising up to a third floor with an elaborate cornice above. There is an additional fourth storey above No. 13 and a fifth storey in the sloping roof, which looks fairly new. These semi-detached houses, in fact, have connections to the terraces on either side and to each other. There is a particularly elaborate connection at third storey level with an oriel window between Nos. 13 and 14.

Stanley Crescent Garden

This half-moon communal garden of 1.68 acres lies between the east side of Ladbroke Grove (p. 81) and the west side of Stanley Crescent (p. 94), in the section between Ladbroke Gardens (p. 91) and Kensington Park Gardens (p. 99). It still retains the original features and design from when the houses were constructed in the 1850s. There is a gravel path along the straight west side, running between gated entrances in Kensington Park Gardens and Ladbroke Gardens. The garden is made up of three large lawns edged with trees and shrubs and separated by gravel paths. There are also further areas of shrubbery where paths meet. In the middle of the garden is a large Victorian decorative urn. The trees include ash, horse chestnut, beech, lime and plane. (See p. 180 for more information on communal gardens.)

Blake sold the remaining land around Stanley Crescent to H and W Gardner, who were brewers, and in 1862 they granted leases of the remaining plots to the north, which were Nos. 14-23, to another builder, William Wheeler. He apparently used Allom's designs too, but in fact they look a very different style of property. Nos. 14-17 are conjoined semi-detached houses on basement, ground and three very grand upper storeys beneath a prominent cornice, and then topped by a final smaller fourth storey. The windows are triples and are stuccoed and painted, but the facade above ground level is bare brick. The same style applies for Nos. 18-23, which is a terrace running round the corner into Ladbroke Gardens. These are all on six storeys, including a basement and a fourth floor above the cornice.

If you have a property in Stanley Crescent you may have rights of access to Stanley Crescent Garden (p. 95) and/or Stanley Garden North (p. 92) and/or Stanley Garden South (p. 97). But to find out if your property does have any such rights, you need to check with the garden committee. (See p. 180 for more information on communal gardens.)

We are unaware of any sales in Stanley Crescent since 2004, when a flat at No. 20 was sold for £1,310,000.

Thomas Allom

Thomas Allom was a founder member of the Royal Institute of British Architects. He was also a recognised artist who exhibited at the Royal Academy. Allom's involvement with the Ladbroke Estate was mainly as the architect for Charles Blake (p. 98). But he also designed houses for Richard Roy (p. 53) and Dr Walker (p. 71) and his designs were used by Felix Ladbroke (p. 61) as blue-prints which houses builders were expected to follow. Allom also designed St Peter's Church, which was built on Blake's land in 1855-7. Apart from houses, Allom also contributed some of the street layout plans, and he designed Stanley Crescent and Stanley Gardens. He broke with the traditional formal house design and adopted a more naturalistic approach, with trees and gardens to break up the formal layout. His terrace designs were noted for adding bow windows and other projections at the ends of terraces to make them more interesting. His designs mainly used paired houses with a considerable amount of ornamentation in the favoured Victorian fashion. He did not ignore the backs of his houses where they faced the gardens. They all have interesting facades. He died in 1872 – the same year as Blake.

Stanley Gardens took its name from Lord Stanley, a member of the House of Lords when the Ladbroke Estate was being developed. The land on which it was built belonged to Charles Blake (p. 98) and in 1853 he granted leases to David Ramsay (p. 65) for the construction of houses on both sides of the street. The houses themselves were designed by Thomas Allom (p. 96). Ramsey went bankrupt in 1854 and Blake then split up the work among various builders. Nos. 1-11, on the north side of Stanley Gardens, is a terrace running from Stanley Crescent to Kensington Park Road (with No. 1 facing onto Stanley Crescent and No. 11 onto Kensington Park Road). These houses were built by a firm of builders called Locke and Nesham.

Stanley Garden South

This communal garden of one and a half acres lies behind the south side of Stanley Gardens (p. 97) and the north side of Kensington Park Gardens (p. 99). There is a gated entrance on the north side of Kensington Park Gardens. The original network of paths still exists. A children's play area has replaced one of the original circular flower beds. (See p. 180 for more information on communal gardens.)

On the south side of Stanley Gardens, the street numbers start with Nos. 12-15, but the houses of this terrace are, in fact, entirely on Kensington Park Road. The houses were built by the firm of J W Sanders. They are on five storeys (including the basement) with a central structure topped at third-floor level with an enormous triangular pediment. The next series of houses, Nos. 16-29, were built by Philip Rainey, who was Charles Blake's clerk of works. Nos. 16 and 17 turn the corner into Stanley Gardens proper and are distinguished by large bow window structures up to the second storey. The terrace proper then continues with Nos. 18-27. At No. 22 is The Portobello Hotel, a well known boutique hotel. Nos. 28 and 29, turning the corner, have a similar bow window construction as the earlier houses. The houses of the main terraces have basement, ground and three upper main storeys, with additional rooms in the side of the pitched roofs. The houses all have large entrance doors in a columned porch, usually between a pair of round-headed windows, set in a plasterwork design of radiating grooves. There is a railed balcony right along the front of the terrace outside the first floor windows, which are tall, usually grouped in threes, and decorated with the heads of Greek columns. The second floor windows are almost as impressive and come with nicely designed window bars radiating at the top for the circular heads, and a coiled plasterwork design underneath the sills (which is repeated in other nearby streets). There's a pronounced cornice and then a third storey, and finally rooms in the sloping roof. The houses are all stucco-faced and painted.

If you have a property in Stanley Gardens you may have rights of access to Stanley Garden South (p. 97) and/or Stanley Garden North (p. 92). But to find out if your property does have any such rights, you need to check with the relevant garden committee. (See p. 180 for more information on communal gardens.)

Stanley Gardens saw a variety of flat sales in 2010, ranging from a flat at Gregory House, which changed hands at £285,000, up to a flat at No. 15, which sold for £1,595,000.

Charles Blake

Charles Blake became the most successful developer in Notting Hill, although he had some close shaves along the way. Blake was an indigo plantation owner in Bengal. He left India for England in 1842 and went into property development. In the 1850s Blake bought and sold various chunks of the Ladbroke Estate. It was knife's edge stuff. He bought the land north of Lansdowne Rise and Crescent, then sold it to Dr Walker (p. 71) for what he had paid for it – which was a smart deal because the market then collapsed. He left part of the price outstanding, but when he demanded the money, Walker went bust. So Blake bought the land back from the trustees in bankruptcy - effectively buying from himself – gambling that the market was picking up and he could build and sell the houses at a profit. By the late 1850s land values were beginning to rise again in Notting Hill, and Blake made a fortune. When the houses were built, Blake bought them back from the builders and sold them at a profit to investors. He kept his Stanley Gardens and Stanley Crescent houses for rental income. He died in Bournemouth in 1872, a very rich man.

Kensington Park Gardens is one of the best addresses in Notting Hill, despite the lack of private parking, and it contains many single-family houses. Houses on the south side are generally larger than those on the north side. Nos. 1-9 on the south side of the road, starting on the corner with Kensington Park Road, were built by William Drew (p. 101) on land allocated to him by Felix Ladbroke (p. 61) in 1949-50. Nos. 1-3 Kensington Park Gardens is a huge brick and stuccoed building, containing a number of flats. Nos. 4 and 6 are traditional cream-painted houses. No. 5 was later demolished and replaced by a huge red-brick Edwardian building containing eight flats on six storeys with improbable bays and decorated with terracotta tiles. Nos. 7 and 8 are another pair of large houses on five storeys. In 1880, when it was occupied by a scientist, William Crookes, No. 7 was the first house in England to use electricity. Most of the rest of the south side is occupied by Nos. 10-22, which were built in 1852 by David Ramsay (p. 65) to designs by Thomas Allom (p. 96). These are quite wide houses on five main storeys (including basements). The entrance structures are unusual, with the porches sunk into the front of the buildings and the doors set back. (Nos. 12 and 13, where the terraces meet, have entrances in a conjoined side porch structure.) Each house has a balcony, mostly separate, outside the very tall first-floor windows, which are extravagantly decorated with an impressed design like a triumphant Roman arch, topped with an architrave. There are smaller balconies outside the second-floor windows, which are decorated with a plaster pattern, almost like Celtic lettering. Most houses have one more storey above the cornice with smaller windows, although Nos. 16 and 17 have two storeys above the cornice. Up to ground floor level, the plaster is incised to look like stonework, and the houses are stuccoed and painted cream or pastel colours.

On the south side, the street starts, on the corner with Ladbroke Grove, with a big mansion block called The Lodge, a 1930s-style building on six storeys, containing 23 flats. The original terraces on the north side then begin with No. 24. Ladbroke allocated the whole of this side of the road to Charles Blake (p. 98) in 1852 for the construction of more terraces to designs by Thomas Allom (p. 96). Blake built Nos. 24 and 25 and Nos. 32-35 – he actually kept No. 24 as his own home. But he arranged for David Ramsay (p. 65), his fellow developer, to build Nos. 26-31 and Nos. 36-47. (No. 26 and Nos. 28-30 were completed by J D Cowland.) The houses on the north side of Kensington Park Gardens are not quite as grand as on the south side. They generally have five storeys (including basements) with the top (third) floor above a cornice. But Nos. 29-31 and Nos. 36-40 have tiled mansard roofs with windows let into them instead. No. 40 has two main storeys above the cornice. Nos. 41-45 have the more usual one main storey above the cornice, but in addition have mansard roofs with rooms in them above that. The first terrace ends with No. 33, and a new terrace begins with No. 34; between them is an arched entrance into the private gardens of Stanley Garden South (p. 97) at the back. The terrace runs round the corner to No. 47, into Kensington Park Road, with bow window structures facing out on each of the two sides. There is a long balcony running along the length of each terrace at first-floor level, and widening out over the house porches. The first-floor windows are tall but narrow, sometimes separate, sometimes forming a triple structure topped with a semicircular pediment, but nothing like as elaborate as the first floor windows of the southern houses.

If you have a property in Kensington Park Gardens you may have rights of access to Ladbroke Square Garden (p. 87) and/or Stanley Garden South (p. 97). But to find out if your property does have any such rights, you need to check with the relevant garden committee. (See p. 180 for more information on communal gardens.)

There were a number of sales in 2010 at The Lodge, Kensington Park Gardens, for prices between £1,000,000 and £2,950,000. There were two sales at 5 Kensington Park Gardens for £1,850,000 and £950,000. No. 47 is a freehold house, which was sold for £5,700,000.

William John Drew

In the 1830s William John Drew entered into a building agreement with James Ladbroke (p. 61), the owner of the Ladbroke Estate (p. 61), to take an area of building land on either side of Ladbroke Road, between Ladbroke Grove and Portland Road. Drew built about 50 houses during the 1840s. Most of Drew's houses were designed by Thomas Allason (p. 78). Drew did not build any more houses after 1851, but he lived until 1878.

Ladbroke Square is not a square – it's just a single street; in fact, it only has houses along the southern side of the street. But there is the very large Ladbroke Square Garden (p. 87) at the front. The house numbers start at Ladbroke Grove and then run to Kensington Park Road. No. 1, on the corner of Ladbroke Grove, is slightly out of place because it was built as a single house by W H Rowlings, a builder from Theobalds Road, in 1851, and it is smaller than the rest of the terrace. It has four main storeys, with rooms in the attic, and canted bays up to first-floor level. Ladbroke Square House, at Nos. 2-3, is a large double-fronted building on seven storeys (including mansard rooms), which was presumably built as a block of flats, and it contains 19 flats.

There is then a range of houses from Nos. 4-22, which runs to the corner of Ladbroke Terrace. Nos. 4-17 were built in 1856-60 by William Wheeler. These houses have stuccoed basement and ground storeys, with a single porched entrance for the raised main door, and a single ground floor window beside it. Above, there is a wrought-iron railed balcony running right along the terrace. There are first, second and third storeys with a cornice above, and a smaller fourth storey below the top of the facade. These floors are brick-faced but the window surrounds are stuccoed and painted cream. The central houses, Nos. 10-13, are slightly grander, with triple windows and taller rooms. Nos. 20-22 are slightly different, with shared porches, stone balustrades for the first-floor balconies, and they lack a fourth storey. Nos. 20-22 were built first in 1844 by John Brown, a St Marylebone builder.

On the other side of Ladbroke Terrace is a range of houses, Nos. 23-47, which run to the corner with Kensington Park Road. In the early 1840s, Jacob Connop owned the lease on this part of the estate, which had been part of Whyte's racecourse. In 1843, Connop arranged for James Ladbroke (p. 61) to grant leases of the plots for Nos. 23-27 Ladbroke Square to his solicitor, William Parkin. (Parkin may have been trying his hand at speculative building on his own account or it may have been security for a loan to Connop.) Nos. 23-27 are a simpler design than the previous terrace; they are more severe and less decorated. The houses are stuccoed up to ground floor level and bare brick above. French windows open onto a balcony at first level and there is a second and third storey above. The next group, Nos. 28-31, were leased to C H Grove, another solicitor, at Connop's request in 1844, and possibly also as security for loans. Nos. 33-37 went to Connop's architect, John Stevens. In 1846 Ladbroke allocated No. 38 direct to Henry Monson, a St Marylebone builder, and Nos. 39-47 were allocated to J T Crossthwaite, a builder from Addiscombe. Between them they created the terrace which runs from Nos. 28-40A. These houses are stuccoed at basement and ground level, but otherwise they are not particularly decorated. They have balconies above the porches, some of which are single and some conjoined, many of which are walled in like lobbies with the entrance door at the front. These houses have higher, taller first-floor windows than the previous ones, with a second storey above that, then a deep cornice, and finally a third storey. (No. 40 lacks the third storey above the cornice.) Nos. 41-46 make up the final terrace, also with walled-in lobby porches, and are also stuccoed up to ground floor level. They have tall first floors with French doors opening onto a continuous balcony, quite wide second floor windows above, and a third floor above the cornice. No. 47, round the corner, faces onto Kensington Park Road.

If you have a property in Ladbroke Square you may have rights of access to Ladbroke Square Garden (p. 87). But to find out if your property does have any such rights, you need to check with the garden committee. (See p. 180 for more information on communal gardens.)

In 2010, two houses were sold in Ladbroke Square: No. 47 for £5,750,000 and No. 26 for £6,200,000. Among the flat sales, a flat at No. 5 sold for £1,475,000, a flat at No. 14 for £840,000, a flat at No. 12 for £635,000 and a flat at No. 29 for £583,500.

Wilby Mews is right next to the Ladbroke Arms. It is a very wide cobbled yard and it contains a variety of old and new mews properties. On the west side there are some original mews houses. No. 2 onwards form a single terrace of two-storey properties, with a larger central house. There are newer mews houses at the end and on the east side. Nos. 15-16A were clearly built as a group after the 1970s, with garages, one main upper storey and rooms in the roof.

There is no record of any sales in Wilby Mews since No. 4 was bought in 2006 for £770,000.

Notting Hill Gate

Notting Hill Gate is a modern name for what the Victorians called 'Kensington Gravel Pits'. Present-day Notting Hill Gate is the site of one of the earliest toll gates, where travellers along Bayswater Road and Holland Park Avenue (as they are today) were taxed. In the 18th and 19th centuries, 'turnpike trusts' were set up to take tolls from users of roads to pay for their upkeep. Streets off the main road were barricaded to make sure people didn't get round the tollgate. The tollgate wasn't abolished till 1864.

Ladbroke Terrace starts on the east side with Nos. 3 and 4, which are a pair of conjoined, very wide, low-rise villas set back behind front gardens. These were built in 1826 by Robert Cantwell (p. 36) an architect and builder. These join No. 5, which is a much larger white-painted house on four main storeys, also built by Cantwell in 1833. Above Ladbroke Road, Nos. 7-9 are very wide double-fronted detached villas with basements, very high raised ground floors, two upper storeys and additional rooms in the sloping roof. Nos. 7 and 8 may have been built by Cantwell, but he may have given the building work to William Drew (p. 101). Either Cantwell or Drew built Nos. 10 and 11. Cantwell arranged for Drew to take the lease of No. 12 and for William Liddard to take the lease of No. 13 in 1838.

The numbers go up to Ladbroke Square and come back again on the west side of Ladbroke Terrace, so the houses opposite, between Ladbroke Road and Ladbroke Walk, are Nos. 14-17. This is an extremely tall terrace on basement, ground, three upper storeys and then additional rooms in the gable ends. It is brick-faced except for the white painted plaster of the window and door surrounds and the quoins. Balconies run along the front of the building at first floor level. On the west side also is Chartwell House, an extremely large 1980s development, with plenty of parking at the front, and five main storeys and a penthouse storey. The building contains 31 flats, with a resident warden, next to a nursing home.

In Ladbroke Terrace, all the 2010 sales were of flats in No. 12 Chartwell House. (It was the same in 2009). Prices ranged from £595,000 to £700,000.

Ladbroke Walk is quite a wide cobbled street, which actually looks like a village street because there's very little uniformity. All the houses look as if they were individually built, and they display a mixture of bare brick or painted facades. Most of the houses are on two storeys, with the traditional garage entrance at ground floor level and an entrance door beside it to the first-floor living accommodation. Most of the houses also have additional mansard rooms in the sloping roofs. Nos. 25-29 (continuous) on the north side seem to have been built as a single terrace, judging by the identical window heads and brick cornices. The houses are most individualistic on the south side. No. 10, rather strangely, has a blank wall where you would expect a ground floor window. Many of the houses have steeply sloping tiled roofs, so that the second floors there are more full-scale storeys than you normally see in a mansard roof, particularly Nos. 13-15. No. 16 looks as if it could be some kind of church - or prison.

No. 18 Ladbroke Walk was sold in 2010 for £2,565,000.

Victoria Gardens is a cul-de-sac off Ladbroke Road. On the west side, Nos. 1-7 is a terrace of rather nice looking small houses, on ground and two upper storeys, which are painted white at ground floor level and generally bare brick above. Each house has a large canted bay next to the simple entrance door. The first-floor windows are quite tall and each has an ornamental black wrought-iron railing to protect the plant holders. The east side of the road is mainly taken up with a car park, but there still remain three houses, Nos. 15-17, which are in exactly the same style as those opposite.

In 2010 No. 7 Victoria Gardens was sold for £1,600,000.

Horbury Mews is the most popular residential mews in Notting Hill by a long way. It was built in 1877-8 on the grounds of a former market garden. It is a wide cobbled place, twice as wide as a normal mews. Nos. 1-4 on the west side and Nos. 9-12 on the east side are virtually identical in construction, although some houses have been altered subsequently. Each house has a garage at ground floor level, and most of these still retain the opening double wooden doors, not the horrible up-and-over metal ones many mews have. Next to the garage is a narrow front door. Above, is a single storey with a cornice or parapet above that, and then there are some additional rooms in the sloping tiled roof. Some houses, such as Nos. 2 and 10, are double-fronted, with living room windows on either side of the main door. Others are single-width. They all have the same style of window heads, created by placing rubbed bricks on edge, and they all have painted brickwork. Nos. 5-8 is a terrace which is surmounted in the middle by a large triangular pediment headed 'Horbury Mews 1878'. The houses look very much the same as the previous terraces, but this terrace is not painted but bare brick, revealing that the shaped bricks in the window arches are multi-coloured, which is an attractive effect. Many of the houses have tubs for shrubs or plants outside, but are kept quite close to the houses behind the council's yellow lines.

There were no sales in Horbury Mews in 2010. The most recent sale was of No. 9 for £2,440,000 in 2007.

Felix Ladbroke (p. 61) leased the site for **Horbury Crescent** to William Chadwick (p. 80) in 1848. Building was commenced in 1855 by his son, W W Chadwick, who employed a builder, William Wheeler, to construct sixteen houses. On the west side, No. 2, which faces onto Kensington Park Road, is the start of a terrace of even-numbered houses of Horbury Crescent, running up to No. 18. Each house has a basement and a raised ground floor, with a single large living room window next to the individual porches. There's a continuous balcony along the front of the first-floor windows, opening out above the porches. There's no decoration other than curved brackets supporting a simple architrave. Then there are second and third storeys above that. Nos. 22-28 are without the third storey or the shared balcony.

On the east side, No. 1, at the start of the terrace, looks like an individually built house. It's on four storeys and stucco-faced. Nos. 3-13 is a terrace of houses on four storeys. There are simple architraves on brackets over the raised ground floor entrance doors, and all the houses have stone effect incising in the plaster work at ground floor level. The houses are mainly bare-brick faced for the first and second storeys, although the window surrounds are stuccoed-painted, and the whole of the facade of Nos. 11 and 13 is painted. There are no balconies, but the first-floor windows have little ledges for plant pots. They are relatively small houses (for the area).

There have apparently been no sales in Horbury Crescent since the sale of No. 1 for £4,500,000 in 2008.

Nos. 9-13 **Portobello Road** on the west side were built in 1852 by William Chadwick, who owned the area between Pembridge Road and Holland Park Avenue. These were generally small terraced houses, brick-faced but with stucco architraves. Nos. 65-105 comprise a terrace between Chepstow Villas and Westbourne Grove. Thomas Pocock owned this part of the area and he allocated individual plots to various local builders in 1848-9. From 1852-3 he similarly granted leases of plots for Nos. 115-175, from Westbourne Grove up to Elgin Crescent. William and Henry Cullingford (p. 118) were the builders of Nos. 2-80 (even) between 1854 and 1858, under leases from the executors of W K Jenkins (p. 114). Portobello Road today contains the Portobello Road market, which is famous as a tourist attraction.

There were three house sales in Portobello Road in 2010: No. 22 for £1,325,000, No. 14 for £1,775,000 and No. 193 for £1,675,000 (although there is some uncertainty about whether the whole building was included). A flat at No. 222A was sold for £605,000 and one at 305A for £840,000.

Notting Hill: Ladbroke Grove to Portobello Road

Notting Hill: Portobello Road to Chepstow Place

QUICK REFERENCE							
STREET	PAGE	STREET	PAGE	STREET	PAGE
Chepstow Crescent	115	Denbigh Close	111	Pembridge Mews	119
		Denbigh Road	110	Pembridge Place	120
Chepstow Place	124	Denbigh Terrace	111	Pembridge Square	121
Chepstow Villas	112	Linden Gardens	126		
Clanricarde Gardens	125	Pembridge Crescent	116	Pembridge Villas	118
		Pembridge Gardens	122	Westbourne Grove	109
Dawson Place	119				

Westbourne Grove runs as far as Queensway, and it is mainly retail, not residential, so we are not going to attempt to describe the individual properties.

Westbourne Grove was just a country track near the river until it was developed in the 1850s. On the north side, James Bennett built Nos. 122-152 (even) in 1847-9. In 1850 James Hall (p. 29) built Nos. 154-164 (even). Nos. 166 and 168 were built by John Foster of Paddington in 1847. John Maidlow built Nos. 170-176 (even) in 1852, and T J Bolton of Paddington built Nos. 178-192 in 1848. On the south side, James Hall built Nos. 155-169 (odd) from 1848-50. Bolton built Nos. 207-22, and J D Cowland built Nos. 243 and 245 in 1856-9.

Thomas Pocock owned the land on either side of Westbourne Grove near the Kensington Park Road junction. Nos. 282-304 (even) on the north side and 283-303 (odd) on the south side were built by, or for, him in 1851-2. On the north side are the council blocks of Ashton House, Archer House and Denbigh House. They are fairly low rise, on four storeys. On the south side is the six storey block of Longlands Court.

There were three house sales in Westbourne Grove in 2010: No. 215 for £1,475,000, No. 213 for £3,350,000 and No. 209 for £3,750,000. These were all outmatched by the price of £4,200,000, achieved for a single flat at 288A Westbourne Grove. There were several flat sales at No. 47-49 Westbourne Grove: £1,825,000 and £1,850,000 being the high prices, but also £440,000 and £390,000. A flat at Bayswater Mansions went for £412,500 and two flats at Longlands Court went for £450,000 and £435,000.

The Westbourne

The Westbourne was a river which ran through Paddington, Bayswater and Hyde Park to eventually join up with the Thames. It was dammed up in 1730 by George II to create the Serpentine. The rest of the river lives on as a sewer which runs through a pipe above the platform at Sloane Square Tube Station.

Denbigh Road begins on the east side, with a few shops with flats above. Westhill Court, at No. 5, is a courtyard of flats, with a four-storey block facing onto the road, but with a large arched passageway through the middle to low-rise flats at the back, all in modern brick, but with some parts plastered and painted cream. Nos. 9-11 is a short terrace of attractive houses on three storeys built by J D Cowland in 1856-9. (No. 9 has a basement.) Pencombe Mews has the date 1984 over the entrance arch. Inside it is an attractive terrace of 14 three-storey houses in nice brick with simple painted window and door surrounds. Round the corner there is a second leg which is profuse with shrubs and climbing flowering plants. Most of the houses have a garage in the ground storey, but some garages are next to the houses. The houses seem larger and wider than the typical townhouse, and it's a very attractive enclave. Back on the main road, Nos. 11 and 15 have been slotted into the narrow gap between the remaining terraces and the mews entrance. Nos. 17-23 are part of a terrace, although they give the impression of being two semi-detached buildings because the entrances to Nos. 19 and 21 are set well back from the main facades.

These are charming pastel-painted houses on three storeys, with small balconies at first floor level, with very tall French doors opening onto them. Henry and William Cullingford built these houses in 1851.

On the west side is Longlands Court, a post-war estate in cheap brick, with six storeys of flats and external corridor entrances, typical of council developments. It is part of a larger complex along Westbourne Grove. Henry and William Cullingford built Nos. 12-24 in about 1853. Nos. 12-16 is a threesome, with No. 12 crammed later onto the side of the semi-detached Nos. 14 and 16. Nos. 18-24 are semi-detached houses. Unlike the houses on the east, they have very raised ground floors, up steep steps; they are stucco-faced and painted light pastel colours. They have very tall first-floor windows with triangular pediments and brackets, and an attractive wrought-iron balcony between them. The second-floor windows are less decorated.

The only sale in Denbigh Road in 2010 was the sale of a second-floor flat at No. 22 for £1,100,000.

The north side of **Denbigh Terrace** is taken up by Longlands Court Estate. Nos. 13-26 is a terrace of houses on the south side, beginning at the Portobello Road end. The houses in this terrace were built by a variety of local builders in 1852-5. Most of the houses have basement and ground floors, and one upper storey, but the central houses, Nos. 18-20, have an additional second storey. Many of the house owners have converted their lofts to create additional rooms with Velux windows. The houses have raised front doors, without a porch structure. There is an architrave on brackets above the ground floor windows. The first-floor windows are plain, but above is a cornice which is usually painted white. The facades are mainly painted stucco.

There has apparently not been a sale in Denbigh Terrace since a basement flat at No. 18 was sold for £1,808,000 in 2009.

Denbigh Close, off Portobello Road, used to be called Denbigh Mews, according to the huge sign in the gable of the house at the end. It's quite a narrow cobbled mews and it contains about 20 small houses. The houses are on two main storeys, consisting of a ground floor (mainly taken up with the garage door), then quite a low first floor, and then a second floor in the sides of the tiled roof and the gable ends. Nos. 6-8 are more modern and luxurious-looking houses, but still making the most of the same fairly limited height as the original houses.

There have apparently been no sales in Denbigh Close since No. 4 was purchased for £1,600,000 in 2007.

On the south side, at the corner with Pembridge Villas, **Chepstow Villas** starts with Ashdown Lodge, a post-war block, which has seven flats on three upper main storeys. This is followed by several low-rise red-brick post-war buildings. Little Chepstow at No. 1E is the nicest looking, with a small garage on the ground floor and living accommodation on the first floor, set back behind a railings to provide a terrace. No. 1 itself is further along and is the start of a Victorian terrace running up to No. 11, all of which were built in 1847-9 by George Passmore, a plumber from Edgware Road. These houses have forecourts large enough for cars. The accommodation is on basement, raised ground, and two upper storeys (with an additional storey on the two end houses and mansard rooms in the sloping roofs of the houses in between).

The north side of the road up to Ledbury Road is a series of semi-detached houses. They have a basement, ground floor, and two upper storeys. Nos. 2-8 were built by William Reynolds in 1846, and they have identical columned porches, wide first-floor windows and a cornice, but they have been quite heavily altered in some cases. No. 2, rather incongruously, has a balcony outside a window at second floor level, and a couple of houses have modern windows in place of the original sashes (not so much incongruous as ugly). Nos. 10-16 were built in 1850 by John Wadge. They all have side entrances, 'stone work' around the ground floor windows, and stylised architraves on columns for the first-floor windows. Nos. 18-24, built by William Judd in 1846, are joined in the middle by a ground floor structure, but seem to have been considerably altered. Nos. 22 and 24 have enormous Greek column heads with sprouting leaves set into the plasterwork near the top of the house (for which 'incongruous' would be way too inadequate).

On the other side of Ledbury Road and Chepstow Crescent, the south side continues with a series of semi-detached and detached houses from Nos. 13-23. Of these, Nos. 17-23 were built by William Cullingford in 1847-50. Most of these houses are on ground and two upper storeys (although some of the houses have basements) and they are all stucco-faced and painted, and have strongly defined quoins at the corners. They also share the feature of tiny brackets, with little token scrolls under the window sills. On the north side, William Cullingford also built Nos. 26-32 in 1847-50. They are semi-detached houses, with basement, ground and two upper storeys. The dominating structure is the massive red-brick construction of Thornbury Court, with 45 flats on five main storeys (including a lower ground storey) and additional flats in the mansard roof. Thornbury Court used to be a convent of 'Our Lady of Sion'. With its church-like entrance porch, it still has a religious quality about it. It has massive curved first-floor windows with terracotta carvings of heads at the apexes. There is further decoration between the second and third floors, although the major impact is created by the sheer size and redness of the place.

Chepstow Villas continues from Pembridge Crescent. In 1850-53 James Hall (p. 29) built Nos. 25-33 on the south side, and Nos. 42-52 on the north side. These are all detached houses with central raised entrances and plain pillared porches, but without balconies above. On the south side, most of the houses are quite low-built with a lower ground floor, a very raised ground floor, and only one storey above. On the north side, most of the houses have an additional storey. They all mainly share the layout of a window on either side of the central entrance porch and three windows in the storey above (including one small one over the balcony).

In the final section, leading up to Kensington Park Road, there are much larger terraced houses on either side. Thomas Pocock owned the land on which this part of Chepstow Villas was built. He used his own contractors to construct these houses in 1851. On the south side, Nos. 35-41 have basement, raised ground, and three upper floors. Nos. 35 and 41 stand forward slightly and a balcony runs at first-floor level between them for No. 37 and No. 39. These houses have quite large front garden areas, compared with the houses opposite. On the north side, Nos. 54-62 are houses similar in size with basement, ground (only slightly raised) and then three upper storeys. They differ from the south side by having canted bays at basement to first-floor level, and they seem narrower and more cramped, and closer to the street. They are stucco-faced and painted.

We are not aware of any sales in Chepstow Villas in 2010. A price of £1,270,000 was achieved for a flat at Thornbury Court, No. 36-38, in 2009 and £1,051,000 for a flat at No. 2 also that year.

William Kinnaird Jenkins

James Ladbroke (p. 61) owned two separate 'islands' of land to the west of the main estate. In 1844 Ladbroke entered into a building agreement with William Henry Jenkins for the development of 28 acres in the north east of the Notting Hill area. Jenkins was a civil engineer working in Lincolns Inn Fields. After only a few months, Jenkins assigned his interest to a relative, William Kinnaird Jenkins, who was already a successful building speculator in the Paddington area. He proceeded to develop the 28 acres successfully, despite the economic downturn in the mid-1840s. The main new road which Jenkins constructed was Pembridge Villas. Westbourne Grove, which started in Paddington, was extended through the land to join in Portobello Lane. But Chepstow Villas and Chepstow Crescent were also built partly on this land. Jenkins' principal contractor was William Judd. In 1846 Jenkins leased a further 10 acres to the west from Robert Hall so he could extend Chepstow Villas to Portobello Lane and build Denbigh Road and Pembridge Crescent. The builders he used here were mainly James Hall (p. 29) and the Cullingford (p. 118) and Maidlow families.

Notting Hill: Portobello Road to Chepstow Place

The land on which **Chepstow Crescent** was built was part of the Ladbroke Estate until 1847 when James Ladbroke (p. 61) sold it to W K Jenkins (p. 114). Nos. 3-7, on the east side, are all that remains of Nos. 1-13, a terrace built by Frederick Woods and William Wheeler, who were the largest builders in this street. It is a stucco-faced terrace of Victorian houses in a restrained style on basement, ground and two upper storeys. The first-floor windows are particularly tall sash windows with little metal balconies outside. No. 11 is a post-war brick block of flats with nine flats in a fairly basic style. No. 15 is a modern commercial property. Nos. 17-25 form a terrace of four-storey stuccoed Victorian houses in a similar restrained style to the earlier ones, and they were also built by Woods and Wheeler, apart from No. 17, which was built by Henry Beedle, a Paddington plasterer. Nos. 19 and 21 are taller than the others. No. 29 is another block of flats, double-fronted with eight flats. No. 35 and No. 37 (round the corner in Chepstow Villas) are Victorian properties similar to the earlier ones, but in fact built by Joseph Clutterbuck (p. 158), the brick maker.

On the east side of the road, properties are more of a mix and match. No. 2 (on the corner with Pembridge Villas) and No. 4 are contained in a tall five-storey building, stuccoed up to ground level and brick-faced above. These were built by George Stevenson, a Paddington plumber. No. 6, built by James Swinburn, a carpenter from St Marylebone, is one-storey lower, but has rooms in the mansard roof. No. 8, built by Thomas Aitchison, another St Marylebone carpenter, is an extremely tall and thin building on six storeys with a totally out of proportion pediment on brackets on top. Nos. 10 and 12 are a semi-detached pair with nicer proportions, on basement, ground and two upper storeys, with attractive balcony rails outside the first-floor windows. No. 10 was built by Thomas Bryan. Nos. 14-20 consist of a terrace of large properties, again with basement, raised ground floor storey and three upper storeys. The main doors are at the front of the porches (turned into lobbies), so the ground-floor windows are set back and have their own balconies. Nos. 14-20 could be the centre of a single terrace starting at No. 10, because the same first-floor railing design runs right through to No. 24. Nos. 22 and 24 have basement, ground and two upper storeys. In fact, the plots for Nos. 16-22 were allocated to John Powell, but George Stevenson definitely built Nos. 14, 22 and 24, so possibly he built the whole terrace. Chepstow Court then goes up to the corner with Chepstow Villas; this is a pre-war block containing 34 flats on six storeys, in a dark red brick and white painted windows.

Flat sales in Chepstow Crescent in 2010 were all low value. There were three sales in Chepstow Court, at prices from £350,000 to £445,000. The lowest sale price in the street was £270,000 at No. 11D, while another flat there sold for £377,000. A flat at No. 16 sold for £470,000.

Pembridge Conservation Area and Association

The council created the Pembridge Conservation Area in 1969. The council has increased powers in a conservation area to require approval for works, and can also issue directions suspending automatic approvals for some kinds of works. The Pembridge Association was set up by residents in 1972 to represent local residents' interests. The conservation area runs from Portobello Road to Chepstow Place and Ossington Street, and goes down to Notting Hill Gate and up to Westbourne Grove. This is only a rough description and if you are interested in a particular property, you need to check specifically – some streets are excluded. It can have a significant effect on property values. You can look on the Association's website which is pembridgeassociation.org.

Pembridge Crescent is a charming tree-lined crescent, although the trees are actually mainly in the houses own front gardens. The overall impression is of large detached double-fronted houses, stuccoed and painted white or cream, although the houses are fairly individual in style. For the most part, they are on basement, raised ground and two upper storeys, with either an additional smaller third storey above the cornice, or a roof above the cornice, with rooms in the sloping front edge. They generally have nice front gardens with stone pilaster walls. The east side of the road was controlled by Charles Maidlow, an auctioneer, who acquired the rights to many of the building plots in about 1853. In 1854 various members of the Maidlow family carried out most of the building works. No. 1, built by Henry Cullingford in 1859, is a slightly lopsided-looking house with a single storey extension, and the upper windows have a rope decoration. Nos. 2-5 form a small terrace, with Nos. 3 and 4 in the centre having an additional storey (the difference due presumably to the fact that Cullingford built the outer houses, but Jane and Francis Maidlow built Nos. 3-4). No. 6, again by Cullingford, is a detached house, whose principal feature is elaborate church-like surrounds to the ground-floor windows. Nos. 7 and 8 are a semi-detached pair sharing a first-floor balcony, and these were built by Christopher Garwood, a Paddington builder, who acquired the building rights from Maidlow. Nos. 9 and 10 are detached houses built by Cullingford. No. 11, built by William Maidlow, has a strangely recessed ground floor bow window, with pillars in front supporting an overhanging first floor balcony above. There is a modern block at Nos. 12-13, but the cement facing is painted cream, so it actually fits in quite well in the landscape. This has a little front garden down to the main entrance and it contains 17 flats. Finally, No. 14 was also built by William Maidlow.

There is a lot more uniformity on the west side. No. 15A is a detached house, but Nos. 15-17 are a short terrace of houses on five storeys, with a basement, ground, two upper main storeys, and a third storey above the cornice. These are followed by the pair of Nos. 18 and 19. All these houses were built by Henry Cullingford in 1854. Nos. 20-22 are double fronted, with a basement and then stairs up to a raised ground floor. There are two main storeys below the cornice and a third storey above. The first and second storeys are rather interesting; the first floors windows have the same excessive church-like surrounds for the outer pair as for No. 6 on the north side. Cullingford built these houses in 1859. Nos. 23-25, which Cullingford built in 1854 with the earlier houses, again have four main storeys, but this time the third floor consists of rooms let into the sloping roof rather than a floor in the main structure. Nos. 26 and 27, built by Cullingford in 1858, are detached single-fronted houses with high first-floor windows (plus a second storey and rooms in the mansard roof). Nos. 28 and 29, built by James Hall (p. 29) in 1854, are a semi-detached pair, also on four main storeys with rooms in the mansard roof, and with triangular pediments above the first-floor windows which open onto a metal railed balcony in each case. No. 30 is a very narrow property on the side, built later.

There were three flat sales above the £1 million mark in Pembridge Crescent in 2010: £1,208,450 at No. 9, £1,200,000 at No. 32 and £1,225,000 at No. 24. A flat at 18B was sold for £910,000, one at No. 23 for £747,121 and a flat at No. 7 for £661,000.

William Cullingford

The main builders in the Pembridge Crescent area were two families, the Cullingfords and the Maidlows. William Cullingford was the head of his family's building firm.

Nos. 2-20 **Pembridge Villas** were built in the section of the road which becomes Chepstow Villas. James Hall (p. 29) was involved in most of them in one capacity or another. James Ladbroke granted him a lease of No. 4, at the direction of T W Budd in 1846, which Hall kept as his home. In 1847 Ladbroke granted him a direct lease of No. 6. No. 8 was granted to him, again at the direction of Budd. It appears that T W Budd had the rights to the rest of the houses and in 1848 he granted leases to Hall of Nos. 14-20. At Hall's request, he granted leases of No. 10 and 12 to C Hedge, a coal merchant of Pimlico.

In Pembridge Villas proper, George Stevenson, a Paddington plumber, took the corner plot for No. 22 on the west side in 1845. He also took Nos. 24 and 26. The rest of the range, as far as Chepstow Crescent, was divided up among various builders: J D Bishop of Brewer Street, Soho took No. 28 and Henry Sherlock, a plumber from Paddington, took number 30, both in 1847. Nos. 32-40 (even) were built by William Weston, a builder.

Below Chepstow Crescent, Charles Maidlow, an auctioneer, leased Nos. 50-56 from the executors of R Hall in 1852. Below Pembridge Crescent, James Hall (p. 29) took Nos. 58-66 from Hall's executors in 1851-5.

On the east side, James Hall also built Nos. 9 and 11 in 1849. The main builder of the early houses was George Trigg, a Paddington builder. Between 1846 and 1852 he took Nos. 13-23. Nos. 33-55 were built by William Radford between 1849 and 1855.

The sale which dwarfed all others in Pembridge Villas in 2010 was the sale of a detached house at No. 18A for £10,250,000. Four flats changed hands in Viscount Court, No. 1 Pembridge Villas: at prices between £440,000 and £500,000 and one stand-out flat at £1,194,000. At No. 28, there were sales for £860,000 and £912,500. Other flat sales included £1,225,000 for a flat at No. 32, £730,000 for a flat at No. 38 and £785,000 for a flat at No. 50.

Pembridge Mews was constructed by William Cullingford (p. 118) between 1849 and 1851. There's a long track or narrow road before you reach the cobbled mews. The houses are all two-storey cottages, many of which have been quite extensively redeveloped, so there is little uniformity any more in the appearance of the houses. The brick facades have been painted in many colours.

There does not appear to have been a sale in Pembridge Mews since the sale of No. 14 for £1,655,000 in 2007.

The start of **Dawson Place**, at the eastern end, is in a small stretch, from Prince's Square to Chepstow Place. No. 1, on the south side, is an extremely tall house with basement, ground and four upper storeys. On the north side, Nos. 2-4 are part of a terrace, and the houses are much smaller in scale, with one less upper storey (but No. 4 also has some rooms in the mansard roof). The main part of Dawson Place begins on the other side of Chepstow Place. Most of the houses were built by William Radford or Francis Radford (or both of them) between 1851 and 1852, so they share the same basic layout. They also share individual design features, such as the entwined circles which form the wall of the balcony above the entrance porch outside the first-floor windows of almost every house. The Radfords built Nos. 6-14 on the north side and Nos. 7-11 on the south side. Most of these houses differ in size from those, such as No. 9, which has a basement, ground and one upper storey, to much larger ones, such as No. 14, which has a basement, raised ground, two upper main storeys and then large room,s nearly as high as the second storey in an almost vertical tiled roof. They all have nice front gardens.

Beyond Pembridge Place, the Radfords built Nos. 16-30 on the north and Nos. 13-29 on the south side of Dawson Place. The houses on the south side continue to be mainly detached and double-fronted. On the north side, many of the houses' front doors have curved heads to the entrance surrounds, and some of the houses are joined. On the south side, many of the houses have attractive metal canopies from the front gate to the main door, with glazed pitched roofs. The houses on the south side have very raised ground floors, but on the north side they are generally close to ground level.

There were two very large house sales in Dawson Place in 2010: £13,000,000 for No. 10 and £10,500,000 for No. 5. There were also several relatively small flat sales, including three flats at No. 1 for prices from £575,000 up to £641,000. A flat at No. 15 sold for £450,000 and one at No. 2B for £840,000.

Pembridge Place runs north of Pembridge Square, and its houses are mainly north of Dawson Place. No. 10 on the east and Nos. 11 and 12 on the west are very similar in style to those in Dawson Place, no doubt because they too were built by the Radfords. Francis Radford built No. 10 in 1851. William Radford had an interest in the plots for Nos. 11 and 12 but arranged for the houses to be built by H Pook of Old Kent Road in 1850, presumably to standard Radford designs. James Hall (p. 29) built No. 1 and Nos. 3-9 on the east side between

1849 and 1851, and he also built Nos. 14-18 on the west side. No. 2 was built by Benjamin Broadbridge, an architect, in 1846. Nearly all the houses are large double-fronted detached houses with raised ground floors behind pillared entrances, which are usually undecorated. Some of the houses are on three main storeys and are flat fronted, but others have canted bays (in the case of No. 6 going up four storeys). It's a nice tree-lined street, and the houses all have front gardens.

Two houses changed hands in Pembridge Place in 2010: No. 3 for £616,000 and No. 2 for £600,000.

William and Francis Radford (p. 13) built the houses of **Pembridge Square** between 1856 and 1864. This is a lovely residential square, although there are still many houses which need to be refurbished, and there are still some hotels as well as the houses. Nos. 1-3 are on the short stretch from Pembridge Villas to Pembridge Gardens. The main range of houses begins on the south side of Pembridge Square with Nos. 6-18 (Nos. 4 and 5 were later demolished.) The houses of the square are all very similar and have a view over the long and narrow central gardens. Each house is double fronted. There is a basement, raised ground, first and second storeys, and additional rooms in the roof space. There is a very wide set of steps up to the central entrance door, which has a very restrained shallow porch. On either side are large canted bays, which run up from basement to first-floor level. Most of the houses have a small balcony outside the raised ground-floor bow windows, supported on rather ornate brackets from the basement, with metal rails similar to those lining the entrance stairs. The first-floor windows have a decorative structure which looks like a balcony (but isn't) of linked circles of different sizes in plaster or stone. The second floor has smaller windows, decorated with Greek heads and brackets supporting an architrave, which open onto balconies with stone pilasters topped with metal railings on top of the canted bays. Each house has a strong cornice on brackets, with a dentil decoration underneath, topped with elaborate arch-like structures, which frame the windows into attic rooms behind. They look - the little central one particularly - like mini Marble Arches. There are three of them, with a balustrade in between. These were a model for the designs of Holland Park (the road) houses which the Radfords went on to build.

Pembridge Square Garden

This is a long and narrow communal garden in the centre of Pembridge Square. It was designed by Francis Radford (p. 13) and laid out between 1856 and 1864 as part of the Radfords' construction of Pembridge Square. The original railings were taken down to be turned into armaments in the second world war, and the Pembridge Association finally succeeded in having them replaced in 2008. (See p. 180 for more information on communal gardens.)

The east side of the square contains Nos. 19-22. A rather charming difference from the houses just described is that the houses here all have a metal canopy with a pitched glazed roof leading from the street to the main door. They look rather rustic. The northern range of the square starts at No. 23, also with a metal canopy, and runs to No. 26 on the corner with Pembridge Place. Nos. 25 and 26 are joined together. The longer range on this side of the square then runs from Nos. 27-35, back at Pembridge Villas.

If you have a property in Pembridge Square you may have rights of access to Pembridge Square Garden (p. 122). But to find out if your property does have any such rights, you need to check with the garden committee. (See p. 180 for more information on communal gardens.)

The largest flat sale in Pembridge Square in 2010 was £3,137,500 for a flat at No. 19. Another flat at No. 17 went for £1,300,000 and one at No. 20 for £1,030,000. Bringing up the rear was a flat at No. 1 which sold for £400,000.

William and Francis Radford (p. 13) laid out **Pembridge Gardens** and built all the houses in 1857-9. Pembridge Gardens starts on the east side with a terrace of grand houses converted into a single apartment building called Radford House, which contains 76 flats (of which ten are basement flats). The separate pillared entrances for the original houses have been retained. Large first-floor French windows open onto a continuous balcony, and there are two more main storeys, and rooms in the attic. From No. 11 the houses are mainly detached. Nos. 11-15 are on basement, ground, two upper main storeys beneath a cornice, and then a smaller third storey above it. (No. 15 has an additional set of rooms in a mansard roof). These all have large porches on the left side of the frontage, next to a very large single ground-floor window, and the facade at this level is incised to look like stonework. The continuous metal balcony above the porches is in the same style as Radford House. The first-floor windows are tall but relatively undecorated. Nos. 17-29 are detached houses with a grander double-fronted large entrance and a high porch, and they have basement, ground and three upper storeys. Instead of metal railings, there is a solid balustrade outside the balcony; the balcony itself is only found in front of the central first-floor window, but the balcony wall pattern is reproduced underneath the first-floor windows on either side.

There is more uniformity on the west side of the road. Numbers start at No. 2 and the houses are almost all detached, although some such as No. 6 and No. 10 are, in fact, joined a fair way back from the frontage at the back of a short passage. The first few houses are relatively narrow, with two windows on each of the upper storeys. From No. 10, they become wider houses, with three windows on each of the upper floors. The houses are on basement, ground, and three upper storeys. There is a metal balcony outside the tall French windows at first-floor level. The plasterwork at ground floor level is incised to look like stonework. From No. 18 up to No. 34, at the corner with Pembridge Square, the houses change and adopt the design of Nos. 17-29 opposite. The same balustrade decoration of the porch is repeated under the first-floor windows. These houses also have a first and second upper storey, but not a third floor. Nos. 30 and 32 are slightly different in having an additional third floor, and No. 34 has a great deal of classical Greek decoration added to the façade. These houses are all stuccoed and cream- or white-painted.

In 2010, three flats in Radford House, No. 1 Pembridge Gardens, sold at prices from £358,000 to £395,000. A flat at No. 22 went for £400,000.

Chepstow Place is very literally the dividing line between Notting Hill and Bayswater, with the west side of the street being in W11 and the Royal Borough of Kensington and Chelsea, and the east side being in the W2 postal district and the City of Westminster. Starting at the top of Chepstow Place, there is a red-brick mansion block called Chepstow Mansions on the west side, with four main storeys of flats above ground-floor shops, and a further storey in the gables and mansard roof. After Chepstow Mansions, Nos. 2-8 is a short terrace of three-storey, white-painted houses, close to the road. Nos. 12-28 are similar but larger, and are set further back with large front areas for parking. The houses are flat-fronted and undecorated, and they have boxed-in porches. Nos. 32 to 34 are modern infills. Nos. 36-44 are similar to Nos. 12-28. No. 46 is a detached, double-fronted, two-storey house.

On the east side (which I will mention briefly for completeness), there is the extensive flat development of Baynards and Rede Place behind it. Then Nos. 15-49 is a charming terrace of houses on four storeys (including basements) with additional rooms in the mansard roof for Nos. 41-49. They have an almost villagey feel to them, possibly because the entrances are at street level, rather than the usual raised entrances up a flight of steps. At No. 39 is the well regarded Italian restaurant, Assaggi, which is on the first floor. The entrance is accessed in a small alleyway. Nos. 51-59 are larger stucco-faced houses on five storeys with raised ground floor entrances.

Three builders undertook the construction of the range of houses on the east side. Nos. 2-8 have shorter gardens than the rest. The leases were granted by T W Budd to the builder, James Hall (p. 29), in 1850. The rest of the range, from Nos. 10-44, were built in about 1850 by John Maidlow, a builder from St John's Wood, who was much involved in the construction of Pembridge Crescent. The very end house was built on land owned by Robert Hall and that plot was taken in 1852 by Francis Radford (p. 13).

George Treadaway, a Paddington draper, built most of the west range. He took leases of Nos. 15 and 17 from James Ladbroke (p. 61) in 1847, and leases of Nos. 23-33 from T W Budd, the adjoining landowner, in 1849. For some reason, John Lawrence, a St Pancras carpenter, took No. 21, the house in the middle of Treadaway's two ranges in 1847. James Herd of Paddington built the houses on either side of the Dawson Place junction, Nos. 51-69.

No. 61-69 Chepstow Place saw the most sales action in 2010, with flats going for prices from £834,500 to £1,920,000. A basement flat at No. 33 was sold for £625,000 and a flat at No. 1 for £495,000. There was a single house sale of No. 47 for £3,700,000.

Clanricarde Gardens appears on the map as completing the line of Chepstow Place to Notting Hill Gate, but in fact it is a cul-de-sac entered from Notting Hill Gate, but there is a narrow passage for pedestrians into Moscow Road. It's mainly flats, with a smattering of hotels, and despite its proximity to Notting Hill Gate, it has somehow evaded gentrification. The buildings start with Apsley Mansions on the east and Clanricarde Mansions on the west, which consist of flats in the three upper storeys of buildings fronting onto Notting Hill Gate itself. There are then almost identical terraces on either side of the street, running north towards Pembridge Square. The terraces comprise Nos. 2-50 on the west and Nos. 1-51 on the east, and the entrances of the end houses are diagonally placed. The terraces were designed and built as a unit, rather than pieced together by different builders in different styles. They were constructed between 1869 and 1873 by two builders, Thomas Goodwin and William White. The buildings are on basement, ground and three upper main storeys, with flats also in the roofs above the parapet wall. There are differences in these roof level flats: some of the buildings have flats in gable ends and others are attic conversions in the sloping mansard roofs. The houses have individual pillared porches and a balustraded balcony structure runs right along the terraces, opening out over the porches (but the porches are unusually not in front of the first-floor windows). The first-floor windows have pediments and elaborate coats-of-arms designs, and there is a frieze below the balustrade at the top. In the central and end sections of the terraces, the houses have triple windows at all upper levels (otherwise, there are two single windows per floor), and also stand forward slightly, with quoins for emphasis.

The highest price achieved in Clanricarde Gardens in 2010 was £715,000 paid for a flat at No. 42. There was a sale at No. 20 for £692,000 and for £650,100 at No. 29B. There were four other sales in the low £600,000s, and five sales prices below £600,000 (the cheapest being £301,000).

Linden Gardens is a series of connected streets, entered off Notting Hill Gate. The style of the houses is very similar throughout. They are brick-faced at ground floor level, in a brick which is grey or dull yellow (possibly depending on whether the facades have been sandblasted or not). Basements and ground storeys are stucco-faced, but with indentations to make it look like stonework, and they are generally painted a uniform light cream. The houses have almost classical porched entrances, with balustraded balconies above for the first floors. Some of these buildings have canted bays, which generally run up to first floor level, and these are also stuccoed and lined to look like stonework. These have balustraded balconies on top for the second floors. This uniform layout is, in fact, broken at the very start by No. 1 on the west side, which is a wide double fronted red-brick building in Dutch style, on basement, ground and two upper main storeys, with extra rooms in the gable ends and sloping roof. The building has been converted into flats. Nos. 2 and 6 opposite have the standard construction. There is then a cul-de-sac to the east for Nos. 6-24, with standard houses, generally with two upper storeys and more rooms in the sloping roof above the parapet wall. The parapet wall has an interesting wave-like frieze underneath. The main road then continues onwards with Nos. 26-32. This is a tall terrace with three upper storeys (and rooms in the sloping mansard roof). The first-floor windows have elaborate pediments, and the second-floor windows are almost as tall.

This is then followed by a post-war concrete construction at No. 34-36 Linden Gardens, called The Limes, which consists of some low-rise sections on two storeys and then a block of seven storeys. It contains 33 flats and five houses, and has car parking next to it. There are then two Edwardian semi-detached houses on two storeys at Nos. 38-38B and Nos. 40 and 42, both with distinctive curved bays.

Opposite, on the west side, again is a terrace, Nos. 77-99, which runs to the end of the street, with No. 99 facing onto the top of the side section of Linden Gardens, described next. This is a very similar terrace to Nos. 26-32, but with more elaborate decoration above the first-floor windows and more elaborate second-floor windows, which have decorations with scallops and quite deep hoods. Each building has a single porch with simple pillars and steps up to the main door and a balustraded balcony above.

Linden Gardens branches off to the east between No. 7 and No. 77. The terrace, containing Nos. 9-23 on the south side, has houses in the style of Nos. 77-97. However, most of the houses in this side section have stone-effect plaster decoration round the ground-floor windows, intended to look like stone. On the north side, Nos. 73 and 75 have been converted into mansion flats.

At the south western corner is the entrance to **Linden Mews**. This is a short cobbled mews of seven houses built in the same grey or yellow brick as the main terraces, with houses on two storeys, with rows of red bricks for decoration. Some of the houses seem to have been quite extensively redesigned.

Linden Gardens begins again with No. 25, just past Linden Mews and running up to No. 35. The houses are similar to those previously described. There is an open cutting above the Underground rail track at this point. Garden Mews is a gated mews, with a handful of traditional little mews houses, which look relatively unspoiled, but it is almost over the top of the open rail track section. On the opposite east side are Nos. 57-71 (the numbers are running back the upper way) and the houses are of similar size, but less decorative, with fairly rudimentary work above the windows in comparison to the previous houses.

Continuing past Garden Mews on the west side is another terrace, curving this time, is Nos. 37-53. These houses are similar to Nos. 25-35, but this time with slightly less decorated windows. Opposite, on the inside of the curve, there is a short terrace which is, in fact, No. 55, a single-doored building with flats.

The highest sale price achieved in Linden Gardens in 2010 was £1,800,000 for Flat 2 at No. 57. There were no other sales above the million pound mark. £965,000 was paid for a flat at No. 83, and £870,000 for a flat at No. 89. There were three sales of around the £800,000 mark at Nos. 9, 12, and 39A. There were two sales in the low £700,000s, at Nos. 79 and 16A, and a sale for £665,000 at No. 51. There were three for less than £500,000.

Notting Hill: The North East frontier

QUICK REFERENCE					
STREET	PAGE	STREET	PAGE	STREET	PAGE
Alba Place	139	Dunworth Mews	139	Powis Square	144
Aldridge Road Villas	135	Hayden's Place	139	Powis Terrace	146
		Lancaster Road	138	St Luke's Mews	138
Artesian Road	129	Ledbury Road	147	St Luke's Road	137
Chepstow Road	133	Leamington Road Villas	136	St Stephen's Crescent	135
Colville Gardens	143				
Colville Houses	142	McGregor Road	138	St Stephen's Gardens	135
Colville Road	143	Moorhouse Road	131		
Colville Square	141	Northumberland Place	133	Sutherland Place	132
Colville Terrace	140			Talbot Road	134
Courtnell Street	130	Powis Gardens	144		

This is an area which was, in the past, considered to be beyond traditional Notting Hill. But Notting Hill is now pushing up towards the Westway and many Victorian houses, in formerly despised streets, are being brought back into family occupation.

Artesian Village

The area nowadays called 'Artesian Village' begins just north of Westbourne Grove. The long south side of **Artesian Road** begins after the shopping centre, Whiteleys, and a block of flats. Nos. 7-37 is a terrace of Victorian four-storey houses with stuccoed ground floor and basement storeys, and two brick-faced storeys above (plus some additional attic rooms). The houses have a continuous wrought-iron balcony at first-floor level. Nos. 15-23 stand slightly forward from the main terrace. The houses have enough room for a small garden or an area for a single car. There is a break for Needham Road. Nos. 39-67 form a new terrace, starting just past the Cock and Bottle pub. These are smaller three-storey houses without basements, porches or balconies (although there is a little cantilevered balcony outside each first-floor window, suitable to put potted plants on). They have smaller front gardens than the previous terrace. Nos. 49-53 stand slightly forward. Then there is Artesian House, a mansion block built in 1937, with eight flats on four storeys. No. 73 is a rather interesting looking house, originally similar to the other terraced houses, but now with massive metal front doors with animal representations, and metal pillars holding up a first-floor balcony.

The northern side of Artesian Road starts near Chepstow Road with Nos. 2-6, which is a short terrace of brick-faced houses on basement, ground and one upper storey. Nos. 8-12, up to the corner with Northumberland Place, have basement, ground and two upper storeys, with individual balconies for the first-floor windows. The lower two storeys are stuccoed, and the upper floors are brick-faced. On the west side of Northumberland Place, Nos. 14-18 Artesian Road reproduce the distinctive style of the Northumberland Place houses. Nos. 20-24, on the corner with Sutherland Place, are much taller buildings with a basement and a very raised ground storey. The Catholic church of St Mary of the Angels takes up the next section to Moorhouse Road. From Moorhouse Road to Courtnell Street, the road is taken up with the back gardens of the houses of those streets. There are a couple of cottages in the stretch from Courtnell Road to Ledbury Road.

Several houses changed hands in Artesian Road in 2010. No. 8 was sold for £2,550,000 and No. 59 for £1,998,950. A ground floor flat at No. 35 sold for £450,000.

The house numbers in **Courtnell Street** start with No. 3, on the west side. Nos. 3-23 are all three-storey houses (no basements), some with porches up to the street edge, and some with little areas and ordinary entrance doors. Some also have mansard rooms created in the sloping roofs. They have stuccoed ground floors, grooved to look like stone and then painted, and are bare-brick above (or painted in some cases). Nos. 25-37 is a terrace of larger houses with basements, and raised ground floors with porches. These also have stuccoed stone-effect basements and ground floors, but the two upper storeys are bare brick-faced with white painted window surrounds. There is a continuous balcony running along in front of the first-floor sash windows. Nos. 39-45 return back to the former style of houses starting on the ground floor and with two smaller floors above. Finally, on the corner, at the Talbot Road end is a larger house with canted bays.

On the east side of Courtnell Street, the house numbers start with No. 4. Nos. 4-16 are all three-storey houses without basements, very similar to Nos. 3-23 opposite. They are stuccoed and painted. They also have mansard rooms in the sloping roofs. Holland Park Motor Services occupies a modern infill building. Houses begin again at Nos. 18B-40. These have ground floors with porches almost onto the street and two additional storeys above. They are all stuccoed at ground floor level but mainly have bare brick above, although the brick work is painted on some of the houses. The first-floor windows are not as tall as on the west side of the road but they are nice looking sash windows. They don't have balconies, just a projecting shelf with an iron railing. All the houses on the road have additional rooms in the sloping roof, whether original or added later. There are a lot of trees and it is all rather charming.

In 2010, No. 11 Courtnell Street was sold for £2,275,000 and No. 9 for £2,100,000. There was also a flat sold at No. 25 for £550,000.

Generally speaking, properties in **Moorhouse Road** are much bigger than in Courtnell Road. Houses start on the west side at the junction with Artesian Road, with an interesting terrace combining Dutch gables with a large dash of Gothic. These houses are on basement, ground and one upper main floor, but with additional rooms in most of the gable ends, which is a particular architectural feature of this street. They have relatively long front areas, and wide entrance stairs up to conjoined porches with church-like curved heads, and there are canted bays at basement and ground floor level. The bays and the porches are stuccoed but otherwise the facades are mainly bare brick. That style runs up roughly to No. 19, although Nos. 17 and 19 are rather bigger houses. A larger, more classical terrace, Nos. 21-41 contains houses on basement, ground and three upper storeys, with entrance porches, and railings outside very ornately decorated first-floor sash windows. These houses are fully stuccoed.

On the east side, much of the start of the road is taken up with one side of the church; the houses then start with No. 2. These are houses on basement, ground, and two upper storeys. They are not particularly decorated, and they have narrow entrance doors, flush with the front of the building. From No. 12-26, there is a terrace of slightly more elaborate houses, also on basement, ground and three upper storeys, but now with raised ground floor doors with porches, and a continuous first-floor balcony. The first-floor windows have decoration matching those on the opposite side of the road in the terrace of Nos. 21-41.

There were no house sales in Moorhouse Road in 2010, but a flat was sold at No. 19 for £750,000, one at No. 37 for 596,950, one at No. 26 for £301,000 and finally one at No. 39F for £338,000.

Sutherland Place is a heavily tree-lined street. The numbering starts at No. 17 for some reason and numbers are consecutive in this street, not odd or even on one side or the other. The houses are four-storey and are set reasonably far back from the street, with a slightly raised ground floor level above the basement and quite a shallow porch, with an equally shallow balcony running right the way along above it and in front of the first-floor sash windows. They are stucco-faced and painted in pastel colours. An odd design feature is that the porches have a very large square block above the top of the columns, supporting the balcony above, as if the builder ordered pillars too short by about 18 inches. This style runs along to No. 31. Nos. 32-33 form a later detached property on basement, ground and one upper storey. Then the former style begins again for Nos. 34-40, but with more normal-shaped porch columns.

The start of the west side is taken up with another side of the church, and the houses begin with No. 41. Up to No. 47, the houses are very plain, with no porches and no real balconies except on the very first house. The houses are on basement, ground (both stuccoed) and two upper brick-faced storeys. From No. 48 there's a new terrace of houses on basement, ground and two upper storeys, with distinctive window surrounds and porches, and a balcony running along above the porches. (No. 48 is the exception, without a porch and without balconies). These houses are mainly fully-stuccoed with painted facades, and have a single wide ground-floor window next to each porch. That terrace runs up to No. 59. No. 61 is part of a large corner building in Talbot Road.

No. 21 Sutherland Place was sold for £2,850,000 in 2010, and a flat at No. 29 Sutherland Place was sold for £1,695,000.

Most of the houses in **Northumberland Place** have large trees in their front gardens which help to make the street very attractive. Numbers start on the east side at No. 1 with a four-storey terrace (basement, slightly raised ground, and two upper storeys). The style changes slightly from No. 5, where there is a distinctive patterned wrought-iron railing outside the first-floor windows, giving an individual little balcony. From No. 5 onwards (No. 5 only has a vestige of this) the houses generally have curved hoods over the front doors, or a continuous metal hood for some of them, supported by a metal frame patterned like the balcony railing on edge. This is a highly distinctive design. The only other place it is to be found, as far as I am aware, is in Kensington Park Road. The houses also have little cantilevered balconies outside the ground floor windows with French doors. The first terrace ends at No. 14. Another one begins at No. 15, but with the same style. This charming style runs all the way up to No. 28.

The west side of the road then starts with No. 29 at the Talbot Road end. The houses on this side have a similar style to the opposite terrace, ending at the Artesian Road end with No. 55. Most of the houses have small front gardens which are generally well tended.

Northumberland Place was popular with house buyers in 2010. £3,286,200 was paid for No. 42, £2,650,000 for No. 39 and £2,350,000 for No. 9. There were no flat sales.

The two sides of **Chepstow Road** (south of Talbot Road) must have been designed and built by the same builder because they each have a central section of houses facing each other, with sunken pilasters, with elaborate flowery heads running up the first and second storeys of the facades. On the east side, the terrace starts at No. 22 and runs up to No. 66, and the western terrace starts at No. 7 and runs up to No. 51. Many of the houses on the east side and some on the west side are similar to the houses in Artesian Village, with a distinctive metal framework for ground and first floor balconies and in place of traditional pillars for the porches. No. 11 upwards on the west side are mainly flat-fronted houses on four storeys (including basements) with front gardens. Further up on the east, there are flats above shops. North of Talbot Road, on the east side, there is a range of much larger Victorian houses from No. 82 to No. 100 which are on basement ground and three upper storeys. The upper storeys are in bare brick with white painted window surrounds, and some of the houses have rooms in the mansard roof.

Sale prices seemed to be either big or small in 2010. A flat at No. 58 Chepstow Road was sold for £2,200,000; another at No. 44A went for £1,495,000; a flat at Gate Apartments, No. 2 Chepstow Road, was sold for £1,300,000, and finally a flat at No. 59A changed hands for £1,100,000. Then, with no sales in the centre ground, there were six sales at prices from £425,000 down to £368,000.

Talbot Road starts at the Chepstow Road end with a terrace, Nos. 20-42. The buildings are on five storeys (including a basement). The nicest housing is on the south side and it is made up of small numbers of Victorian semi-detached houses and short terraces, because the road is interrupted by the Artesian Village roads running north. These houses generally have a country town air to them and are on basement, ground and two upper storeys; many have rooms which have been added in the pitched roofs. The houses are generally painted in pastel shades and many of them have attractive rounded windows.

Maisonette sales topped the sale prices in 2010. At No. 28 the third and fourth floor maisonette sold for £980,000, and the first and second floor maisonette went for £852,000. A second and third floor maisonette at No. 40 sold for £920,000. There were fourteen other flat sales at prices from £565,000, at No 73, down to £240,000, at No. 90.

Over Talbot Road, **St Stephen's Crescent** is a fairly short crescent of fully stuccoed, cream-painted houses, opposite St Stephen's Church. Nos. 1-10 are a single terrace, with flats on basement, ground, and three main upper storeys. There are large balconies above the pillared entrances and an elaborate parapet wall at the top of the building.

There were no sales in St Stephen's Crescent in 2010. Two flats changed hands in 2009, at No. 2 for £485,000 and £399,950 respectively.

The first stretch of **St Stephen's Gardens**, between Westbourne Park Road and Chepstow Road, has terraced houses on each side. On the north side, Nos. 4-34 are in a terrace of brick-faced houses (some bare brick and some painted). The houses are on basement, ground and three upper storeys, and they have rather block-like porches on bare pillars which support large balconies outside the first-floor windows. The houses in the terrace on the south side (Nos. 1-27) are similar in size but much more elaborate; they are fully stuccoed, with decorated first-floor windows, and more ornate (but shallower) porches. St Stephen's Gardens continues on the west side of Chepstow Road, but now with a central garden. Nos. 36-62, on the north side, are very similar to Nos. 1-27, but the houses seem to get more ornate on this side of Chepstow Road, with a lot of plaster decoration under the second-floor windows and all kinds of scrollwork round the first-floor windows. Nos. 29-53 on the south side continue the process of increased decoration with plasterwork designed to look like blocks of stone round the ground-floor windows.

There were 11 sales in St Stephen's Gardens in 2010, ranging from £815,000 for a flat at No. 4A down to £280,000 for a flat at No. 17. Most of the sale prices were £500,000 or under.

Westbourne Park Road to Westway

North of Westbourne Park Road, **Aldridge Road Villas** has Nos. 1-53 on the east side and Nos. 2-48A on the west side. These are mainly semi-detached houses on four main storeys with additional rooms in the mansard roofs. They are all brick faced with canted bays up to second-floor level and windows with rounded heads above the side entrances. (In some cases the construction differs so that the entrances are in the middle.) On the west side, after No. 8 is Aldridge Court, which is a flat-roofed 1960s building on four storeys, containing 8 flats. The original buildings begin again with Nos. 20 and 22 which are stuccoed semi-detached houses with paired central entrances, and with No. 24 attached to it. Apart from that, the houses proceed regularly up the road on either side with attractive trees in the front areas of many of the houses.

There were 2 house sales in Aldridge Road Villas in 2010, with £3,775,000 being paid for No. 8 and £3,050,000 for No. 31, both semi-detached houses. There were also 8 flat sales. The highest price achieved was £535,000 for a flat at No. 49, and the remaining prices were mostly in the £400,000s, between £493,970 at No. 4 and £425,000 at No. 19, with £395,000 being the lowest price paid for a flat at No. 44.

On the west side of **Leamington Road Villas**, Nos. 2-12 form a terrace of basic Victorian houses on basement, raised ground and two upper storeys, with shallow porches and canted bays up to first-floor level. Nos. 14-40 are terraces of rather nicely proportioned houses on basement, ground and two upper storeys, and for the most part with first-floor terraces above canted bay ground-floor windows. Nos. 42-52 are on basement, ground and three upper storeys and they are brick-faced but stuccoed up to ground floor level. These are much larger houses with relatively grand ground and first storeys with triangular and curved pediments above the windows. They have paired porches and a continuous balcony, with metal railings running along the terrace at first floor level, widening out into terraces above the porches. The east side of Leamington Road Villas begins with No. 1 and the houses up to No. 11 follow an identical design to those opposite. Nos. 13-19 are more elaborate semi-detached houses on basement, ground and two upper storeys, with stone effect balconies outside the first-floor windows. The terrace, comprising Nos. 21-35, was designed in a very individual style. The houses are on basement, ground and two upper storeys. The ground-floor windows have curved heads, which makes them rather attractive, but they also sport a very dramatic plaster design with an Art Deco look to it, in contrast to the traditional Victorian decoration of the first-floor windows and above. Nos. 37-49 are another standard terrace of houses on basement, ground and two upper floors, with canted bays up to first-floor level, and very little decoration.

Leamington Road Villas did not see quite as much sale activity as Aldridge Road Villas in 2010. However, it achieved a higher price for the only house sale: £3,240,000 for No. 11. The remaining six transactions were flat sales. The highest price achieved was £500,000 for a flat at No. 22. The remaining sales were all in the £400,000s, with the lowest price being £419,000 for a flat at No. 37A.

St Luke's Road begins on the east side with a brick-built block called St Luke's Court. Nos. 9-31 are traditional terraced houses on four storeys (including a basement) with a simple porched entrance and canted bays at ground and first floor levels. Nos 33-47 are quite large terraced houses, also on four storeys (including a basement) and, in some cases, rooms in the gable ends. They have canted bays up to ground floor level and rather elaborately decorated first-floor windows – mostly triple windows. Tavistock Mansions at No. 49 is quite a pleasant looking post-war brick-built block with car parking underneath and containing 22 flats. On the west side of the road, Nos. 2-12 form a rather motley collection of terraced houses of differing heights. There is a short terrace, Nos. 18-24, between McGregor Road and Lancaster Road, with houses on basement, ground and two upper storeys and elaborate first-floor triple windows. There's another short terrace from No. 30 to No. 36, also on four storeys, with rooms in the mansard roof as well. St Luke's Road goes north over Tavistock Road. At the end near the Westway, there's a little clutch of houses from No. 42 to No. 50, which have the potential to be rather nice. The houses are brick-faced with shallow canted bays, and they are on four storeys, including a relatively high basement storey. They have tall first-floor windows and smaller second-floor windows, and the windows have rounded heads and are attractively decorated.

In 2010 a buyer paid £840,000 for No. 3 St Luke's Road. A flat at No. 33 sold for £605,000; there was also a sale for £377,000 of a flat in Tavistock Mansions, and £355,000 was paid for a flat at No. 50.

On each side of **Lancaster Road** there are terraced houses of very similar design. The typical house has a basement which is only partly below ground floor level and is set well back from the front railings. Then there is a very raised ground floor with canted bays, and then two storeys above that. The first-floor windows are quite tall. Some of the houses have porches with columns, but others do not. There are no balconies. The houses west of All Saints Road are often painted in very strong colours.

There were two house sales in Lancaster Road in 2010, with No. 37 selling for £3,100,000 and No. 13 for £2,650,000. The highest price paid for a flat was £785,000, at No. 190. A flat at No. 172-174 was sold for £615,000 and another at No. 61 for £537,500. The lowest price was £360,000 at No. 160

McGregor Road contains terraces of fairly similar houses on either side: Nos. 1-25 on the north side and Nos. 2-24 on the south side. They have basements, raised ground floors and two upper storeys, and a parapet wall at the top. There is room for pots on top of the shallow porches of the main entrances, but no room for balconies as such. The houses have fairly tall and decorated first-floor windows and shorter second floors. There are canted bays up to ground floor level.

There have been no transactions in McGregor Road since 2007, when No. 12 changed hands for £3,225,000.

St Luke's Mews is entered via a passage between Nos. 4 and 6 St Luke's Road. The mews is a cobbled road which runs right through to Basing Street, crossing All Saints Road in the middle, so it's more of a proper street than a normal mews. It contains charming two-storey houses in a variety of styles, so it avoids the uniformity of many mews. Several of the little houses are left unpainted, and some have been painted. There are some attractively original looking garage doors. It is partly residential and partly business, including some very attractive little shops and galleries. The section of St Luke's Mews running to

Basing Street is mainly taken up with more modern, 1970s style, mews houses on two storeys.

In 2010 No. 21 St Luke's Mews was purchased for £1,325,000. There was a flat sale at No. 12 for £470,000.

Portobello Road to Ledbury Road

Portobello Road has several mews off it which deserve some comment. The first two are north of Westbourne Park Road, but they belong in this section.

Hayden's Place on the west contains a gated development at No. 5, called Portobello Studios. There are five modern houses, which are white-painted with bathroom tiles round some of the windows. It's more Portmeirion than Portobello. If only the address had been No. 6!

One property in the development sold for £2,500,000 in 2010.

Alba Place, on the east side of Portobello Road, is a gated development of what look like original, but heavily, redeveloped mews houses all in bright colours. There are 12 dwellings, and they are mostly flat-faced with individual metal balconies outside a first-floor door leading nowhere.

There were no sales in Alba Place in 2010. In fact, there have been no sales since 2008, when No. 7 was sold for £636,000.

Dunworth Mews is a rather charming mews off Portobello Road. On the north side, there are bare brick-faced houses on two storeys which all still look fairly original, some with authentic-looking garage doors. Then there is a section running off it containing a modern set of 18 two-storey houses with large windows, most of which are part of a gated development with a paved courtyard with trees. Three additional houses are outside the gated part.

The only property sold in 2010 was No. 8 which changed hands for £1,200,000.

The battle of Puerto Bello

Admiral Vernon captured a town called Puerto Bello in Mexico from the Spaniards in 1739. Some now-forgotten but patriotic Englishman named his Notting Hill farm 'Porto Bello Farm', and Porto Bello Road became the name of the track leading to it.

Most of the houses in **Colville Terrace** are on the south side of the road, in a single terrace which runs from No. 1 up to No. 18 (consecutive). These are tall buildings on basement (which is really almost ground floor), very raised ground floor with a canted bay, and three main upper storeys. Flats have later been added in the mansard roof. On top of the porch structures, which most of the houses have, there are balustraded balconies outside first-floor windows, and there are also smaller balconies with metal railings outside first-floor windows above the ground floor bays. At the start, the houses are quite brightly painted, but they generally become cream-coloured towards the end of the terrace. Most of the houses have surprisingly narrow windows on the upper floors, with three windows per floor, and they have rather Aztec-looking decorations, like plumed birds heads above the windows. On the east side of the Colville Road junction, there is another long terrace on the south side of very similar design, beginning with No. 19 and running up to No. 38. The porches are possibly more pronounced and with more ornate column heads. The balustrade walls of the balconies are semi-circles piled on top of each other. Some of the later houses have sets of windows joined together in threes. As the terrace develops, several of the houses have canted bays running right up to the top of the buildings. There is a short terrace on the north side of the road at that point, comprising Nos. 39-42. These houses are similar to the houses opposite and also have canted bays running right up to the fifth storey.

George Tippett (p. 142) probably built most of the houses in Colville Terrace, but he also allocated plots to his relative, Thomas

Sheade Tippett, and to Henry Saunders and Walter Blackett, who were builders he worked with.

No. 15 Colville Terrace was sold for £1,620,000 in 2010. A ground floor flat at No. 21 went for £530,000. The remaining sales were at very similar prices: a flat at No. 41 for £620,000, another at No. 11 for £615,000, and one at No. 36 for £610,000.

The Talbot Estate

Portobello Farm covered 170 acres of land. In 1755 it was bought by Charles Henry Talbot, a barrister. The Talbot family let it to farmers until the second half of the 19th century when the farm tenancies ran out and the property became available for development. At the time it was owned by Sir George Talbot, and when he died in 1850, he left it to his two daughters, Mary Anne and Georgina Charlotte Talbot. They immediately sold part of the land to the Great Western Railway, and in 1853 they sold 17½ acres to Dr Samuel Walker (p. 71) who began work on All Saints Church. The Talbots sold the rest of their estate to Charles Blake (p. 98) in 1862.

Colville Square is the name given to the actual square, but also to one side of the road behind the square where Nos. 1-13 have their entrances. The long terrace of original houses have been converted to flats with stair structures added where the porches used to be. The buildings are on six storeys (including a basement) and some of the buildings have extra rooms in the mansard roof. On the other side, Nos. 1-13 have access directly onto the square itself, and this is a combination of garden beds, tarmac paths and a playground for children. Nos. 14-26, on the other side of the square, face the gardens across the road in the traditional manner. These are smaller houses on ground and basement, and with three main upper storeys. The upper floors each have three narrow windows with rounded heads. All the houses in Colville Square are painted in cream. The north of the square is a brick-built post-war mansion block called Twisaday House, owned by a housing trust.

George Tippett (p. 142) may have designed the houses in Colville Square but he didn't build any of them himself. The houses were built by builders he worked with on projects: John Wicking Phillips, Edward Gurling, and John May.

There was one sale in 2009, when a flat at No. 23 changed hands for £800,000 but there were no sales in 2010.

George Tippett

Dr Samuel Walker (p. 71) bought the land for the streets around All Saints Church in 1853, but there was a property crash and he had to sell. In 1860 the land was bought by George Tippett. Although he was still in his early thirties, he had built up a large building firm and was already building terraces in Princes Square and Leinster Square in Paddington. Between 1860 and 1875, he developed his Notting Hill estate, which included the Colville and Powis streets. Tippett probably designed the houses.

Tippett held onto what he regarded as the best properties to let, but when the area began to lose popularity with potential tenants his rental income couldn't cover his loan interest payments, and he went bankrupt in 1885. Bankrupty was the depressing fate of a large proportion of the entrepreneurs who built Victorian London.

Colville Houses is mostly taken up by modern housing association flats. But there's an interesting terrace on the east side, Nos. 1-8 (consecutive), which are large Victorian houses on five storeys (including basement). Between the porches, the houses have canted bays running right up to the fifth floor. They are all painted in different pastel shades and the first-floor windows have interesting painted plasterwork decoration above them in place of normal pediments.

A flat at No. 6A was purchased in 2010 for £650,000 – the only sale that year.

Colville Road begins at the Westbourne Grove End with a brick-built council block called Portobello Court. On the east side of the road, Nos. 2-8 comprise a short Victorian terrace of four storey houses (including a basement). North of Lonsdale Road, there are similar terraces: Nos. 10-14 on the east and Nos. 19-23 on the west. These are followed by more extravagant Victorian buildings, which are Nos. 16-28 on the east and Nos. 25-35 on the west side. The houses on the west are semi-detached houses on basement, ground and three upper storeys, with canted bays running the full height of the building on either side of the central porches. They are painted in various colours but with white plastered window surrounds. The first-floor windows are unusually tall. The houses on the east side have a slightly Italian feel to them. Everything is built in threes. Each terrace has three houses, the central porches share three columns, and all the windows are built as three units on the upper floors. The houses are all reasonably well set back from the road with front areas, they have five storeys in all (including a basement), and they are painted like those opposite.

In 2010 a flat at No. 33 was sold for £1,075,000, and a flat at No. 29 was sold for £655,000.

Colville Gardens is a continuation of Colville Road, running up to All Saints Church. On the east side, Nos. 31-53 are houses very similar in style to those on the west side of Colville Road. The difference is that these have unusually deep porch structures leading up to raised ground floor entrances, and these porches support balconies large enough to seat several people comfortably in the summer. On the west side is a long terrace of very tall properties which have been combined into Pinehurst Court, No. 1-3 Colville Gardens. They sit back a good 20 yards from the road behind a communal garden, and it was probably constructed as a single mansion block. There are seven storeys (including basements and mansard roofs flats). The whole terrace is painted cream with white window surrounds. The backs of the properties overlook Colville Square.

A flat in No. 37-39 changed hands for £650,000 in 2010. Otherwise, all the sales were in Pinehurst Court, where one flat was sold for £630,000 but the other four flat sales were at prices between £399,999 and £288,000.

On the east side of **Powis Gardens**. there is a stepped terrace of houses running uphill from No. 2 to No. 11 (consecutive). These are houses on basement, raised ground and two upper storeys. They generally have canted bays up to first-floor level, next to porch entrances which provide small balconies for the first-floor occupiers.. There is a council-built block of flats brick on the west side.

There was one notable sale in 2010 of a top floor flat at No. 9 for £1,200,000 but otherwise sales were are at the lower end of the price spectrum, with one sale at No. 10 for £610,000 and four sales for less than £500,000 - £480,000 for a basement flat also at No. 10, £492,500 and £480,000 for two flats at No. 31, and £495,000 for a ground floor flat at No. 20

On the east side of **Powis Square** there is a terrace of houses, Nos. 42-47 (consecutive). Nos. 46 and 47 are similar to the houses at the end of Colville Terrace. Nos. 42-45 are of a rather strange design. These houses are on five storeys (including a basement); the basement, ground and first storeys are rendered and painted. The two upper storeys are run-of-the-mill flat-fronted and brick-faced, with three windows per storey of a very basic design. But the basement, ground and first storeys contain unusual giant canted bays within which the porch structure is inserted at ground level. Finally, on the east side, there are two more modest houses at Nos. 49 and 50, which appear to have been inserted much later and on quite a small scale, with low floors, and very narrow windows. The west side of the square is occupied entirely by a post-war, brick-built mansion block on ground, raised ground and two upper storeys, which must be a council block. The block backs onto Powis Square, the communal garden, which contains grass areas but also a playing area for children. The northern side of Powis Square is a series of terraced houses, Nos. 29-41, which are on basement, ground and three upper storeys, with additional rooms in the roof above the parapet wall. These houses are painted in pastel colours, with canted bays up to first-floor level between the porches. Each has a small balcony for the second-floor flats above the bays. There are similar houses at Nos. 31-33, on the other side of the beautiful red-brick Tabernacle. Powis Court, at No. 29-30 Powis Square, is a post-war concrete block with balconies at each level containing 30 flats. The main part of Powis Square is the western section. Houses run round the corner towards the church up to No. 28. The houses on the west side start at No. 15. The main terrace runs up to No. 24 and these houses are on five storeys (including basement) and, on either side of the paired entrances, they have canted bays right up to the top of the building. They have unusually tall first-floor windows. The entrance doors have no porches. They are all rendered and painted in light colours. No. 25 is the start of a short terrace which in fact runs round the corner of the square. These properties are on basement, ground and three upper storeys.

George Tippett (p. 142) built 13 of the houses in Powis Square himself, and the others were built by John Tippett (a relative of his) and Thomas Basset May (a relative of John May who built houses in Colville Square). In the 1920s, Kensington Borough Council bought Nos. 1 to 13 Powis Square and converted them into 68 flats.

The highest price achieved in the square in 2010 was £795,000 for a first and second floor maisonette at No. 43. Other flat sales were for £630,000 at No. 92, £610,000 at No. 50, and £470,000 at No. 49.

Tippett's gardens

In most Kensington squares, the terraces faced across streets towards central gardens. In Notting Hill, this was reversed and many of the terraces were constructed so as to back onto hidden communal round gardens. George Tippett (p. 142) adopted something in between, which he used in Prince's and Leinster

Squares in Bayswater, and also in Colville Square, Colville Gardens and Powis Square. In his squares, one side of the square opened directly onto communal gardens, while the other side of the square faced them across the street. It was either the best or worst compromise – depending on which side of the street you live.

Powis Terrace contains a series of Victorian terraces on either side all having 'Hedgegate Court' written over the central porches. These buildings run from No. 1 to No. 17 from the east, and from No. 2 to No. 16 on the west. They are all on basement, ground and three upper storeys, with large canted bays on either side of the porch structures running right up to the top of the building. The facades are fairly ornate, with friezes and parapet walls, and they are all generally painted white. There are smaller terraced houses at the north end of the road which are more traditional in design and flat-fronted, all with shops on the ground floors, but with flats on the two upper floors.

George Tippett (p. 142) built nine of the houses in Powis Terrace himself, and it is not known who constructed the rest.

There were no sales in Powis Terrace in 2010. (In fact, there have been none since 2003!)

Why the area went downhill

On the face of it, there was no particular reason why this area should not have been just as successful as Bayswater, where George Tippett (p. 142) built very similar terraces. But the area found itself right next to a market in Portobello Road, and it became hemmed in by the Hammersmith & City Railway which opened in 1864. A lot of lower middle-class folk moved into the area, which caused the rich to move away as soon as their leases came to an end. (Many of the houses were let for 21 years.) In the 1880s houses began to be subdivided. By the turn of the century nearly half the houses had been converted into flats or boarding houses.

South of Artesian Road, **Ledbury Road** is mainly a shopping area but there are some flats in the upper storeys above ground floor shops. The main residential part of the street starts after the junction with Colville Terrace, where Nos. 101-117 form a terrace on the west side of the street. The houses have various designs - plots must have been allocated to different builders – but basically these houses are on four storeys (including a basement). The ground floor façade has been made to look like painted stonework, but the walls are bare brick above. On the east side of the road, starting at the junction with Artesian Road, Nos. 70-100 comprise a terrace of much more uniform houses on basement, ground, and two upper storeys. The central section has much more ornate upper parts than the outer houses, including pilasters sunk into the front of the building and pediments for the window heads. The rest of the terrace has brick-faced upper parts and fairly restrained and undecorated windows. The houses all have similar porch structures and there is a long metal railing running right along the terrace at first-floor level and opening out to form balconies above the porches

North of Talbot Road, there is a long terrace on the west side comprising Nos. 129-161. These properties are on basement, ground and three upper storeys. They are stuccoed and cream-painted up to ground floor and bare brick above. They have very ornate, painted first and second floor windows (and, in the central section, third floor windows) with a distinctly 'Art Deco' feel to it. On the other side of the road, there is a long council-built block of flats on three and four storeys behind small gardens.

Ledbury Road was built by other member of Cullingford's family during the 1840s and 1850s.

On the west side, Ladbroke granted William Cullingford leases of the plots of Nos. 39-43 (odd) and Nos. 32-36 (even) opposite.

William Judd took No. 38, the remaining house on the east side.

On the west side in 1846, John Snook, a Paddington builder, built Nos. 47-51, and John Pilkington, a St Marylebone builder, built Nos. 53 and 55. Four years later, William Turner built Nos. 57-61.

There was one house sale in Ledbury Road in 2009: No. 117, which was bought for £2,820,000. A flat at No. 129 was sold for £920,000, a top floor maisonette at No. 47 for £795,000 and a flat at No. 60 for £680,000.

Campden Hill Square area

QUICK REFERENCE						
STREET	PAGE	STREET	PAGE	STREET	PAGE
Aubrey Road	151	Campden Hill Place	155	Hillsleigh Road	154
Aubrey Walk	152	Campden Hill Square	149	Wycombe Square	153
Campden Hill Gardens	155				

Campden Hill Square, the central garden square, which slopes downhill, is large and rather lovely, with plenty of natural looking groups of shrubs and trees, as well as a nice lawn and flower beds. There is a good view looking north towards Holland Park, especially from the south side of the square.

On the east side of the square, Nos. 1 and 2 are probably 20th-century buildings, which are bigger and wider than the other houses but with only two main storeys above ground floor level. Nos. 3-12 are all very similar as they step up the hill. Most, but not all, have basements. The ground floor levels are stuccoed with horizontal banding. There are generally three brick-faced storeys above. The windows have no particular decoration and are all the more charming for it. The two windows above the main door at first-floor level have individual balconies and the second-floor windows usually have balconettes. The houses have quite well grown front gardens.

The houses on the south side of the square have a fantastic view from the top of the hill. The houses are set well back from the pavement, with front gardens. Nos. 14-25 – the first range of houses – have basements, raised ground floors, and above that, three and in some cases four storeys. They were not all built together so there are all kinds of first-floor balcony railings. The houses are mainly Victorian and stucco-faced up to ground level and with bare brick above. No. 18 is very different; it is faced in red brick and has almost a Bramham Gardens style to it. Nos. 26-29 are early 20th-century additions to the terrace, which to some extent mimic the style of the existing houses, but on a much smaller scale. They all rise to second floor level, but otherwise are completely different from each other.

The houses on the west side of the square are rather more varied than on the east side. There are some Victorian houses with basement, ground and two upper floors. Nos. 50-52 share a similar design in which the whole of the front wall of the building on either side of the entrance doors is curved to create a bow, within which sits a completely flat window. They each have a main ground and first floor. No. 50 seems to have been converted to provide fairly modern French doors and a garage at the bottom level, but No. 51 looks very original, with a scarily diagonal door top, indicating settlement in the past, and it retains its basement. No. 52 is double-fronted, with a big entrance porch and two curved bow wings. No. 53 is a more conventional flat-faced house on basement, ground and two upper storeys. The basement and ground are stucco-faced and it is brick faced above.

The square was designed by Joshua Flesher Hanson, following the style of Regency Square, which he had built in Brighton in 1818. Hanson may have built some of the houses in Campden Hill Square himself but he generally granted the leases to other builders. Campden Hill Square was originally called Notting Hill Square but the name was changed to its present name in 1893.

There were some chunky sales in Campden Hill Square in 2010. The highest price was £7,500,000 for No. 3, followed by £6,041,999 for No. 47, £5,431,646 for No. 48 and £5,150,000 for No. 10. There were no flat sales.

Joshua Flesher Hanson

Joshua Flesher Hanson seems to pop up as a middle-man in property deals all through the Notting Hill area. He built extensively in Brighton, in Hyde Park Gate, and also in the Ladbroke Estate (p. 61). In 1823 he entered into an agreement with James Ladbroke (p. 61) to develop the area between

Ladbroke Grove and Ladbroke Terrace, and he also built along Holland Park Avenue.

Aubrey Road is steep, as are the prices for its houses. The house numbers run downhill to Holland Park Avenue on the west side and run up from Holland Park Avenue on the east side of the road. The road starts with Aubrey Lodge, a rather 1920s school-like building on five large storeys, containing seven flats (including the caretaker's). No. 1 is a nice little house which looks very 'Regency' in style, built in grey brick but with red bricks for quoins and window heads. Other features include the porch hood on enormous brackets, an ornate oriel window at first-floor level, and the rather 'un-Regency' mansard windows in the steep tiled roof. No. 2 has a mixed look to it - Gothic battlements, little arrow slit windows and some church-like windows, but also a protruding Tudor-style wooden canted bay at first-floor level. It looks a bit bizarre. Nos. 3 and 4 look like they were originally designed as a prison, in grey brick, with gable ends and a Gothic look. No. 5 is a big cream-faced building on four storeys. No. 6, in a mushroom colour, is on three storeys. Nos. 5 and 6 have diagonally placed windows, as if on a chessboard. No. 6 is the most natural-looking house, on two main storeys, with two single windows on either side of the raised main door, a very wide frontage, and mansard windows in the roof. No. 7 is a more modern building on two storeys with a mansard roof.

On the east side, Nos. 8 and 9 are more modern houses on three main storeys, plus rooms in the mansard roof, and garages on the ground floor level. Nos. 10 and 11 are pebble-dashed houses on three storeys, looking as if they were built in the 1930s. No. 12 is a modern house, as are Nos. 13 and 14. They all look architecturally designed and are built with plenty of windows.

Aubrey Road was originally designed by Joshua Flesher Hanson (p. 150) as a service road for his new houses on the west side of Campden Hill Square. In 1841 this piece of land was all that still remained of the land Hanson had bought from the Lloyd family in 1823. Instead of building onto it, he sold it on to a surgeon called James Hora. Hora died shortly afterwards but his widow employed Henry Wyatt, an architect, to carry out the development. Wyatt built six Gothic-style villas between 1843 and 1847. These were originally called Aubrey Villas, but are now numbered 1-6 Aubrey Road. The road was named Aubrey Road in the 1840s.

There was only one sale in Aubrey Road in 2010: No. 6A was bought for £4,400,000.

The Lloyd family estate

In Tudor times, there was a 20 acre farm called Stonehills, south of what is now Holland Park Avenue. In 1750 it came into the possession of the Lloyd Family. The site of Campden Hill Place was sold off in 1820 to Thomas Brace, a solicitor. The site of Campden Hill Gardens was sold to Evan Evans, a Bond Street grocer. But 13 acres remained, including the rest of the Campden Hill Square area. This was sold in 1823 to Joshua Flesher Hanson (p. 150), a substantial developer in the Notting Hill and Holland Park area.

Aubrey Walk runs along the top of the hill. Most of the south side of Aubrey Walk is occupied by Wycombe Square. But near Aubrey Road, No. 13 is a 1950s block with three flats. Nos. 15-19 are Edwardian-looking houses in a yellowish brick on three storeys; but strangely many of the windows have been bricked in. At the western end of the street stands Aubrey House, which is one of the largest private houses in Kensington and has a blue plaque referring to four famous former residents. It also has one of the largest private gardens in Kensington. Aubrey Walk was originally an approach road to Aubrey House. Its name was originally Notting Hill Grove but it was renamed Aubrey Walk in 1893. When Campden Hill Square was constructed by Joshua Flesher Hanson, coach houses and stables were built in Aubrey

Walk. These were later converted into residential accommodation.

At No. 9 Aubrey Walk is the Campden Hill Tennis Club, which is the biggest private tennis club in Central London. It was founded in 1884. There are six indoor and six outdoor courts.

On the northern side, at the Hillsleigh Road end, Nos. 2-4 are rather charming Victorian houses on three storeys with tall first-floor French doors opening onto little balconettes. Properties in Aubrey Walk were built by Joshua Hanson and by a coal merchant called John Cowmeadow, who constructed Nos. 2-6 (even) Aubrey Walk. It seems he went out of business shortly afterwards. Nearby is St George's Church which looks like a building designed by Escher. Nos. 8-16 is a run of 1930s-style cottages on three main storeys with additional rooms in the very steep hipped roof. The cottages have shallow canted bay windows next to the entrance doors, and little front gardens. Then there is a series of individual houses built together as a terrace, but in different styles and clearly from different eras. No. 30 is a three-storey house in Canary Wharf-style. No. 26 is a rather attractively quirky Edwardian four-storey building with different sized arches and stairs that look as if the same 'Escher' influence was in play as in the nearby church. Finally, Nos. 46-50 are '70s-style townhouses on three storeys with garages.

No sales occurred in Aubrey Walk in 2010. The most recent sale was of No. 12, which changed hands for £2,810,000 in 2009.

Opposite St George's Church, on Aubrey Walk, is the entrance to **Wycombe Square** which takes up most of the south side of Aubrey Walk. This is an extensive development of quality houses and flats constructed by St James Homes in 2003. The main block of flats is No. 1 Wycombe Square, which contains 27 flats on four main storeys. The low-built buildings bordering Aubrey Walk are also flats, Nos. 27-43. (The security guards assure me that this numbering is correct even though there are 27 flats in No. 1 Wycombe Square.) Then there are 19 town houses running back from the road, round a garden square, and four further flats attached to that. There is also underground car parking. The ground floors of the houses are attractively stone-faced and so are the window surrounds; the rest of the facades are faced in yellow brick. Many of the houses have bow windows either at ground and first floor to break up the view. Many of the houses are built around the square and these have very weighty square-columned stone porches with balconies above. The whole thing looks very classy, and even the trees seem to be perfectly barbered. The gardens in the centre of the square have manicured lawns in lozenge-shaped brick enclosures, and there are a lot of beautifully shaped privets and similar shrubs round the lawns and in the front gardens of some of the houses as well.

There were no sales in Wycombe Square in 2010, in contrast with 2009 when there were five sales, including £9,557,500 paid for No. 19.

Hillsleigh Road runs uphill from Holland Park Avenue. The first property on the east side is a big block of flats called Linton House, which contains 38 flats on six main storeys and a slightly recessed penthouse floor, all built in a severe red brick with white-painted balconies. (It's address is No. 11 Holland Park Avenue, but it goes well back up Hillsleigh Road.) Hillsleigh Road houses begin on the west side of the road, with No. 1 on the corner, and running up to No. 12. These are individual houses, some Victorian and some quite modern. What they all seem to share is that they are on two main floors with some kind of attic conversion above. There seems to have been a competition in the size and variety of their attic second-floor conversions, because they are of unusual shapes and sizes. After No. 12, the housing switches to the east side of the road with a two-storey house, painted flamingo pink, called Ness Cottage (although it looks more like a fort than a cottage with its central turret and battlements). Next to it is Essex House, a two-storey red brick house with very ornate windows, which has the look of a Victorian rectory with its large gables and wide front door. Hill Lodge at the top of the road is a big house with a large annex behind a high wall.

Hillsleigh Road was originally called New Road but was renamed Hillsleigh Road in 1910. It was constructed on the east side of Campden Hill Square to give access to stables and coach houses behind the main houses in the square. On some unused land, Hanson built several additional houses. There has been considerable rebuilding since.

£4,350,000 was paid for No. 1 Hillsleigh Road in 2010.

Campden Hill Place is a private road next to Hillsleigh Road, containing four rather attractive houses facing onto a large central flowerbed with a drive around it. There are three houses on the east side. No. 1 appears to be a late Victorian brick-faced house on two main storeys with prominent gables. Nos. 2 and 3 are large detached houses on two storeys with canted bays beside the main doors. No. 4 is tucked away at the top on the west side.

We could not find a record of any sales in Camden Hill Place.

Campden Hill Gardens runs from Aubrey Walk going northwards, with a branch to the west. The buildings are mainly typical Victorian houses on four storeys and they are generally brick-faced with white-painted stucco up to first floor, with protruding ground-floor and first-floor windows

Evan Evans, a New Bond Street grocer, bought part of the Lloyd Estate. He died in 1825 and his great nephew, Robert Evans, inherited it. It was only in 1870 that Robert Evans decided to join in the general development in the area. He granted leases to John Reeves and George Butt, who were local builders. The next year, they bought the freeholds of most of the plots from him and they built most of the houses.

Nos. 4-10 on the west side form a big terrace with basement, ground and three quite large upper storeys, shared recessed entrances, and canted bay windows. The houses are built in grey brick, although the basement and ground storeys are stuccoed. Nos. 12-18 and Nos. 22-26 are similar terraces. No. 28 is much wider, with huge canted bays and extraordinarily large sash windows at ground floor and first floor levels, almost like an art studio. Nos. 32-34 are a post-war brick-faced block, on three main storeys, with mansard rooms but no basement. There are bay-fronted houses on either side. Nos. 4-18 may have been built by William Childhouse, a Paddington builder, and Jonathan Pearson, an ironmonger from Notting Hill. Nos. 28-36 were built by Alfred Little, the son of the well-known Kensington builder, Jeremiah

Little, between 1871 and 1874.

On the eastern side of the street there is a long terrace of virtually identical double-fronted houses, from Nos. 5-23, which are on lower ground, raised ground and two upper storeys. They have canted bays on either side of the entrance door running up to the first-floor level, and a little balcony outside the second-floor windows on top. The houses have recessed entrances. The ground-floor windows have curved tops, but the first-floor windows are square headed. Some of the houses have mansard rooms in the attic. These were also built by Alfred Little between 1871 and 1874.

No. 32A Camden Hill Gardens was sold for £1,625,000 in 2010. Otherwise there were only flat sales, at prices from £485,000 at No. 9, up to £670,000 at No. 24.

Hillgate Village

QUICK REFERENCE					
STREET	PAGE	STREET	PAGE	STREET	PAGE
Callcott Street	157	Farm Place	157	Jameson Street	159
Campden Hill Road	164	Farmer Street	159	Kensington Place	161
		Hillgate Place	160	Peel Street	162
Campden Street	164	Hillgate Street	158		
Edge Street	162				

Farm Place is a short street running between Hillgate Place and Uxbridge Street. The area itself is known as 'Hillgate Village'. At the end of the street is a small old-fashioned neighbourhood pub called the Uxbridge Arms.

All the house numbers in this street are consecutive, as opposed to odd on one side and even on the other side. Nos. 1-8 Farm Place is a terrace of plain brick-faced, three-storey houses (including basements) painted in vibrant colours, with slightly raised ground floor entrances, normal sash windows next to the entrance door and one or two bedroom windows above. No. 10, which turns the corner into Hillgate Place and has its entrance there, is one storey higher. On the east side of the road Nos. 11-18 are three-storey houses (including basements). The houses are much more uniform on this side of the road, with very similar entrance doors with architraves above, and two first-floor windows. Nos. 19 and 20 at the corner with Hillgate Street are larger and have an additional second storey.

There were no sales in Farm Place in 2010, in contrast with 2009 when four houses changed hands.

Callcott Street is a small tree-lined street between Uxbridge Street and Hillgate Place. The house numbers start at the Uxbridge Street end on the west with a fairly large (for this part of town) four storey house (including basement) with a central raised main door and a side extension. The main terrace is Nos. 2-10, which is a rather nice series of houses on three storeys (including basements) with matching raised entrance doors, ground- floor windows with a bracketed architrave, and two attractively designed first-floor windows above.

On the east side, Nos. 11-17 is also a terrace of houses on three storeys (including basements), but they are somewhat smaller than the houses on the west side. Certainly they don't have such high raised ground floors, although they are slightly raised. The houses on the west side are generally stucco-faced and scored to look like brickwork and then painted. Most of the houses on the east side are painted brick, but some have the scored stucco at least up to ground floor level. All the houses have very similar black railings along the pavement and also leading up to the raised ground floor's main entrance door.

No. 17 Callcott Street was sold for £1,650,000 in 2010.

Joseph Clutterbuck

The area surrounded by Notting Hill Gate, Kensington Church Street, Campden Hill Road and Sheffield Terrace was known as The Racks in earlier centuries. In 1839 the property came into the hands of Benjamin and Joseph Clutterbuck, who were professional brick makers, and the land became their brickfield. Joseph Clutterbuck (or builders appointed by him) was responsible for the construction of the streets between Notting Hill Gate and Hillgate Place (formerly Dartmoor Street). Clutterbuck himself died in about 1851. Most of the houses in this area were put in multiple occupation and it was really close to being a slum.

Hillgate Street is an attractive little street with a restaurant and residential mix. Joseph Clutterbuck, or builders appointed by him, was responsible for the construction of houses in Hillgate Street (formerly Johnson Street). Nos. 8-22 on the west side is a terrace of houses on basement, ground and two upper storeys, painted in a variety of colours, but with not much architectural decoration, and probably not built by a single builder. There is a Greek restaurant and a Japanese restaurant on the ground floor of some former houses. On the east side, it is all residential, with Nos. 9-23 being a charming terrace of little houses on ground and two upper storeys behind small front gardens. Like the houses opposite, these have painted facades and simple doors and windows. In the middle, at No. 13, is Hillgate House, a Victorian municipal-type building, now occupied by businesses. The Hillgate Pub is a rather attractive pub on the corner with Hillgate Place. Hillgate Street continues a short distance beyond Hillgate Place where No. 28 is a simple brick house on four storeys.

No. 25 Hillgate Street was sold for £1,650,000 in 2009 but there were no sales in Hillgate Street in 2010.

Farmer Street is a quiet little road. Joseph Clutterbuck or builders appointed by him were responsible for the construction of houses in Farmer Street (formerly Farm Street). It starts on the east side with Nos. 1A-7, which is a row of small two-storey houses with bow windows. Nos. 9-25 is a terrace of slightly larger houses, but still relatively small, with a basement, raised ground floor and first floor. These houses are mainly painted, some have little canopied door hoods, and some have bow windows. On the west side of the road, past Geales Restaurant, Nos. 6-22 are three-storey houses, but instead of basements, these have normal ground-level entrances and two storeys above. The houses on the east side have room for two first-floor windows, but the west houses only have one central first-floor window. No. 24 is a bigger property with basement, raised ground and first floor, built as part of a terrace in Hillgate Place.

There were no sales in Farmer Street in 2010. The most recent sale was of No. 1 Farmer Street in 2009 for £1,150,000.

Jameson Street runs north of Kensington Place. The street is tree-lined on one side. As with the other streets, Joseph Clutterbuck or builders appointed by him were responsible for the construction of the houses in Jameson Street (formerly St James or James Street). Jameson Street has a single terrace of houses on the west side starting at No. 2 and running up to No. 22. These start as houses on ground and one upper storey, but from No. 16 they have a basement as well. Each house has one sash windows next to the plain entrance door with two first-floor windows above. On the east side of the street, the main terrace begins at No. 11 and runs up to No. 37. These are workers' cottages on three storeys with no basements. There is a simple brick decoration running along below the very top of the facades like a cornice. Most of the windows have slightly curved heads, which is an attractive unifying feature. Most of the houses on the west side are fully painted, but those on the east are usually only painted up to ground floor level with bare brick above.

The most recent sale in Jameson Street was No. 17, sold for £1,200,000 in 2008.

Hillgate Place connects many of the other streets in Hillgate Village. On the north side Nos. 4-10 form a short terrace between Jameson Street and Farmer Street. The houses have basement, ground and first storeys, with paired porches for the raised ground floor entrances. The houses are similar in the next stretch from Farmer Street to Hillgate Street, comprising Nos. 12-30, but the houses may be slightly wider because they have two windows per house at first-floor level, whereas the previous terrace has only one window per house. (No. 20 has canted bays at ground and first floor level, and No. 18 has a bow window at ground floor level.)

On the south side of the road, there is a single terrace of houses running from No. 3 to No. 31, also in a very similar architectural style to those opposite, containing basement, ground and first floors. The style changes slightly from house to house and the different cornices reveal that different builders built individual houses. On the corner with Hillgate Street, No. 25 is a larger house with an additional second-storey.

Beyond Hillgate Street, the houses continue in similar style. The long terrace on the south side runs from No. 33 to No. 71 on the corner, and these are all roughly similar houses on basement, ground and first floors, with very occasional ground floor bay windows (possibly inserted later) and painted facades in various colours. At the very end, standing at right angles, Nos. 73 and 77 are similar, but between them is an entrance to Nos. 75, 75A and 75B, which is a little private mews. On the north side there's a little terrace, Nos. 26-30, starting next to The Hillgate pub with houses on basement, raised ground and first floors only, and with two first floor windows. From Callcott Street, the terrace of Nos. 36-44 also contains houses on basement, ground and first floors, but they have a slightly different style, with virtually no raise to the ground floor, and with a stuccoed façade which is scored to appear to be stone work and then painted. (Most other houses in the street are brick faced.)

As with elsewhere in Hillgate Village, Clutterbuck or builders appointed by him built the houses in Hillgate Place (formerly named Dartmoor Street because John Jones, who sold the land to the Johnsons, had apparently quarried stone on Dartmoor for Clutterbuck's construction business).

In Hillgate Place, No. 41 was sold for £1,550,000 in 2010. There were also flat sales at No. 42 for £315,000 and at No. 15 for £530,000.

Kensington Place runs between Campden Hill Road and Kensington Church Street, and is on a slight incline. There are a few houses on the south side of Kensington Place near the Kensington Church Street end, but mainly this side is taken up by garages or the backs of properties in the main street. Kensington Place has terraces of houses, such as Nos. 7-23 on the north side, beginning at Jameson Street, on three storeys (including basements) with triangular pediments above the ground-floor windows. At the start of the terrace the houses are brick-faced, but from No. 17 onwards they are rather roughly plastered and painted. From Hillgate Street, the houses run from No. 24 to No. 46, in a similar style. The earlier houses are brick-faced but painted, and from No. 33 they are bare-brick faced for the most part. These houses have rather ornate ground-floor windows with triangular pediments on brackets next to raised ground floors, contrasted with fairly plain first-floor windows, and they have an architrave above. There's a reasonable amount of area in front of the basement windows.

On the south side of the street, near the Campden Hill Road end, there is an extensive post-war estate, which is reasonably attractive, built in dark bricks. It starts with an attractively creeper-covered seven-storey block on the corner of the main road, called Melbourne House. Then there's a row of two-storey townhouses, Nos. 51-59, running along Kensington Place, also with plants growing up the brickwork and pleasantly overgrown front gardens. This is followed by Palmerston House at No. 60, which is another block of flats, this time on eight storeys and containing 59 flats. The blocks of flats have extensive underground parking areas.

In Kensington Place, No. 35 was purchased for £2,100,000 and No. 28 for £1,891,850. There was also a flat sold at No. 6 for £795,000.

Edge Street is a cul-de-sac which runs west of Kensington Church Street. The West Middlesex Water Works Co. bought land south of Kensington Place in 1809, where they built a reservoir. Some of the land was not needed and they rented it out. After 1825, they built a road and a sewer through this land and sold it off for development. The road now known as Edge Street was then known as Sheffield Street. It took its later name from Andrew Edge, who was one of the purchasers. This was a cul-de-sac and small houses were built here similar to those in Peel Street. Many of them were knocked down to make way for the Circle line in 1865, and later for the construction of a mansion block.

On the north side, there is a mixture of brick-faced houses in an assortment of architectural styles. Nos. 18-36 on the north side are mainly on two storeys. Nos. 40-42 look like they were originally a school. Some of the houses have attractive trellised roof gardens, or bay windows, all different. On the south side the properties are now mainly commercial (such as 'The Studios' at No. 170) or schools. There's a large Victorian red-brick mansion block called Campden Hill Mansions just off the main road on the south side with 22 flats. Edge Street and Peel Street are the outer boundary of the Hillgate Village area.

The only sales in Edge Street in 2010 were two flats at Campden Hill Mansions, which went for £595,000 and £550,500.

Peel Street runs between Campden Hill Road and Kensington

Church Street, and is on a slight gradient. Most of the north side is taken up with Campden Houses, early 20th century blocks on six storeys, then there is a higgledy-piggledy mix of mainly three storey houses. The houses are mainly two or three-storeys and both sides of the street are terraced. Some houses are painted and some are just bare brick. On the south side, halfway along the road, is an old pub called the Peel Arms which is now a private house. The north side on the west end of the street is a large six storey terraced mansion block built in 1877. On the south side of the street, halfway along, is a rather attractive, very narrow street called Peel Passage, linking the street with Campden Street.

Peel Cottage on the north side has a blue plaque naming Sir William Russell Flint, the artist who lived there from 1925 to 1969, and the cottage has an unusual tiled frontage.

Only houses changed hands in Peel Street in 2010: £1,775,000 was paid for No. 37, £1,535,000 for No. 51, £1,580,000 for No. 97 and £1,150,000 for No. 39.

Punter and Ward

In 1822, a speculator called Henry Chandless bought the land on which Peel Street and Campden Street were later built. Chandless sold this on to two Marylebone builders, John Punter and William Ward. (It then turned out that Chandless was a minor, so the buyers had to wait until he reached 21 before he could sign over the property to them). Punter took Peel Street for development and Ward took Campden Street. Punter built a number of houses in the area himself, but in 1829 he sold his remaining land to John Herapath, a railway journalist. When the houses were originally built there were no sewers. One house was used to keep pigs. Many of the original houses were knocked down when the Circle Line was constructed. After it was covered over, rebuilding took place in the 1870s.

Campden Street stretches between Campden Hill Road and Kensington Church Street. It is on a slight slope. The north side, at the western end, has a uniform terrace of three-storey houses, stuccoed up to first floor, which abut immediately onto the road. The eastern section of the north side has more varied architecture, mainly houses with attractive ground-floor bay windows in differing styles.

The houses on the south side of the street are slightly smaller, mainly brick, with stucco up to the first floor. On the same side is Byam Shaw House, a particularly attractive and unusual block of flats.

The eastern section of the street has some small specialist antique shops and also the Churchill Arms at the junction with Kensington Church Street.

Campden Street was built by William Ward. It was his portion of the land jointly bought with John Punter in 1822. He constructed houses here in a relatively relaxed way over the next 30 years. In about 1850 he sub-contracted the work of building the remaining houses to Henry Gilbert, who was both a builder and a pub owner, and to William Wheeler, a local builder. Ward died shortly afterwards.

Three houses changed hands in Campden Street in 2010: No. 26 for £1,900,888, No. 29 for £1,650,000 and No. 35 for £1,310,000. At the other end of the scale, a flat at No. 42 was sold for £356,000.

Campden Hill Road extends well beyond this area and into Kensington and so we do not attempt to cover it here. But we provide the following price information.

No. 27 Campden Hill Road changed hands for £3,450,000 in 2010 and No. 142A was sold for £1,500,000. There were also some high-value flat sales, including: £3,100,000, 3,010,000, £2,225,000 and £3,800,000 for flats at Campden Hill Court. At the other end of the scale, £435,000 was paid for a flat at Kensington Heights, No. 91-95.

Flats and houses

Houses

Terraced houses
Houses were built in long terraces, each terrace forming a side of a square. Terraces would be built facing into the square with a road in front. In the centre of the square there would usually be a central communal garden. Later, terraces would often be built facing out, with their backs to the central square, which allowed the occupiers to have direct access to the communal gardens without having to cross a road.

The benefit in building terms of constructing houses in terraces was that side walls could be shared between houses, and the chimney stacks for two houses could be built as one paired unit back to back.

The economic reasons for building terraces were that more houses could be crammed into the land allotted to a builder by the landowner. The more houses, the more rent the land owner would get once they were built. Property speculation in Victorian England was a risky business; most of the builder developers described in this book went bust at some point in their careers. Land owners demanded a payment annual rent after a certain number of years, leaving just enough time for builders to construct the houses and hopefully sell or rent them at a profit.

Mews and stables behind terraces
Until the arrival of the railway, most well-to-do families needed a horse-drawn carriage to take them around. So many terraces were constructed with cobbled mews behind, containing stables and accommodation for stable hands and coachmen. The horses tended to get the better accommodation. They are now all converted into little mews houses, usually on two storeys.

Semi detached and detached houses
Around the 1860s, there was more demand for detached houses. This didn't make economic sense for developers trying to maximise the land

they had been allocated by the land owner. Semi-detached houses were the compromise which was reached. Two houses would be built with a single-storey, entrance and porch structure in the middle for both the houses. Often they were still part of a long terrace.

Since the entrance and hall structure were now built on the side and were not taking up part of the ground floor of the house, the ground floor rooms tended to become the main family rooms, and the first floor became the main bedroom floor. Such houses needed fewer upper floors because there was more living space on each floor.

Flats

Mansion blocks

In the 1870s the demand for huge houses for large families (and for even larger contingents of servants) was falling away. At the same time land was becoming ever more expensive, and builders could only make a profit by building ever higher. Industrial processes and building methods meant that it was becoming feasible to construct mansion blocks (purpose-built blocks of flats). The idea was seen to work in Baron Houseman's Paris that the idea was imported into England. In the 1880s, even developments which started as houses often finished as flats as builders found they could no longer sell large houses. In some very exclusive parts of central London, single family houses remain as houses. But most terraces have now been converted into individual flats on each storey.

Converted flats

It was only after nearly every bit of land in London had been covered with family houses, that everyone decided that actually they preferred flats. So, in the 20th century, many of the family houses in the Notting Hill area, as elsewhere in London, were converted into flats.

Storeys

The number of storeys or floors in a terrace varies considerably from one street to the next, depending on the market the builder was trying to appeal to. In this book, we use the English system of referring to the floor above the ground floor as the 'first floor' and the floor above that as the 'second floor' etc. It's illogical because they obviously aren't the building's first floor, but it has the advantage that all first floors mean the same type of accommodation in different kinds of terraces, as you will see from the explanation below.

Basement. We call any storey whose floor is below street level the 'basement'. Not all houses have basements, but most terraces in London do. This was too damp for occupation by the owner's family, and it was used for the kitchens, store rooms and servants' quarters.

Ground floor. We call the storey above the basement 'the ground floor'. If there is no basement, then the lowest storey of the house is the ground floor. Every house has a ground floor. In terraces, the ground floor was usually raised up several feet from the true ground level, and was reached by going up a flight of steps from the street. If the 'ground' floor is raised up high enough, then it is often referred to also as a 'raised ground floor'. In that case, the 'basement' floor may have its windows almost as street level and may also be referred to as a 'raised basement'. The ground floor was where the family traditionally had their dining room in Victorian times.

First floor. We call the floor above the ground floor, 'the first floor'. The first floor was where the family had their main living rooms. If you look at the front or 'façade' of Georgian or Victorian houses, many of them have large and quite elaborate windows at first storey level, indicating their prime status, often with French windows opening onto a balcony over the street. Although there were usually two rooms (a front and a back room) there would be large double doors between them which could be opened out to turn them into a larger single room for entertaining. The reason for this superior status over the ground floor was that the ground floor rooms were narrower because they had to make space for the hallway from the main door and then the stairs. But on the first floor, the front room could take up the whole of the frontage, and it was only the back room which had to give up some space for the landing.

Second floor. We call the floor two storeys above the ground floor, 'the second floor'. Bedrooms for the family were usually on the second floor, and when you look at the frontage of a terrace you can see that the windows are usually not as tall as the first floor windows because the bedroom floors were not given such grand rooms, and the windows are usually not so ornate.

Third floor. Many houses stopped at the second floor when it came to floors in the main house. But the larger properties might also have a third floor for bedrooms for the family.

Attics and garrets. Quite often the main front wall of the terrace – its façade or front elevation – is topped with a cornice or a balustrade. There is then a roof above, but it is usually set back slightly from the front wall, and may even be entirely invisible from the street. But equally many houses were built with a steep 'hipped' roof, forming an attic, and you can see windows let into the tiled surface. This is where traditionally the servants had their shared rooms, and it is referred to as an attic storey. Sometimes, attic storeys were added decades later in order to extend the living accommodation. In late Victorian terraces, large gables were an architectural effect, and attic rooms were often built into the gable ends. Single rooms are often called garrets.

Architectural Fashions

Palladian or Classical style

The prevailing architectural style of Georgian period was 'Palladianism'. This was invented by Andrea Palladio in Italy and essentially it required houses to copy the appearance of Roman temples. That is the reason why many Georgian and Victorian houses appear to have columns and friezes, much like those of ancient Rome, pressed into the front of the houses. Sometimes – but really only incidentally – these columns also had useful functions, such as holding up the porch outside the main door. Brickwork was covered by a layer of plaster or cement, called 'stucco', to make it all seem like stonework, as in ancient temples. To increase that impression, you will often see lines cut into the stucco plasterwork to make it look as if there are blocks of stone underneath it, but really it's just plain brick.

Neoclassical style

The style went through a number of changes in the 19th century, such as the 'Neoclassical' which substituted Greek for Roman temples as the model for builders to follow. Robert Adam was the major exponent of the style.

Italianate style

John Nash introduced this style in his designs for the terraces of Regent's Park. It combined classical traditional style with the 'picturesque' style based on nature, and the beauty of the natural landscape. However, its exponents didn't admire the actual beauty of the real world. They admired it only if it looked like a painting. In fact, the word Picturesque was taken from pittoresco, the Italian for 'in the manner of a painting'.

Queen Anne style

There was a dramatic shift in style in the 1860s, when white painted stucco suddenly dropped right out of fashion, and everyone wanted buildings in red brick. This is called 'Queen Anne style' named after the queen who came before the Georges, and before stucco. These red-brick buildings often have very elaborate gables, in imitation of the Dutch style of houses along the canals of cities like Amsterdam. One impetus behind the new building style was that it was cheaper. Bricks were cheap. Using cut bricks on end was the cheapest way to form a window head. Since gables were essentially free-standing features above the roof, they were also comparatively cheap to build.

Gothic style

Gothic Revival was a Victorian movement which believed artists should seek inspiration from the works of the medieval church builders rather than from ancient Greece or Rome (and heaven forbid that anyone should simply invent something new).

The obvious effect on domestic architecture was that doors and windows began to be built with pointed arches and stone surrounds.

Domestic Revival style
Under the influence of the Arts and Crafts Movement, architects of the 1870s and 1880s rejected classical and foreign styles in favour of a 'simple' traditional local style. The idea was to build houses which did not look like they had been designed by architects, although of course they were. Mediaeval barns rather than Greek temples or Gothic cathedrals were the inspiration. One of their most unwelcome introductions was pebble dashing.

Copy books not architects
Victorian builders weren't much different from house builders today. They didn't care much about architecture. What they cared about was building houses people would want to buy. So they observed the prevailing taste, and copied it. Copy books were produced telling the builder exactly how to build a typical house and they reproduced them endlessly until the public wanted something else. The public was usually even more conservative than the builders, so decades after pure architects had given up Classical style, Victorian builders kept churning out terraces with columns, stucco and friezes.

Façades

Front elevation
The front wall of a house – the front elevation or façade – is the bit everyone can see, so it was traditionally given special decorative treatment. This was partly to make it look more attractive and partly to cover up cheap building materials.

Stuccoed façades
The best 18th century houses were faced in blocks of stone. That appearance remained the ideal. One way to make brickwork look like stonework was to cover it with stucco. A 'stuccoed façade' refers to a front elevation of a house completely covered in stucco.

Rustification. Sometimes vertical and horizontal lines were scored into the stucco to make it appear like the joins between blocks of stone underneath. The process of making cuts in the plaster to make it look like the joints between 'ashlar' (shaped stone) blocks is called rustification. It was often so good that it is hard to tell stucco from genuine stone-fronted buildings, particularly when they have been painted.

Vermiculation. Another fashionable effect was vermiculation – digging an irregular texture into the plaster to give the effect of roughly cut stone. This was often used in the surrounds of doors or in fake quoins on the corners of buildings.

Most houses were stuccoed up to and including ground floor level. In some cases, the whole façade was stuccoed. But usually the brickwork was bare above – although you might not notice that because window architraves and cornices and other features were covered in stucco dressings.

Cornices. At the top of the facade was the cornice, a plaster structure running along the top of the wall, or sometimes above the second floor where there were further storeys above.

Quoins. Blocks of stone were often used to form the corners of buildings, often as rectangular pieces, using alternating long and short edges to give a ladder effect. Builders often used them to emphasise the points at which a long terrace façade might be broken up by causing the central and end houses to project slightly.

Rear elevation

The back of the house was usually totally practical and undecorated. There were often small windows on the half-landings. In later Victorian houses built with large gardens, it became the norm to give the back of a house a façade almost as elaborate as on the street side.

Windows

Types of windows

Sash windows. The sash window consisted of two windows or sashes, one above the other, known as a 'double-hung sash'. Each sash could be moved up or down on pulleys and counter-weights concealed in the window frames. The lead counter-weights caused the window to stay in place once it was opened. The entire cased window frame was then recessed behind the brick-work so as to be invisible when viewed from outside. Windows up to the first floor usually had panelled shutters internally, which folded back into cased reveals, and could be secured across the opening with an iron bar.

French windows. Windows were often built which could open out like casement windows. They were called 'French windows' or 'French doors' although there is not really a French connection. They were particularly used to give access at the front onto the first floor balcony.

Casement windows. Casement windows are windows which are hinged on the side and then open inwards or outwards as a single unit. Most windows open outwards.

Dormer windows. These were originally windows for the rooms of servants in the attic, and they were let into the roof surface. Sometimes roofs were raised after construction of the original buildings to create additional living space.

Canted bays. Bay windows are windows in a group of three, roughly forming a bow. Victorian builders took that idea further, and built houses with a window unit standing forward of the main wall. The main window is parallel with the wall, and the two side windows are at an angle – hence 'canted' bay. The purpose of the bay was to increase light in the front room of the ground floor. The bay had to start at basement level for support. A canted bay would also conveniently form the floor of a balcony outside a first floor French window. In later houses, canted bay structures were often carried up to second floor or even higher storeys.

Proportions

Rules of design, derived from Palladian architecture, set down the appropriate proportions for the windows on different storeys. The windows from the main floor upwards would usually be the same width. The main floor windows would be twice as high as they were wide; the bedroom windows would be only one and a half times as high; and the servants' quarters in the attic would have windows only as high as they were wide.

Architraves and surrounds
Where a façade was brick-faced, it was customary to apply stucco rendering to the architraves or surrounds of the window openings. The heads of the windows were spanned by flat arches of brick applied as a facing with a timber 'bressumer' or lintel behind.

Pediments
A gable or head above a window was called a pediment. If it was in a curved shape, like part of a circle, it was called a 'segmental' head.

Paint colour
Windows were often painted in dark colours, particularly to contrast with a stucco façade. It was a late Victorian fad to repaint them white.

Glass
The design of windows was dictated by the quality of glass. '4-over-4' and '2-over-2' (the number of panes in the top and bottom sash windows) became standard arrangements for sash windows. One Victorian practice was to have glazing bars in the top sash, and a single pane of glass in the lower sash.

Blocked windows
If a real window would have been structurally impossible because of some internal feature like a flue behind it, a blind window in the form of a recess was often built into the façade to maintain the harmony with the real windows.

Main entrance

Porches
Most Victorian houses have porches or porticoed entrances, surrounding the main front doors. In essence, the porch is a small roofed structure, a few feet deep, supported by walls or columns on either side of the doorway. The porch might be at the top of a set of

steps up from the street or the area, or be at ground level with perhaps one or two steps up to the main door. Porches basically had two purposes, apart from the obvious one of providing a shelter from the rain. Architecturally, they fitted into the Palladium or classical architectural scheme for the façades of houses. They gave the appearance of being little Roman or Greek temples with their columns and porticos. (The principal column types are detailed below.) Even when the porch was quite shallow, so that full columns were not required, half columns would be let into the wall surface to maintain the appearance. Even with plain brick walls, you will often see a design which echoes the traditional columns on the facing edge of the wall. More practically, the porch provided the floor for a terrace outside the main first-floor room above. Often the window above the porch would have French doors which opened on to it. It allowed for a larger terrace space than could be obtained from the balconies which often run along the front of a building, supported on brackets.

Paired porches

When semi-detached houses came into fashion, houses would be built in mirror fashion, so that the porches would be side-by-side.

Columns

The ancient Greeks loved columns. The Romans loved whatever the Greeks loved. But ancient architects were not free to invent their own columns. There were accepted types or 'orders' which had to be adhered to. An order is not merely a column. It is the whole of the column and the structure it supports. Both have to comply with the rules of the particular order they belong to. The rules specify the parts and also the proportions they must have to each other. There are two main parts of every order: the column and the entablature. The column is fairly obvious. The entablature is what lies on top of the column.

Doric columns. These are the simplest, with plain or slightly fluted columns and little or no decoration on top

Ionic columns. These have fluted columns and a decorative top (or 'volute' like a length of material rolled up at both ends.

Corinthian columns. These are the most ornate, with fluted columns and a volute like a carving of flowers and leaves.

Architraves

It was traditional to cover the door frame with an architrave. Georgian architraves were often fluted rectangular sections with decorated blocks at the corners. Victorian architraves were often in the form of mouldings. The practical purpose was to protect the wood against rainwater dripping onto it.

Hoods

By Queen Anne's day, there was often a curved hood extended over the doorway on beams or brackets projecting from the wall. These were made progressively more decorative. The hood might be covered by a lead sheet.

Consoles

The Georgians replaced the beams or brackets with consoles, which were narrow pilasters or columns running from the ground to the hood.

Door cases

Early Georgian door cases were elaborate, with columns and pediments. Sometimes the approach to the main door was made even more impressive and the main door was surrounded by a porch. The Palladian or neo-Classical styles were able to exploit the porch to mimic the appearance of ancient Roman or Greek temples with columns on either side and a pediment above. The whole arrangement often developed into something akin to a pocket Parthenon.

As the Regency period progressed the style became much more restrained. Typical Regency door cases were flat, with no more than an architrave and front doors were placed within round-headed arches without hoods.

Fanlights

They were called fanlights because originally they were semi-circular, and since early Georgian glass could only be produced in small panes, they were separated by glazing bars radiating from a central point, which gave the appearance of an open fan. Many later fanlights were rectangular, but the name was kept.

Door knockers

The door knocker was an invention of Georgian times. Metal became cheaper in the Regency period and brass door knockers, often in the shape of a lion's head, a sphinx or a crocodile, became usual. Larger houses had bell pulls. The visitor would pull a knob on the door case and a cord buried in the internal wall plaster would pull a bell inside the house.

Boot scrapers

Outside the front door of a Victorian house, you will often see a metal bar suspended a few inches off the ground between two sets of metal legs. This is a boot scraper, designed to get the mud (and presumably the horse manure) of the Victorian street off a visitor's shoes before he entered the house.

Balconies

In London terraced houses, balconies were usually made of stone with cast-iron railings in one of the manufacturers' standard patterns. They were built out from the first floor windows, which often opened onto them with French windows (like patio doors). Most balconies are protected with railings in front, made of wrought-iron or cast-iron. Some balconies have stone or cement balustrades, usually shaped like a row of bowling pins.

Balconies were supported by external brackets but also by iron beams extending into the house. In later Victorian terraces, continuous balconies which ran along the entire front of the terrace, might replace individual balconies. The continuous balcony would usually widen out to go round the top of porches, giving more space for the homeowner at that point. When there were canted bays, balconies were often built on top. Metal balconies (as well as railings at street level), which are now almost always painted black, were in Victorian times painted green. Individual balconies for windows which are not large enough for anyone to walk out onto are usually called balconettes.

Walls

Structural frame
External walls were built of brick. A timber frame formed the internal construction of all but the larger houses. Wooden joists supporting the floors ran between the front and back walls. The framework of the internal partition walls from the ground floor upwards was timber. Brick walls were only used internally at basement level or to support a stone wall-hung staircase, or to give added structural support in particularly large houses.

Bricks
Originally, bricks were made by hand, one by one, in individual wooden moulds. They were made of clay mixed with water. The 'green' bricks were then dried in straw. Once dry, they were fired in a kiln to produce a useable brick. During the 19th century, mechanisation improved production and pressed bricks were produced mechanically.

Till the advent of modern methods, brick firing was a hit-and-miss affair. Bricks were stored in rows with wood, coal or coke laid in the gaps and then the whole thing was set alight. Bricks which were fired evenly were used for exterior walls. Poorly fired bricks were used inside, or covered with stucco. Over-burnt bricks were used for flue linings.

Laying bricks. Various methods were used for laying bricks. The most popular types were English bond (alternating rows of headers and stretchers) and Flemish bond (alternating headers and stretchers in every row).

Types of brick. Bricks are heavy and transport was difficult, so most buildings had to be constructed from locally made bricks. London clay bricks have a slightly yellowish colour. As it became more popular to have brick-faced houses, buyers demanded more interesting bricks. Among the favourites were 'gault' bricks from Suffolk, Staffordshire blues – also called 'engineering bricks – and deep red bricks from Accrington in Lancashire. Particularly in the Queen Anne style houses, much more perfectly shaped bricks were used with a very thin line mortar, barely visible in between the bricks. Many buildings employed moulded bricks and moulded brick panels as decorative features in the heads of windows or porches.

Stucco
Stucco originally meant a particular slow-setting plaster composed of gypsum, sand and lime. The word has been broadened to cover any external cement rendering. A Brick Tax was imposed in 1784 to fund the fight against the Americans in the War of Independence. Builders responded by covering the front of a house in stucco, which became a regular feature of Georgian houses, because it concealed the bricks.

Paint colour
The light white or off-white paint which now covers the stucco in the best squares and terraces of London is a fairly modern invention. In Georgian and Victorian times darker colours were generally used.

Roofs

The roof was either concealed behind a brick parapet or built in the form of a mansard with dormer windows. The front facade of the house would be topped with a parapet wall, which would usually be cement or stone, topped with coping stones.

Pitched roofs
The pitched roof is a roof like a tent, with two sloping sides. The Victorians did not emphasise their roofs because Palladium or classical style used Greek or Roman temples as their model for house façades, and pitched roofs did not fit in with that ideal appearance. A compromise was to build two pitched roofs in the shape of an 'M',

which meant that neither of the peaks was high enough to be visible from the street. The gutter in the middle was called the 'valley gutter', for its obvious similarity to the valley between two mountains. That ran from front to back, and the drainpipes would usually be down the back wall.

Hip roofs and mansard roofs

In the late Victorian housing developments, a form of hip roofs, known as mansard roofs, became more popular. With a hip roof, instead of two sides like a tent, the roof has four sides like a pyramid. With a mansard roof, the straight sides of the hip roof were bent, with the lower halves almost vertical. The benefit of this was that it allowed builders to create proper rooms in the attic, because the outer walls no longer had to slope all the way to the floor.

Gables

The mansard roof fitted in with the Queen Anne (p. **Error! Bookmark not defined.**) and Dutch Revival styles of building, which emphasised gables. Many later Victorian houses are built with gable roofs, where the brick front – what you might regard as the flap of the tent roof construction – was given considerable architectural prominence.

Slates

In Victorian England, slate replaced tiles as the preferred roof covering. Its structure meant that it could easily be split into thin sheets. Most of the slate for house building was brought from quarries in Wales. After a sheet was split from the rock face, it would be cropped to the correct size and shape or 'dressed'. The slates were nailed to the wooden supports of the roof. Each slate would be laid slightly overlapping the one below and the nails would go through both.

Finials

Victorian houses were built with decorative terracotta finials fitted along the top of the roof line.

Chimneys

London chimneys came in all shapes and sizes and are usually constructed of brick. The Victorians often made feature of them, and designed them to look like castle towers. The chimney pots themselves were bedded in mortar known as flaunching.

Rain water pipes

Good taste required that rainwater pipes which would spoil the pure lines of the façade should be confined to the rear walls wherever possible. even the gutter serving the front parapet wall and the drain for the centre valley of M-section roofs were often made to run into a lead-lined trough passing through to the back of the building.

Gardens and areas

Communal gardens and garden squares

The layout plan for most Victorian terraces involved grouping terraces to form the sides of a square. Roads would run in front of the terraces, but in the centre of the square would be a communal garden, usually fenced off from the public with iron railings. The benefit of this arrangement was that the homeowners could look out of their front windows onto the gardens. The drawback was that the houses were physically separated from the gardens by the roads in front. Then they had the idea of reversing this plan. Instead of having houses looking at a central square across a road, they began building the terraces with the houses facing out over the road at the front still, but with the back of the house opening directly onto hidden communal garden. That is the arrangement which makes houses in Notting Hill so attractive. With this plan, people could walk out of the backs of their houses straight into the garden without having to cross a road, and it makes them safer for children.

The management and the right to use communal squares and gardens are usually jealously policed by a committee of the local residents. Your particular property may not have a right to use the garden. Just because a property is close to communal gardens, doesn't mean your property has the right to use them. It often defies common sense. With some gardens, you can use them if they can be viewed from your house; or only if your building backs on to them. In some cases, specific buildings acquired rights in the past and others didn't. Always check.

Areas

The more expensive terraced houses had basement with a small forecourt called the 'area' in the front to allow light to enter the basement windows. To prevent people falling off the pavement into the area, railings were constructed round it at street level, usually with a metal gate leading down steps to a basement door.

Front gardens

Very few Victorian houses have front gardens. Where they exist, they're usually quite small. Most houses were constructed too close to the road to give much scope for gardens.

Railings

Railings are now almost always painted black, but in Victorian times they were painted green. Early Georgian railings had a regular leaf or spear-shaped pattern at the top. Later, more elaborate patterns were created as advances in the manufacture of wrought and cast iron provided opportunities for more inventiveness. Robert Adam introduced anthemion and other floral designs.

Paving

Hard surfaces were more popular than grass. Areas were often paved with flagstones. Or there were paths made of gravel or coal ash. There might be urns or statues decorating the hard surface.

Lawns

By 1810 lawns had become popular. Edwin Budding invented the modern cylinder lawnmower in 1830, but it was not until about 1850 that it came into general use. Flowerbeds were often made into interesting shapes, rather than left with straight edges.

Inside houses

Water supply
In 1817 the Metropolitan Paving Act required water companies to lay cast iron pipes. Companies could provide a low service where the water was only pumped to the ground floor. A high service where water was pumped to upper floors was more expensive. So, for the most part, servants on the upper floors still had to carry their water up the stairs.

Lavatory
In Victorian times lavatory was the word for a wash basin. Modern toilets were not invented till rather later.

Baths
Showers are a modern invention. Georgians and Victorian used baths. But they were not fixed or plumbed into the water supply. Running hot and cold water to a tap was generally unknown. Instead, a moveable bath would be placed in front of a fire in one of the rooms when needed, and filled with water which had to be brought up from the kitchen range (just as in the hotels of countless 'westerns'). Baths were usually made of painted wood. In Victorian times, enamelled cast iron baths came into fashion.

Fireplaces
In London terrace properties, each pair of houses would have the fireplaces and chimney flues built into the shared party walls, culminating in a combined chimney unit on the roof. The chimney flues had to zigzag to get round the fireplace on the floor above. This also avoided rain falling on the fire. Victorians thought it reduced draughts, but that is not so. The bricks lining the flue were covered with plaster rendering.

The design of fireplaces was revolutionised by an American engineer, Benjamin Thompson (who is usually known as Count Rumford, a title given to him by the Elector of Bavaria in 1784). Rumford observed that English fireplaces sent most of the heat up the chimney and most of the smoke into the room and he devised a new design with a narrow opening to the flue, to keep the heat in the room, and various other refinements, such as the use of fire bricks at the back to reflect heat into the room. Rumford grates became a regular feature of Victorian houses.

Floors

Floorboards. Oak would only be used for floors in very expensive households and then only in main rooms. Georgian houses usually had pine floorboards. But they were often painted to make them look like more valuable hardwoods. Floorboards were often lime-washed to clean them, and to give them a silver colour, and painted to resemble marble blocks. By the 1820s it was fashionable to stencil patterns onto floorboards. Parquetry was only used round the edges.

Carpets. Fitted carpets became popular in the Regency period.

Kitchens

Ovens. A Georgian kitchen contained an open fire with a roasting grate with spits. It might also have a bread oven and a range for saucepans heated by the fire. Count Rumford (see fireplaces) invented the closed kitchen range, built round the kitchen fire, with hot plates for pans. This was refined till Dr Gustav Dalen produced the Aga design in 1929, which is still used today.

Scullery. There would usually be a separate scullery for preparing vegetables and for washing dishes.

Pantry. Other provisions and cooking utensils would be in a pantry. In larger households, there might even be a separate game room and flower room. Perishable items would be kept in a separate still-room, on thick stone slabs to keep them cold.

Butlers and housekeepers. In the larger houses there would be separate rooms for the housekeeper and the butler (where the valuables would be locked away).

Laundry

There was a laundry room where clothes could be scrubbed and boiled in a copper pan.

How to buy well

Leasehold and freehold

Ownership of flats and houses
All flats are leasehold. Most houses are freehold, but some are leasehold. What 'freehold' and 'leasehold' mean is explained below

Freehold
'Freehold' is the legal word for full ownership of land and the buildings on it. If you own and occupy a house as a single family home, and you don't have a landlord, then you almost certainly own the freehold.

Leasehold
The owner of a freehold – 'the freeholder' – can let someone else have ownership rights over the property, or part of the property, for a period of time. This is done by giving the other person a 'leasehold' interest in the property. (The document is called a 'lease'.) The person who receives the leasehold interest is a 'lessee', 'leaseholder' or a 'tenant'. The person who gives the leasehold interest is the 'lessor' or 'landlord'. Once created, this leasehold interest can be bought and sold. If you buy a flat from existing flat owners, you become the new owner of their lease.

If you own a leasehold property, your ownership has two limitations compared with owning the freehold. It's for a number of years specified in the lease, not forever. And the leaseholder has to obey obligations to the landlord (which are set out in the lease).

'Leasehold' is the basis on which flats are owned in this country. (Recently, Parliament created a form of ownership called 'commonhold' which is similar to the New York condominium arrangements, but it hasn't really caught on yet.)

The essence of leasehold is that it is a direct contract between the landlord and the individual flat owners. The lease imposes obligations on the flat owner as to how they can use the property, and also imposes obligations on the landlord, such as maintenance of the building, which is paid for in service charge by the various flat owners. Flat owners can get together to purchase the freehold from the original landlord.

Is leasehold ok?
Leasehold doesn't sound as good as freehold. But there are some features which make it fine. First, leases are fairly standardised. For leases to be bought and sold for a purchase price, they have to conform to a standard set of requirements. The market accepts these. Second, in most cases, the leaseholder has a legal right to extend the lease. These things have to be checked by a good lawyer – like us – but if they check out, then it's normal and safe to buy a leasehold property. You have to bear in mind that it is the accepted legal structure, universally used for all flats in England.

Leasehold houses
There are fewer leasehold houses. Single-family houses are usually freehold. However, leasehold houses are often found on the traditional estates, such as the Cadogan estate. These traditional estates are usually still owned or controlled by the families of the original owners of the land when the area was first developed from farmland in the 19th century. They have often provided the excellent service of preserving the uniformity and identity of their areas against piecemeal changes. Among other things, they often insist on their standard colour for all painted façades on their estate.

Flats – management and ownership structures
You will usually find that one of these arrangements applies to the building you buy into.

The simplest ownership scheme for a number of flats is that there is a landlord who owns the freehold. The landlord carries out the services, like repairing the roof, and recovers the cost from the flat owners.

In modern leases, management of the building is often arranged by a separate management company owned by the flat owners. That way, ongoing maintenance and day-to-day services are controlled by the people who actually have an interest in them – the flat owners.

An even better arrangement is that the flat owners buy the freehold of the building so that they become their own landlords. That way they have complete control over the management of their own home. Flat owners often have the right to buy the freehold of their building from the landlord and even if they don't buy the landlord out, they can, in some circumstances, force the landlord at least to hand over management of the building to them.

Service charges

If you live in a block of flats, maintenance, repairs and other services can realistically only be handled by one party (the landlord or a management company) on behalf of the whole building. Works to repair the roof or the foundations, or to keep the communal gardens looking nice, all need to be handled that way. The expense will ultimately be borne by the flat owners. They will each be expected to put up a certain amount of money each year to cover anticipated expenses based roughly on the size of their flats, and then there will be an accounting at the end of the year to work out how much money is left, or whether they have to put up a little bit more to cover a shortfall.

As explained already, either the landlord has the responsibility for looking after the building as a whole, or there may be a management company involving all the flat owners. If the landlord performs services such as maintenance, flat owners are protected by law against the most obvious abuses. Landlords can't carry out substantial works without getting quotes from several builders and consulting the tenants. They have to act in a reasonable way in many situations, or find themselves unable to recover the money.

The simplest service charge arrangement involves flat owners only contributing to costs each year as they are incurred. But replacing lifts or roofs can then be a huge financial burden in the year when the work occurs. The better arrangement is for there to be a 'sinking fund'. This means the flat owners contribute towards future large expenses by putting a proportion of the anticipated costs into a special bank account each year and so spreading the cost over several years.

What a flat owner owns

Usually in a purpose-built block your flat will be limited to the internal plasterwork; the lease wording will specifically exclude from your ownership all main walls and structure. (The structure will usually be part of the 'common parts' maintained by the landlord or management company out of the service charge fund.) If you are buying a flat in a converted house, then your lease will probably say that you own the floorboards and the joists underneath, and that you own the ceiling but not the joists to which it is attached (which will usually belong to the flat above). There would usually be some description of whether dividing walls are split between flats or are part of the common parts. I keep saying 'usually' because there are many variations, and these are just examples. You need to look at the actual provisions to make sure they really do make practical sense. That's where we can help. You ought to make sure your surveyor has seen them as well before you buy.

Mutual rights and obligations

Mutual rights. When you own one flat among many (or even one of two) you need various rights over the other flats and over the common parts. For example, you need the right to cross the front path and the internal halls, landings and stairs to reach your flat. You need a right to have water and other utilities passing to and from your premises through other parts of the building. You need there to be some rights of support from the rest of the building structure. Other flat owners will want similar rights, – e.g. in respect of pipes passing under your floorboards to reach their flats.

Mutual obligations. Most of the pages of the lease will be taken up with a long catalogue of your obligations. Other flat owners should be subject to similar obligations so that everyone operates under the same set of rules.

Landlords' obligations

Most leases will contain clauses saying that the landlords will carry out the services, including maintenance of the structure and insurance of the building (while of course recovering the cost in the service charge). The lease should also say that the landlord will make sure that all leases in the building are in a similar form, so that everyone knows they are obeying the same rules as everyone else.

Alterations

If you want to carry out any alterations in your flat, you will need to check the wording of your lease carefully. Individual flat owners usually can't do works to the exterior or structure of the building, but they should be allowed to alter the interior. But it is rare for a lease to give the flat owner an unrestricted right to alter the interior. Usually leases forbid any alterations at all unless you first get the landlord's consent. This is fine if it also says that the landlord's consent cannot be unreasonably withheld, because then the landlord can only refuse permission if there is a good reason – e.g. your works would damage the ceiling below. But without that 'not to be unreasonably withheld' wording, you could find yourself unable to carry out even minor changes to the internal layout. This is less of an issue if the flat owners as a group own the building, and are therefore the landlords, because neighbours may be sympathetic to reasonable changes which they might want to make themselves.

When you buy a flat, you should always check the layout plan in the lease against the actual layout to check for unauthorised alterations in the past.

Insurance

The landlord or the management company will usually maintain buildings insurance on the entire building under a single policy. The premium cost is then billed to the individual flat owners in the same proportion as they pay service charge. The alternative – each flat owner insuring their own flat – isn't practical, because if someone forgot to insure a flat in the middle there wouldn't be enough money in total to rebuild the building if it burnt down. Flat owners have a legal right to receive copies of the block policy and to receive evidence of policy renewal each year.

Extending the length of the lease term

Leases are often granted for 99 years. I have no idea why 99 appeals so much to landlords! If you buy a lease which was created when the house was converted into flats in the 1970s, then there may now only be about 70 years left. Most flat owners (but not all) have a legal right to extend their leases by another 90 years. You have to pay the freeholder something for this. Once the lease term dips under the 80 year mark, the price for a lease extension goes up dramatically.

You can't apply for an extension lease until you have owned the flat for at least two years, so if you are about to buy a flat and you want the lease term extended, you need to arrange for the seller to start the process by serving a notice on the landlord before you buy. The right can then be passed on to you without there being a two-year delay.

Buying the freehold

Flat owners can band together to buy the freehold of the building from their landlord. This is technically referred to as 'collective enfranchisement'. Most flat owners in most residential buildings have the right to make the landlord sell the freehold to them. But the conditions which have to be met are quite detailed.

The procedure is rather more complicated than getting an individual extension lease on a flat. But ultimately it is usually beneficial for the flat owners to join together to buy the freehold so that they have control of their building.

Finding a property

Selling agents

You are most likely to find properties from estate agents – their shop window, mailing list or website. Most property owners use an estate agent to sell their properties, and they generally use a local firm with expert knowledge of the local property market. The firms specialising in selling properties in the area covered by this book are listed on page 241.

Some sellers place their properties with several estate agents, so you may end up getting details of the same property from several of the firms you contact. But many sellers put the property with one firm of estate agents only – they pay less commission that way – so you need to register your interest with all the local agents in an area if you want to make sure you're going to find out about all the properties coming onto the market. You don't have to pay anything to the agents for this. Their fees are paid by the seller. So there is really no downside to registering with all the local agents.

The estate agent is working for the seller. The way the system works is that estate agents are instructed by the property owner to sell the property and it's the seller who pays the estate agent's fees. But estate agents' obligations are not all one-sided. They have a legal duty to you to ensure that their sales particulars are accurate. They also have a legal duty to deal with you in an honest and fair way, and not to mislead you.

Be the first person the estate agent calls

The estate agents get quite a big fee – from 1% up to 3% of the sale price – but they get nothing unless they sell the property. So they have quite a lot riding on achieving a sale, especially if there are other competing estate agents trying to sell the property who might snatch their commission away. So you as a potential buyer really matter to the estate agents.

If they think you are serious, they may devote a lot of time and trouble to helping you (because helping you ultimately helps them). If you've got a good relationship with an estate agent who treats you as a serious buyer, then he may ring you up with details of a property as soon as — or hopefully just before – it goes on the market. If he doesn't think you are serious, you may quickly find yourself getting a very peremptory service, while he concentrates on people he sees as better prospects. How you handle the estate agents can make a big difference to how successful you are at securing the home you want. These are suggestions to bear in mind.

- Don't ask estate agents to send you details of all their properties. If you are looking for a two-bedroom flat, be clear

- Be clear about how much money you can afford. This will be a combination of the cash you have saved and the mortgage you can raise. If your budget is unrealistic for the type of property you are looking for, the agent will soon realise that and lose interest.
- Line up a mortgage in principle. This shows you are a serious buyer, that you are organised, and that you can go ahead as soon as a deal is agreed in principle.
- Don't be unnecessarily negative about viewings. Give the estate agent proper feed-back as to why a particular property was not suitable.
- Make sure estate agents have telephone numbers on which you can be contacted at any time of day. Respond quickly. Ring estate agent couple of times a week to prove you are a serious buyer.

Viewings

Things to consider on a first viewing

Take the estate agent's particulars. You may need to consult them. They may list what fixtures and fittings are included or excluded, and they should have a layout plan with room sizes. It's worth taking a torch and a tape measure.

These are some basic issues to consider on a first viewing. They are things which for the most part you would have to live with.

- Check the basic measurements of the room.
- Measure the height of the rooms
- Check if rooms have attractive looking windows.
- Check features you will have to live with, such as wooden floors, staircases, cornices, and fireplaces.
- What are the views like out of the windows?
- If a garden is included, note down which way it faces. Is the garden south facing, and is it as big as you want? To catch the sun, the garden needs to be south or west facing.

How to buy well

- When viewing in daylight, make sure all lights are turned off so you can see how much sunlight there is in each room.
- Don't be put off by bad decor, but equally don't be charmed by exquisite furniture, all of which will be removed.
- Is there off road parking?

Things to note down on the first visit

Here are some suggestions on things to note down on your first visit to a property. They are things to look at again closely if you decide you are interested.

- Ask when the central heating boiler was last serviced.
- Turn the shower on to check the water pressure.
- Look for gaps in the roof covering (daylight visible through the attic).
- Check what condition the garden walls or fences are in.
- Peeling wallpaper may indicate a damp problem.
- Damp patches or stains on the ceiling could indicate leaking pipes.
- Condensation on windows may mean a condensation problem. The sellers will have taken steps to reduce it as far as possible, so it will probably be worse when you move in.
- Check what storage room there is.
- Do the floors feels springy? – this can indicate a problem with the joists below.
- Are there enough electrical sockets for your needs?
- Is there a damp proof course? – this is a row of slates or pitch in the brickwork about 6 inches off the ground level.
- Is the guttering damaged or blocked? – signs would be water on the wall or moss growing on the wall.
- Do any walls bulge or have obvious cracks?
- Are there any missing roof tiles? – bring binoculars.
- Is there any fresh paint? – this could conceal damp problems.

Specifically for flats

- Are there names on the doorbells? That indicates home owners. Blank spaces indicate renters. (Obviously this is not scientific!)

- Look at the state of the common parts – entrance walls and stairs etc – which will indicate how effectively the building is being managed. Also look out for heaps of uncollected junk mail which is an indication of neglect and poor management.
- Check that the lift works.
- Ask about noise from neighbouring flats, and try to listen out for any. This can be a problem, particularly in converted houses where there may be no soundproofing between floors. In a single home, that isn't a problem, because the whole family is usually either upstairs or downstairs. But in a converted house, where one family is permanently above another it can matter a lot.
- Test for how solid the walls are between this flat and the next-door flat. If they sound particularly flimsy, you may have noise problems.
- Check if there is a car parking space allocated to the owner of the flat.
- Check what access you have to the gardens, and rights to use them.
- Find out how long previous owners have lived at the flat. If there have been frequent changes of ownership that may indicate that it's not a good place to live.
- Make sure that you are told exactly how long the lease is. This will affect value.
- Find out what the service charges are.

Second viewings

If you have narrowed down your search to a particular property or couple of properties which you then go back to for a second visit, there are some more detailed considerations you should think about.

Cupboard space. See if there is enough cupboard space for your family's needs. In particular, look for built-in wardrobes in the bedrooms. Remember that installing new cupboards or wardrobes in a room will make it even smaller. So if you are being shown a tiny bedroom don't just imagine putting in a bed, but also putting in wardrobes. If it doesn't work comfortably, then you would be overpaying if you price the house on the number of bedrooms.

Check doors. You should open and shut all cupboard doors, and pull out all drawers to see how they work. This will tell you whether you're going to have to replace kitchen and bathroom units. It is also a good indication of the quality of the kitchen units.

Walk round the block. Walk down the street and round neighbouring streets to get a feel for security, lighting, and noise. Much of the year you are likely to be coming home to the property in the evening when it's dark, so you need to feel secure.

Go at a different time of day. If you visited the first time in the daytime, then come back when it's dark for the second viewing, or the other way round. A room that may seem cosy with lamps on, may seem dark in daylight. A quiet street by day may be dangerous by night.

Binoculars. We recommend you should take binoculars and look carefully at the roof. Obviously, you are not a surveyor, but it is worth noting if a lot of slates or tiles are slipping or if there is a bow in the roof, since that would indicate that there may be some major building work you will have to carry out.

Damp. Look out for any signs of damp. This could be in the form of wet patches on a wall or condensation round window sills. You would want to know the cause before you buy, and make sure it can be remedied easily.

The outside. On the first viewing, you probably concentrated on the house itself. On the second viewing, have a look round the outside, at the state of the garden and at any sheds and paving. Check if the property can be overlooked by the neighbours. Check the state of fences to see if they don't need to be repaired or replaced. Are there trees in the neighbours' garden which will block out sunlight from your garden?

Questions to ask

These are questions we would suggest you ask the sellers. You can ask the estate agents as well.

Why are you moving? If it's because of the unreasonable neighbours, then you need to know that. They probably have a perfectly good reason for moving. They want a bigger house, or they want to be nearer their children etc. But if the sellers seem to be totally taken by surprise by your question and thrown into confusion, you may need to consider their answer quite carefully. What you are trying to identify is whether there is something wrong with the property, the neighbours, or the area which is causing the sellers to move out. They may have heard about a proposed development which will affect values.

How long have you lived here? If the seller only moved in six months earlier, that's a sign there is something wrong with the property, the area or the neighbours which is driving the seller out again. They will probably give you a true answer to this one, since it's easy to check. But if they have only lived at the property for a few months, you certainly want to listen carefully to their explanations for moving on. The problems you are trying to identify are very much as for the previous question.

How long has the property been on the market? If a property has been on the market for a long time while other properties are shifting quickly, it's a sign that there is something wrong with the property which previous buyers have found.

Have any previous sales fallen through and, if so, why? A seller won't want to tell you the answer to that one, but it's really quite a reasonable thing to ask. If there is some problem – a problem with the title of the property, or something which would only be revealed by a detailed survey, such as subsidence – you need to know it now before you invest time and money in the purchase. Sellers can be unlucky and have a series of bad buyers, but equally the buyers may have withdrawn because they kept receiving adverse surveys, or discovered legal problems. You need to be given the full picture to avoid wasting your time, if there is a problem which is going to put you off when you find out about it.

What items are included in the sale? There have been cases where the seller has even dug up the concrete base and pole for the washing line and taken them away in the removal van! You need to clarify upfront that all the light fittings, carpets, curtains, and kitchen equipment will be left and included in the price. Otherwise, the seller may try to add something to the price for those items later. You also want to make sure about bathroom and kitchen units. They may look fixed but often they are easily removable and you don't want to have an argument about that when the moving day arrives.

What are the neighbours like? That's a fair question. You aren't buying a property in a vacuum. You need to know that you aren't taking on difficult or noisy neighbours.

Have you done any works to the property? You want to know exactly what work has been done since the sellers moved in. Your surveyor and solicitor will need to check that they did the work properly and complied with local authority requirements. Even if all they have done is redecoration work, you want to know about it because they may have done it to conceal a problem, such as papering a wall to cover up a crack or damp. If the sellers have redecorated the whole place, that is not terribly suspicious because people are advised to do that before they put the property on the market. If they have done something specific in one area, then you want to know exactly why that was.

When can you move? Hopefully the seller has already found a property to buy so that any deal would go through in a reasonable time frame. But if the seller has not yet found a property to buy, that may affect your decision, especially if you need to move in quickly to meet some deadline like getting your children into the local school. But if they give you a particular week day or month by which they say they can move, you should take that with a pinch of salt because it all depends on external factors, especially when you are all in a chain of transactions.

What is the parking situation like? You definitely want to know how easy it is to park in the street and whether there are any residents' parking permits.

Do you have the right to use communal gardens? Just because the communal gardens (p. 180) are right across the street, doesn't mean this property has the right to use them. Always check.

What is shared? You need to know if there is a shared garden, a shared driveway, or shared services.

What are the outgoings? Council tax, payments under the lease such as service charges, and power bills.

Is the area noisy?

When was the boiler and central heating system installed?

What improvements would you make if you were staying?

When does the garden get the sun?

Have you ever been burgled?

What are local schools like?

Agreeing a deal

Handling sellers
There is a bit of a balancing act here. When viewing, you should avoid being too critical of the property – particularly in matters relating to the current owners' taste (or lack of). You may not admire the three plaster ducks on the wall, but don't laugh out loud at them. Even though the sellers want to sell, they can easily take against anyone who they think has insulted them, and you would be surprised how big a part seemingly miniscule issues of good manners can play.

On the other hand, you mustn't sound too enthusiastic about the property if you are going to try to negotiate the asking price. It will do no harm to leave the sellers slightly anxious as to whether you are totally in love with their property.

So don't give too much away. Even if you love the property, don't say you definitely want to buy it. If they know you are really keen, that may embolden them to refuse an offer below the asking price.

Negotiating the price when there is competition
If you are trying to buy a particularly desirable property and there is a lot of competition for it, then you may have to simply accept a seller's asking price if you want to be sure of getting your offer accepted and moving on with the deal. The problem may be that other prospective

buyers also offer the asking price – or more. (Even after your offer has been accepted, the estate agent is under a legal duty to pass on other offers to the seller.) The seller is in a comfortable position, faced with multiple offers. When buyers simply keep upping their prices in competition, it is known in the trade as a 'bidding war'. One option the seller may adopt is to have a 'Dutch auction' in which competing prospective purchasers outbid each other until someone emerges as the highest paying one. A seller may even formalise this by having 'sealed bids' or 'best offers' organised by the estate agents.

Another option for the sellers is to opt for a contract race. Papers are sent out to two or more buyers: the first to be ready to exchange contracts gets the property. (That's the theory — but the sellers can still go with someone else.) If the sellers like you but are tempted to have a contract race, offer to exchange within a fixed period and ask them to give you a clear run just for that period, such as two weeks.

Negotiating in a buyers' market

If the seller is not being besieged by prospective buyers, you may be able to negotiate a reduction in the asking price. Sellers used to put properties on the market at slightly inflated prices simply because they expected buyers to try and knock the price. That is not so often the case nowadays. But it is quite probable that when the sellers put the property on the market they went to several estate agents who each gave them different possible sale prices. Human nature being what it is, they probably chose the agent who proposed the highest price. But if you make an offer which is in line with the lower part of the band of suggested prices, there is a good chance that the sellers will be able to reconcile themselves to a sale at the lower price.

You may also be able to knock something off the asking price on the basis of physical defects or a bad layout. A similar property up the road may have gone for a good price because it has been beautifully restored. So it would be quite reasonable to offer less if you are going to have to carry out work yourself to put this property in the same price bracket.

Advantages you may have other than price

Sellers probably have to buy another property and will be worried about losing their new dream house if the buyer of the property they are selling messes them around or the deal falls through. So even if you do not offer the highest price, you may pip other competitors to the post if you have another advantage. For example, having a mortgage lined up in principle may be an advantage – also not having a property to sell, or being prepared to fit in with the seller's needs about the completion date.

Deciding what to offer

One maxim is: Decide the top price you would go to, and then offer 10% less. That gives you some scope for negotiation. Even if the estate agent thinks your offer is ridiculous, he is under a legal duty to pass it on to the seller.

If you don't have money for new curtains or furniture, it is a good idea to ask the seller to include those items at the time you're agreeing the price. If you agree a price and then later ask about them, the seller will want extra. If it is all part of agreeing the property price at the outset he is more likely to just throw them in.

Estate agents are negotiating for the sellers so it is part of their job to try to persuade applicants that their offers are too low and get them to increase them. Ask them to justify their argument by reference to other recent sales. But they do know their market, so you should take note if what they are telling you makes sense.

Making the offer

You are usually better off making the offer to the estate agents, not to the seller direct. We are not a nation used to bartering, so an attempt to negotiate a price direct with the seller can result in a confrontation and a lot of emotion. If you make the offer to the agents, then the sellers can let off steam to the agent, without the whole deal collapsing in recriminations and insults. Once the seller calms down, the agent can then come back with any counter offer. The agent can also attempt to reason with the seller (and with you) to arrive at a figure you can both accept. That may mean you never become best buddies with the seller, but do you really care?

Generally it is a bad idea to make an offer while you are viewing the property. Certainly avoid getting into a handshake with the seller, because, if you later need to pull out or want to modify your offer in any way, you will be treated as if you've broken some mediaeval rule of chivalry.

If you offer a lot less than the asking price, always give reasons to the estate agents to pass on to the sellers. If the sellers just think you are trying to be clever or trying to take advantage of them, they may dig their heels in. If they can see that there is some reason behind your proposal, they may be prepared to take it into account. Even if they don't agree with what you say, at least they are more likely to stay in negotiation with you than pull out abruptly, and this gives you scope to back down if you have to.

When it comes to making an offer, here are some pointers to bear in mind. Don't reveal you're too keen. Make it clear you are looking at other properties you are interested in as well (even if you aren't). Don't keep ringing the estate agent for an answer. Act cool! Don't get too emotionally invested in the particular property. It's worth what it's worth and you mustn't get into a frame of mind where you must have it at all costs. You have to accept that you may not get the property and then you will have to look for something else. Even if your offer is accepted, the deal may still falls through. Emphasise the advantages of selling to you. If any of these apply to you, make sure the seller knows: you have a mortgage in principle, you have a buyer for your home, you are a first-time buyer, or you are a cash buyer.

The buying process

Once a deal is agreed, you move forward to the stage of detailed investigations. You instruct your solicitor and your surveyor. The mortgage process starts. But remember that nothing is certain until contracts are exchanged.

Make sure the estate agents take the property off the market. Check whether the agent is the sole agent. If several firms of agents had the property on their books, the other ones will want to find an alternative buyer, so it is particularly important to make sure they are also instructed to take it off the market. Ask the various agents for details of available properties anonymously a few days later to make sure.

Timescale

There are several factors which can contribute to the time it takes to find a property and move in. The legal work itself shouldn't take more than 2 to 3 weeks to reach exchange of contracts, if there is nothing legally wrong with what the current owner is selling. Then a further 2 weeks is needed between exchange of contracts and completion to make the necessary arrangements. (If necessary, that period can be reduced.) These are factors which can change that timescale:

Legal problems. If there is something wrong with the sellers' lease, or the sellers have carried out alteration works without the necessary consents from the landlords or the council, it can take extra time to solve those issues. But that's rare.

Landlords and management companies. Information is often needed from the landlords or management companies about the running of the building. In a small number of cases, it is necessary to get written approval from the landlord for a sale to the new buyer. This can add time depending on how fast the landlord and management company are prepared to move.

Chains. If the sellers do not need to buy another property to move into and if you are a cash buyer with nothing to sell, then everything can go through quickly. But sometimes, the sellers will be planning to use the sale proceeds to buy a new home, and often buyers are also selling a property to finance their new purchase. You can end up with quite a few buyers and sellers linked together in that way, each needing the money from their sale to finance their purchase. Because of this, everyone has to exchange contracts on the same day, and arrange for completion to take place on a mutually agreed completion date, so that they can all move at the same time. Until everyone in the chain is ready, no one can exchange contracts. If someone is falling behind, because of problems on their particular purchase, it holds everyone up.

Instruct solicitors

The legal side of buying or selling a property is called 'conveyancing'. It is done by solicitors like us. Solicitors are all regulated by the Solicitors Regulation Authority.

The solicitors' job is to organise the purchase of the property for you. At its most basic, we check that the seller owns the property and we make sure ownership is transferred to you. We also have to check for a variety of practical and legal issues which commonly affect properties.

Buying a property may be one of your most important financial transactions, so you won't want to take risks. Things can get complicated, and there are lots of potential pitfalls. You want to enjoy your new home without problems or anxiety, and you want to be able to sell it easily again. It always pays to use an expert.

When your offer on a property is accepted, the estate agents will send your solicitors confirmation of the deal and details of the sellers' solicitors, so they can make contact and start work. You should appoint your solicitors before you make an offer on a property, so that when the offer is accepted you can immediately give the selling agents your solicitors' details.

Anti-money laundering

Your solicitors also have to carry out 'anti-money laundering' checks on you. Usually this consists of taking copies of your passport and some recent utility bills or credit card statements so that the file contains written evidence of your identity. They have to do this even if they know you. It's a legal requirement.

Arrange your mortgage

If you need a mortgage loan it is a good idea to arrange a mortgage in principle before you start looking for a property. Once you have agreed a deal, you now need to action the second half of the mortgage process and get your lenders to value the property. (Although they have confirmed how much they will lend you based on your income, they will still only lend you an agreed percentage of the value of the property, if that turns out to be less.) They will choose a surveyor to do their valuation. If you have a surveyor you plan to use for your structural survey, the lenders may agree to use your surveyor. You need to get the lenders to organise their valuation as soon as possible, because delays in this can hold up the mortgage offer. Also, the sellers will understandably get anxious if there is a long delay before a surveyor arrives; that is often taken as evidence that a buyer is not serious.

Arrange your survey
You need to arrange for a surveyor to carry out a 'home buyers' report' or a 'full structural survey' of the property.

We can recommend surveyors

Ring us if you need a surveyor. We know some good ones who will give you a good practical report.

Full structural survey. The traditional structural survey is the most detailed form of survey for the job. The surveyor will carry out a physical inspection of the property and produce a report which will be fairly comprehensive (but not totally comprehensive – the surveyor will not normally investigate services such as water, drainage and electrical systems). It will also be limited by the amount of access the surveyor has. If the sellers won't let him pull up fitted carpet and poke under floorboards he may not be able to discover damp problems underneath. You should check in advance whether the sellers intend to impose any restrictions on access and discuss the issue with the surveyor.

If you are buying a flat in a converted Victorian house, for example, you really should have a proper survey. Conversions have often been carried out by amateurs or by developers trying to make the most money out of the least work, so you need to make sure you're not buying into a load of problems.

Homebuyer's report. The home buyers' report is a more limited type of survey than a structural survey. A homebuyer's report is a printed form which the surveyor fills in, as opposed to a full structural survey report which will be drafted by the surveyor from scratch.

A homebuyer's report would be most appropriate when you are dealing with a modern straightforward home. But if you are buying anything old or odd, then you should consider a full structural survey.

Local authority searches

The local authority search – or 'local search' as it is usually called – is a questionnaire sent to the local council, which it completes and sends back with information about the property and the area.

The local search is important because it can provide crucial information which could affect your decision whether to buy or not. It can tell you if the property is in breach of any public regulations or if a major road is about to be put through the back garden.

The contract

You are ready for exchange of contracts when you have your mortgage offer and your solicitors have approved the contract. If there is a need for speed, or you are abroad, your solicitors may sign it for you if you give them written authority.

A property contract has to be in writing and the contract has to set out all the agreed terms, and be signed by all contracting parties. The contract can be signed as one document, or as two identical documents. For convenience, that is normally how it is done – the sellers sign one copy and the buyers sign an identical copy. Then the parts are exchanged – hence 'exchange of contracts'.

Property contracts are in a more or less standard form. There are so many relevant issues which can arise that the Law Society has devised a set of standard conditions which will govern most circumstances. These are part of a printed form called 'the standard conditions of sale'.

Deposit

You have to pay a deposit at exchange of contracts. This is traditionally 10% of the purchase price. The deposit is usually held by the sellers' solicitors until completion as 'stakeholder'. This means that the sellers' solicitors must hold the money as middlemen between the two sides. They can only release the money to the sellers after completion of the sale has taken place. If the sellers fail to complete, then the deposit would be returned to you.

There is one practical exception to the rule that the deposit money is held by the solicitors. If the sellers are themselves buying a property, then the normal rules allow them to use your deposit as part of their deposit on their purchase. (Similarly, if you are selling as well as buying, you may be able to use your buyers' deposit towards the deposit on your new home.)

Mortgage offer
You need to make sure you have your mortgage offer. This is a formal document from your lender's head office, confirming the terms of the loan and setting out any special conditions, such as a requirement that you repay a hire purchase debt, or that you have life insurance. It is important that you do not exchange contracts until you have this offer, because you need to make sure you can comply with the conditions and requirements in it.

Buildings insurance
You should check with your solicitors whether you need buildings insurance to be in force at exchange of contracts. The issue is who takes the 'risk' on the property between exchange of contracts and completion. In the past, if the property burnt down before completion, the buyers still had to buy it – they took the risk – and they had to have a buildings insurance policy in force before exchange of contracts to protect them from that date. Nowadays it is more usual for the contract to say that the sellers must hand over the property at completion in more or less its state on the date when contracts were exchanged. If it burns down, the buyers can cancel the contract. So the sellers retain the risk, and there is no need for the buyers to insure the property until completion. You need to make sure you know which of those two scenarios actually applies in your case. If you do have to take on the risk

at exchange of contracts, then you must have insurance in force before exchange of contracts.

Even if you don't have to take on the risk at exchange, you must still make sure you have an insurance offer before you exchange, although you will not put the policy in force until just before the completion date. You can't risk finding you can't insure the property after you have agreed to buy it – e.g. because the insurance company knows there is a subsidence problem in the street.

Remember that if you are buying in a block of flats, then it is probable that buildings insurance is maintained on the whole building by the landlord or management company, in which case you don't have to arrange buildings insurance at all. You will still need your own contents insurance policy.

Completion

Completion means turning the contract into reality. Exchange of contracts merely imposes an obligation on the parties to buy and sell the property at a date in the future. It states the date on which the obligation has to be fulfilled – the completion date. Traditionally, that used to be one month after exchange of contracts, to allow time for the legal work to be done. Now that we no longer rely on the post for everything, that time can be cut back to two weeks relatively comfortably, or even to a matter of days if necessary.

Service charge apportionments

If you are buying a freehold house, then the purchase price is all you pay the seller. If you buy a flat, where there are rent and service charges, then these have to be split or 'apportioned' between you and the seller as at the day of completion. For example, rent and service charge are usually demanded by the management company in instalments every half-year, or perhaps every three months, depending on the wording of the lease.

If your completion date falls in the middle of one of these periods, then the sellers only have to pay for the part of the period up to the completion date, and you are responsible after that. If the sellers have already paid for the whole period, they will want a refund for the period after completion, and this must be taken into account in the completion figures.

As a buyer, you may be worried that when the management company does its full accounts for the year, it may find some further amount due from the flat owner. Since some of that responsibility will relate to the sellers' period of ownership, you may want some assurance that the sellers will meet their bit of the debt. So sometimes it is agreed that one of the firms of solicitors will hold back a retention of a few hundred pounds as security for the potential liability. If there is a liability, then the sellers' share comes out of that retention, and any balance is then released to them.

Money needed for completion
Your solicitors will ask your lenders to send the mortgage loan to them by bank transfer on the completion date. They will ask you to send them any balance you are providing. That will include stamp duty land tax, Land Registry fees and legal fees. You normally have to give your solicitors the funds for those items before completion. Funds should be provided by bank transfer.

Stamp duty land tax
Stamp duty land tax ('SDLT') is a tax you have to pay when you buy a property. SDLT is a percentage of the property's purchase price. It can be anything from 0% to 4% of the price (5% for prices over £1,000,000 after 1st April 2011), depending on the purchase price. SDLT has to be paid to your solicitor before the completion date because he has to pay it on to HM Revenue & Customs within a month (or else you pay a penalty).

The price you pay for your property determines the rate of SDLT you pay. If you buy a property for less than £125,000 (or £250,000 if you are a first time buyer) you pay no SDLT. If the purchase price of your property is more than £175,000 but less than £250,000, you pay 1% of the whole purchase price. It is 3% on properties between £250,001 and £500,000, and 4% on properties going for more than

£500,000.

What happens on the completion date

Your solicitors send the necessary funds to the sellers' solicitors by bank transfer. Once they get the money, the sellers' solicitors 'complete' the transaction and instruct the seller's agents to release the keys to you, so you can move in. The sellers' solicitors send the title documents to your solicitors so that your ownership is documented. They will use part of the purchase funds to pay off the sellers' mortgage loans on the property. The sellers only receive the balance.

Post completion arrangements

Your solicitors receive the title documents. They have to arrange payment of the stamp duty land tax to HM Revenue & Customs. They then apply to the Land Registry to record the change of ownership, and also to record your lenders' charge on the property. After a few weeks, the registration will be completed and you will be shown on the Land Registry's electronic register as owner of the property. (For more on this, see 'Proof of ownership' later in the book.)

If you are buying a flat, there are some additional steps. Your solicitors have to register the transfer document and the lender's mortgage with the landlord or management company, so that they know to send rent demands and service charge demands to you rather than to the previous owners. If the sellers had a share in the freehold or management company, that has to be transferred into your name; your solicitors will be arranging that too.

How to buy well

How to sell well

These are a few suggestions on how to make the most of your sale, and get it through as successfully and quickly as possible.

Use estate agents

Why you need estate agents

Selling privately sounds like a great idea because you save estate agents' fees of up to 3% of the sale price. The question which always strikes me when someone boasts that they sold their house without an estate agent is this: How many tens of thousands of pounds did you lose by not negotiating the best price? In 2010 we acted for a seller in South Kensington who tried to sell privately, with help from a property expert who wasn't a local professional agent. Fortunately, he pulled out of the sale he had arranged, and instructed one of our recommended agents to market the property – he made an extra £250,000!

These are some of the reasons why you need good estate agents.

Reaching the market. All potential buyers will be approaching the local estate agents. They are not likely to come across your home for sale if you are handling your own sale.

Getting a top price. All the local agents know what properties like yours are going for right now. They can seize on the latest evidence to convince your buyer to pay the top price. You may think it's all the same for them whether you get a good price or an ok price. But it isn't. They want to achieve top prices which they can use to persuade the next potential seller to use them, not a competitor. Markets are about confidence. Estate agents have a vested interest in pushing a market up to encourage more owners to put their properties on the market with them.

Professionalism. Estate agents are professional property sellers. There are a lot of good local estate agents to choose from, and a good agent will be a lot better at selling your property than you could be. Among other things, if you decide to try and sell privately, it will probably be your first sale – the equivalent of your first day in a new job. An experienced estate agent would have dealt with hundreds of sales.

Salesmanship. The agent can explain to buyers why your property is more attractive than others the buyers might be interested in, or why a perceived defect doesn't matter, or has no effect on value.

Speed. You are more likely to reach potential buyers through the local estate agents because potential buyers will already be in touch with them. Getting a quick sale may be important if you want to tie it in with a purchase, or if you want to move by a particular date.

Commission is a good investment. Regard the estate agents' commission as a good investment. Estate agents only get paid by succeeding. They will be working hard for you and also for themselves – and that is the best kind of motivation. The investment will be repaid many times over in thousands of pounds of increased sale price and a quicker sale. Our client who made the extra £250,000 certainly didn't begrudge his agents their fee.

Recommended estate agents

We provide a list of good local estate agents (p. 241 et sec). There is no point instructing an agent who is not local just because you like him or he found you the property you are buying. The right buyers won't be knocking on his door.

Selecting the agents

Make a short-list and get estate agents you have short listed to come round, one by one, and tell you what they think of the property and the price at which they would put it on the market. There are a number of things you need to ask each agent, and you should make notes to compare them at the end.

Selling price. You need to know the price at which they suggest you put the property on the market. That may sound like the beginning and end of it. But many an unscrupulous agent with no instructions (because he is no good) will come and quote an enticingly high price just to get the instruction and then talk you into lowering it again in a few weeks time when no viewings materialise. They will blame the lack of success on 'the market'. You can waste several weeks that way, and when you lower the price the property looks like damaged goods. But if the agent can justify the high price, based on prices he or she has recently achieved, that is another matter!

Marketing proposals. You need to find out exactly how each agent will go about selling the property. Will they advertise it in newspapers and magazines?

Advice on your property. See what they have to say about what you should do to the property. A good agent should give you some clear advice on what to do to make the property appealing.

Fees. Fees will obviously be a factor in your choice. If one firm seems just as good as another and will charge you half a percent less, you will favour them. But usually in an area, most agents charge roughly the same. Anyone seriously undercutting may be doing so because they can't get business on merit. You will be wasting money by saving on commission with that type of agent.

Terms and conditions. Check whether the agents are proposing to get sole selling rights, or an extremely long period as sole agents, or whether they get a fee for finding a 'ready willing and able buyer'. You may want to negotiate such terms, or drop an agent who insists on them. If you're giving an agent a sole agency, the usual fee should be reduced for that. (I explain what all these terms mean next.)

Which agency deal to go for

Sole agency. This is best. A 'sole agency' deal means that you appoint one firm and you agree not to instruct any other estate agents for an agreed period. The advantage is that the agents you have appointed will put real efforts into finding a buyer for you, because they are guaranteed a fee if they do. They should offer you a better commission rate for a sole agency. Agree a reasonable period for them to find a buyer. After that, you should be able to terminate the sole agency by giving them an agreed period of notice.

Joint sole agency. A variant on the sole agency theme is to appoint two firms as joint sole agents. That means that it doesn't matter which of the two firms actually sells the property, they split the fee between them. The only reason to do this is if you want to instruct one specialist agent and one local agent. For example, if you are selling a mews house, you might want to instruct a firm of agents who specialise in mews houses, and also a house agent in the local area. That way, you are not duplicating their efforts, but taking advantage of two potential pools of buyers. Not all estate agents are prepared to work on this basis.

Multiple agency. It's a multiple agency if you appoint several agents to work independently, or if you appoint just one agent but without giving a sole agency commitment (in other words you keep the right to appoint more agents tomorrow). Each agent will charge you a higher fee, because it's a bit of a lottery for them. The ultimate buyer of your property is probably going to be someone who is contacting all the agents in the area for properties on their books, and it's just luck which of the firms you have instructed happens to get phoned first. Multiple agency isn't really a very good idea. You are not doubling the pool of buyers every time you double the number of agents appointed, because the same buyers will be approaching all the local agents. In fact, you are just de-motivating all the agents. They are going to put much more effort into selling properties where they are guaranteed to get a fee, than a situation where they've only got a one in three – or less – chance of winning. You also pay the eventual winner a higher percentage fee because commissions are higher with multiple agencies. If you are dissatisfied with the firm you appoint as sole agents, the better option is to find a new sole agent, not just to adopt the scattergun approach of appointing lots of agents.

If you start with a multiple agency, you will pay higher fees. The individual agents won't be keen on incurring advertising costs because of the reduced chances of their firm getting the commission. Your property will get over-exposed and buyers will wonder if you are desperate, or if there is something wrong with the property which is the reason why everyone has it on their books. You won't necessarily get the best advice from a multiple agent because they will be pressing you to accept even a low offer, because they are frightened of a competing agent coming up with another interested party.

Sole selling rights. You should always scrutinise the estate agents' terms of business closely. Don't assume that just because they come in a printed format that they are either fair or unchangeable. Some estate agents put in their terms that you are giving them 'sole selling rights'. That is very different from sole agency. Sole selling rights means that even if you find a buyer yourself, because someone knocks on your door or sees your advert on the Internet, your estate agents still gets a fee when you exchange contracts. Your estate agents may argue – with some justice – that they are putting a lot of effort into trying to sell the property and you should not be trying to advertise it behind their back. It is not really likely that someone will just knock on your door without already knowing it's on the market with your agents. It's much more likely to be someone who has actually got the details from the agents' website or seen the 'for sale' sign outside. Unscrupulous sellers do sometimes try to evade paying their agents' fees by pretending to find a private buyer, who really came via the 'for sale' board. Potential buyers often bypass the estate agents after getting details off their site, approach the sellers without the agents' knowledge, and offer to split the saved commission with the seller. So I am not actually against sole selling rights as long as they are limited, like a sole agency, to a fixed period.

A 'ready, willing and able' buyer. Another term you sometimes see in estate agents' terms and conditions is that you must pay the agents' fee if they produce a 'ready willing and able buyer'. This means that the estate agent will get his fee by producing a buyer who can purchase the property and who makes an offer at the price you have set for the property. Then if you pull out, you still have to pay the estate agents' fee. (Normally, a fee is only payable if exchange of contracts actually takes place.) Most people frown on this type of contract but I have to say that it seems fair to me. If the agents do their job and get you a buyer, why should they lose their fee because you change your mind and don't sell the property? Of course, it could work out unfairly for you if the reason why you do not go ahead with the deal is because your chain of transactions falls through, or because the seller withdraws on your purchase, for example. So it is in your interests to negotiate to have such a provision removed from the agency terms, or make sure it does not apply if the reason why you cannot go through with the sale is because of problems on your own purchase.

Make sure the property looks its best

You have to bear in mind that when a potential buyer stands in your house of flat, he or she is thinking 'Could I live here?' Most people are not imaginative interior designers. They may try for a moment to see past the flower-patterned flock wallpaper, but they quickly give up the battle and say to themselves – 'I couldn't possibly live here'. So your task is to make it as easy as possible for the unimaginative majority to see themselves happily living in your home. That means playing the percentages and making the property look as appealing as possible to the large middle ground of buyers. Your agents are going to know exactly what buyers expect in your sort of property. You should follow their advice.

These are a few ideas which we have picked up from various 'experts' and which we pass on for your consideration.

The hallway. It seems that it takes very little to switch a viewer from open-mindedness to 'definitely not'. That decision can apparently be made in the hallway, after which your beautifully laid out living room will have no effect at all. The hall has to be light, clean and free from clutter. So everything you normally park there must be removed. Pundits suggest you should put a brighter than usual light bulb in the hall light and replace the lampshade with an attractive new one. Consider putting up a mirror to make the hall seem wider than it is.

Living rooms. The whole point is to convince people that they are getting a lot of property for their money. So they have to feel your living rooms are large and spacious. Doors must open fully. If potential buyers open a door and it only opens three-quarters of the way because there is a settee squeezed in behind it, they get the impression that the house is pokey. Make sure no one has to walk round the back of a large chair to get into a room. Get rid of any furniture you can do without.

Tie back curtains and take down blinds to make rooms brighter.

Dining room. It can often be extremely important to have a dining room. When a family moves in, it will quickly degenerate into a children's play area, but when people are looking for a home they aspire to a formal dining room. Everyone will tell you that the number of bedrooms you have in the property is important, and that is true, but you should not claim every room in the house without a tap in it is a bedroom when marketing a property for sale. Ask your agents what they think. A dining room should look like a dining room. Have a dining table and chairs in it. You may be able to rent them on a short-term basis if necessary.

Bedrooms. Bedrooms should seem as large as possible. Furniture crammed into rooms so that they look impossibly small should be removed. The important thing is to avoid a room looking like a box room; it must convince as a bedroom. Buyers can figure out what to do about their storage once they move in. The 'experts' say that a more feminine style to a bedroom will be most appealing to most buyers; they also say that if you want a bedroom to look chic without spending too much money, simply investing in a co-ordinated set of bed linen can do the trick. I don't know; but that's what 'they' say.

Kitchens. Don't waste money replacing the kitchen units and appliances. People will generally prefer putting in their own new kitchen if they have the option. Money spent on totally upgrading kitchens is usually not recouped in additional purchase price. But there are smaller improvements which may well be worth making, and they won't cost a lot. Consider replacing all the cupboard doors with modern ones, without replacing the carcass of the cupboard itself. Putting on new unit doors is a low-cost option which can dramatically transform the look of the units. Dark-coloured cupboards and units should be converted to light-coloured ones wherever possible. It gives a greater sense of space and it fits in with most people's concepts of an attractive kitchen. Take down any curtains or blinds. They make kitchens seem dark. Spotlights in the ceiling, or up-lighters above units can make the kitchen seem brighter. The kitchen is the one area in the house where a bit of clutter can be a good thing. A few attractive jars, and cooking paraphernalia will make it look like a friendly inviting kitchen, not just an empty room.

Bathrooms. The avocado bathroom suite is a well worn joke, but an awful lot of people bought them. If you have anything coloured in your bathroom, have it replaced by a white suite. It may sound like engaging in major building works, but actually it can be done quite quickly and cheaply. (Even if you don't change the suite, fitting a new wooden toilet seat is said to be a good thing to do.) Take the trouble to remove lime scale from baths and toilets. You can use grout-whitener on tiles to make them seem fresh again. New suites or units may have different footprints, so you may have to change the flooring. Never use carpet. Putting a mirror on one wall can have a dramatically enlarging effect. Some pundits say you should put some new white fluffy towels in the bathroom before a viewing.

Repairs. When you think about it, you may realize that you are putting up with a number of little defects in your home which you have become accustomed to – the toilet cistern which needs a special knack to flush, kitchen drawers which don't quite shut, a dripping tap. These are all things you must put right. Anyone coming round the property won't be doing a detailed survey for major defects, but they will open and shut most cupboard doors and drawers, possibly flush the loo, and if they don't work properly they will think the property hasn't been maintained properly and that there must be much more serious problems they haven't spotted. So everything must work perfectly. If there are any cracks in the walls, these should be repaired. (It's okay to repair and decorate – it's not okay to simply conceal an ongoing problem from buyers.) If tiles on the roof are slipping you should have them re-fixed. A single slipped tile will suggest to buyers and their surveyors that the roof may need replacing, even though in fact it really is just a single slipped tile. So it's extremely important to have your roof checked – you can do it yourself with binoculars from across the street, or by looking for daylight in the attic.

Redecorating. It is definitely worth repainting and decorating before you put your property on the market. It is a relatively cheap way of making your home look as close to new as possible. Another reason for redecorating is to get rid of your personal tastes! It's not because your personal tastes are bad, it's simply that most buyers lack imagination. Buyers need to imagine themselves and their furniture in your property. If everything looks clean, white, and generally neutral in tone, they can probably do that. If you have heavily patterned wallpaper or bedrooms with dark red walls and stars on the ceiling, your buyers may step back in shock instead of seeing the potential for their own equally individual scheme. You should always talk to your chosen estate agents and find out what they recommend. You are selling the property, so it's purely a business decision. You are probably saying to yourself, 'The buyers will repaint anyway, so what's the point?' The point is that you must get them to sign the contract first, and that is usually achieved by presenting them with an attractive but blank canvas. Of course, it must all be done classily and with top quality products – I am not suggesting magnolia emulsion. When you do the repainting, have windowsills checked for rot and have any rotten bits cut out and replaced.

Remove clutter. All the precious things that make your property your home – mementos from a holiday, presents from your aunt, your collection of teapots from around the world – these are what estate agents call 'clutter'. The same considerations apply as with painting and decorating: you need potential buyers to see past your presence to how they would live in the property. You mustn't totally depersonalise the place or it won't seem inviting at all, but you should look at it from an outsider's point of view, and get everything which would detract from a sale out of the way. As always, ask your estate agent.

Furniture. The same applies to furniture. Hulking items of furniture makes rooms seems smaller than they are. If you have needed to cram a double bed into a small bedroom, put the double bed into store and replace it with a single bed. That will make the room seem like a well-proportioned bedroom rather than a converted box room.

Floors and carpeting. Usually it is not worth re-carpeting a property, because it's a huge expense. If the carpet looks a mess, you should bring in commercial carpet cleaners. If it still looks so awful that it seriously detracts from the property, you might consider pulling it up if there is an acceptable wooden floor underneath which could be polished. Or you could look for cheap carpeting. The difference between cheap and expensive is often how long it will last, but since you only need it to look fabulous for a few weeks, cheap should do.

Increasing your lease term. Many banks won't lend on a property with less than 60-70 years left on the lease. A short term can put off a buyer, and it can depress your sale price. Under modern legislation, most flat owners (and most owners of leasehold houses) have the right to extend their leases by another 90 years on top of what remains of their existing term in return for a payment to their landlord. The amount of the payment depends on a number of factors, such as the value of the property, the number of years left on the current lease, and the ground rent. But it may be well worth it. Your estate agent can advise you. There is a chapter on it later in this book (p. 233).

Viewings

Preparing for viewings
These are a few suggestions:
- If it's cold, leave the heating on at a reasonable level for someone coming in from outside (which will be lower than for normal living conditions).
- Turn lights on unless the house is already flooded with sunlight. It makes the house more attractive than available daylight on dull days.
- Turn the television off. It makes people feel they are intruding.
- Make sure the place is clean, tidy and smells fresh.
- Make sure the hall is clear.
- Have music playing in the background, but nothing too heavy.
- Put money, jewellery and valuables out of the way. Thieves view properties.
- Keep out of the way if the agent is doing viewing. Definitely don't be sitting in the rooms that really count, because it will

- be off-putting for viewers who will think they're disturbing you.
- Don't be in the middle of a meal. If you show people round when it is obviously a meal time, they will cut the viewing short.

Let the estate agents show people round
Let the estate agent show people round, if at all possible, rather than doing it yourself. There are a number of advantages.

The potential buyers can be honest with the estate agent about anything they don't like. Since many off-putting features will be obvious from the start, the estate agents can volunteer helpful suggestions. If a room is very small they can say, 'See what a brilliant study this would make'. If there aren't enough bedrooms they can say, 'You could easily extend over the garage. Several people down the street have already done it'. But the buyers probably won't mention the property's short comings to you, because they won't want to offend you.

Estate agents will be more credible when it comes to confirming what can be done with a property. They can refer to other properties they know about, or the attitude of the local planning authority to changes. So their repertoire of weapons in the battle of sales is greater than yours. Despite their supposed bad press, most people do believe what estate agents tell them.

You can give the estate agents some parameters – times when you don't want visitors, such as mealtimes or early mornings. You just get on with your life, and try not to be in the bathroom when the visitors are checking upstairs.

Steps to take if you show people round
There may be situations when you will need to handle viewings yourself – for instance, if a couple can only come in the evening or at the weekend when the estate agents' office is shut. A reasonable split of responsibilities might be that the agent shows people around during the day – when you are at work – and you do viewings at evenings or at

weekends, if buyers can't do any other time. You may have to show viewers round your property if it is a long way from the estate agent's office.

If you do show people round, these are some rules you should observe:

Precautions. If you are on your own, particularly if you are a woman, you should take sensible precautions. You may feel you would want a relative or friend to be present. In any event, make sure someone knows you are doing a viewing at a particular time and who it is with. Get some proof of their identity and address first. You can make sure the agents obtain this and verify it before the viewers come round. You could get a landline number and then ring it back to confirm the viewing time.

One tour guide only. If there are two of you, it's usually best for only one to do the showing. Otherwise, rooms will seem cramped as you all manoeuvre to get out of each other's way.

Prepare. Prepare your comments in advance, by making a number of points on paper. Only note down headings. Never try to write a spiel word for word, or it will come out wooden and unnatural. (Obviously don't have notes with you during the viewing!) You can give your notes to the estate agents as well, so that they can use them with their own viewings. In fact, a good start to the list is to ask the estate agents to tell you what they think are the good points of the property. Also have something to say about the advantages of your property over other similar properties. Have some positive points to make about the street and the immediate area,

Make positives out of negatives. Never volunteer any purely negative comments. There may be features which are negative, but find something positive to say about them. The neighbours have a very high wall? – 'The wall is nice and high. It gives us privacy and it doesn't affect the sun in our garden'. The bathroom is very small? – 'We didn't want a bath, because we like showers. We've been told that if you want to put in a bath, it would be easy to move the internal wall further into the third bedroom which would still be large enough for a double bed'.

That sort of thing.

Have answers for defects. Be ready with answers for obvious defects. You should discuss frankly with the estate agents what objections viewers might have. Once you have had a few viewings, you should ask the estate agents to tell you what the comments were when they rang up the viewers. Based on that feedback, prepare some appropriate comments to make on future viewings.

Show the best first. The general rule is that you should show the living room first, but really you should show the most attractive room first. Then they will not be so put off by the fact that a room they see towards the end is not quite so attractive.

Buyers first. Let the buyers go into a room first, so their impression of it is as empty – and therefore as spacious – as possible.

Give buyers space. Give the buyers space so they can talk between themselves without you overhearing them. When they come out of a room, that's how you know they want to be taken on to the next room.

Protect valuables. Some people like to walk around a house on their own. Obviously, you don't want to let people steal things, but the best precaution is to put away all steal-able items before viewing and then let people walk around reasonably freely.

Don't assault your buyers. Try and remain good-natured and friendly. Some buyers ask what may seem extremely impertinent questions, or they may make very rude comments about your home. They may not realise how rude they are being, and it may be the result of nerves, or because they are trying to talk the price down. Don't take the bait.

Don't negotiate. Don't get involved in talking about a deal or prices. Let them go back to the agents.

Ask them questions. At the end, ask them if they have any questions. Perhaps offer them a drink. This gives them an opportunity to ask questions about the local area. You can ask them if the property is what they expected from the particulars, and ask them how they have found dealing with the estate agents. Those are questions which may give you some useful information affecting your sales strategy. Don't ask them if they like the property – that's really putting them on the spot. You will find out soon enough when they telephone the estate agents. If you start asking, it will look as if you are desperate. They will knock thousands off your price.

The value of feedback from viewings

The best feedback you can get from the viewing is an offer. But even if the viewers are not interested in the property, you can still get some value from the viewing by making sure the estate agents ring them and get their feedback on what they liked and didn't like about the property – or the way you handled the viewing. It may not make pleasant listening, but it is all valuable intelligence which will help you with the next viewing.

If you find that the feedback is something such as the garden faces the wrong way, or there are not enough bedrooms, then you should revise the property particulars – they are probably causing confusion. There is no point showing people round your home if their requirements are quite different from what you have to offer.

If the feedback is something like 'the bedrooms are too dark', you could consider a quick redecoration in white. Never underestimate the lack of imagination of potential buyers. If they say the bedroom is too small, consider getting rid of some of the furniture, and just leaving a small bed. It may be inconvenient, but it's better than not getting a sale.

Answering questions

If visitors are remotely interested, they are bound to ask you some questions, and most of them are fairly predictable. Why are you selling? When can you move? What are the neighbours like? You need to be careful about your answers. Obviously your answers have to be truthful. You can be sued later if you mislead people into buying your home by telling them something untrue. (Whatever you say to them, they may write it down and confirm it via the solicitors.)

In some situations, you have a positive duty to volunteer information. For example, if you are aware of any legal problems which are not obvious, such as the fact that a neighbour is claiming a right of way through your back garden to empty his rubbish bins, that has to be declared before the sale goes through. If you don't do it, the buyer can sue you for damages.

Also, you can't cover up ongoing defects. If you know there is a damp problem in a particular wall, you can't repaint it in order to conceal it. What is perfectly legitimate though – and sensible – is to remedy the defect and then to repaint. Then you're not concealing, you're dealing.

When answering questions, it's best to give confident clear answers, and not to waffle on, or the buyer will think you are trying to cover something up.

Second viewings

On a second viewing the prospective buyers are likely to turn up with measuring tape, binoculars, and even a builder friend, and ask more searching questions. This time, they are more likely to look in cupboards to see how much room there is for their own clutter. Well-advised buyers will also make sure they come back at a different time of day. If the first visit was in the evening or weekend, they will want to come during the day to see if there's too much noise from a local school. If the first visit was during the day, they'll come back in the dark to see if there are dangerous characters lurking at every corner, or a noisy local pub.

How to negotiate the best deal

Negotiate via the agents

Most people aren't going to offer you the price you are asking – even if they are actually willing to pay it – because they will hope to get something off the asking price by negotiating. Unless you are used to negotiating as part of your business life, or even if you are, it's best to do the negotiating through the estate agents. It's easy to get polarised. After all, it's your home – and, by implication, you – that they are insulting by offering less than your asking price. Buyers dealing personally are liable to get aggressive in the same way we British typically mishandle negotiations over carpets in foreign bazaars. If both sides exchange messages via the estate agents, it takes all the shoulder-squaring and eyeballing out of the process.

By using estate agents, the negotiating process can be handled with time for you to think. If you are dealing with a seller face-to-face, snap decisions have to be made, and that's when you find you make concessions that you later regret – such as throwing in all the furniture, or agreeing to a delayed completion period.

The absolutely worst thing you can do is to have a handshake deal with the buyer direct. That tends to turn what is in fact a commercial deal into something to do with honour and word, and you will be accused of all kinds of moral wrongdoing if you later need to alter the terms at all.

Hold your nerve
Do not rush to accept the first offer you get. If it is a lot less than your offering price, wait for a few days to see what other viewings bring. (However, if it is definitely a 'buyer's market', and if you have waited for a long time even for that first offer, then discuss it with the estate agents and accept it if they think it is a fair offer.)

If you immediately get an offer at the asking price, or if the prospective buyers make a lower offer that is easily pushed up to the asking price, you must consider whether you have under-priced the property. In a tough market, prices can become quite volatile and you may have over-reacted in difficult market conditions and priced your property too low. Don't feel you have to accept an offer just because it's the price you are asking. See what a few viewings bring in. If it is clear that several people are prepared to pay the asking price, then you should seriously consider upping the price. It may be that when you interviewed various estate agents before you put the property on the market, some suggested high figures, others suggested lower figures, and you put the property on the market at a price in the middle or near the lower end. If so, it just proves that the higher figures were possibly the ones you should have chosen. You are not doing anything wrong if you don't accept the offer and put the property back on the market at a higher price. Gazumping only occurs if you accept an offer and later pull out and go for a higher price.

How to negotiate with buyers.

If you receive an offer less than the asking price, don't simply refuse it, or even necessarily go back with a counter offer. Ask the buyers to explain how they arrived at their figure. The chances are they have just plucked a figure out of the air because they believe that bartering is the correct thing to do, and because, in a tough market, we all expect sellers to reduce the price if we ask. If that is the case, then asking the buyers for reasons puts them on the defensive. But this ploy only works if they cannot justify their figure. They may come straight back with an explanation that such and such a property is on the market at the same price but has an additional en suite bathroom, or a larger garden. So you must be ready with your own comparable evidence. It is a strategy to adopt if you are confident that you have the evidence to support your price.

Don't start negotiating direct with buyers. If you do that you are losing out on one of the main benefits of employing an estate agent in the first place. Using an estate agent to negotiate gives you an opportunity to consider your response before going back.

Don't necessarily draw conclusions from low offers. Some people make ridiculously low offers just to see if they can pick up a bargain, but without really being interested. Look at other properties being sold and weigh up all the factors before concluding that the market really is much lower than you think.

If you receive an offer well below your asking price, one useful tactic is to go back with a counter offer which is only a very small amount below your original asking price. Negotiators expect parties to start splitting the difference. If a buyer puts in an offer £50,000 lower than the asking price, it is tempting to go back at £15,000 less, then the buyers counter at £35,000 and then you split the difference and do a deal at £25,000 off the price. But that is allowing the buyer to set the parameters. If you go back offering, say, £5,000 off the price you set a more restricted playing field for the negotiating game and make it clear that any reduction is going to be minimal. There is a good chance that the buyer will accept your bluff as evidence of your confidence in your price and settle for £10,000 off the price.

What if you get competing offers

If you are very fortunate, you may receive a number of offers from buyers desperate for the type of home you have, and all competing for a small pool of such properties.

Choosing between buyers. There are a number of ways for you to go. If you are perfectly satisfied with the price, then you need to make a decision based on which buyers would be best for you – e.g. a cash buyer, buyers who have already sold their property or have it under offer, or buyers who have a mortgage arranged.

Bids. If you feel that you may be able to squeeze more money out of the transaction, you can institute a 'bidding war' in which you invite the competing buyers to make higher offers. This is anathema to buyers, of course, because they keep being pushed up. Sometimes they just pull out of the transaction altogether and look elsewhere. One fairly civilised way of dealing with competing bids is to have 'sealed bids'. How this works is that the competing buyers are asked to give the estate agents their highest price. At a particular time, the estate agent will open all the bids and tell you the results. You can then choose the highest bid. (Strictly speaking, you are not bound by this arrangement at all, and you can still choose a lower bid if you think the buyer is more likely to perform, or you can carry on trying to push the price up.)

Contract race. Another way of reacting is to have a contract race. Under this arrangement, you accept offers from two or more buyers, and turn it into a race as to who gets to the point of exchanging contracts first. This would only be of interest to you if your priority is to exchange contracts quickly. In a tough market, this can simply put buyers off.

Time limit on exchange. This is a more civilized approach than the contract race. You select one set of buyers and tell them that you will give them a clear run, provided that they exchange contracts within 14 days, or whatever other period is reasonable. But if they don't meet that deadline, you will switch to the alternative bidders and then give them a clear run.

Compromises which don't cost you money
If you have to compromise, try to give something up which does not actually cost you money. These are some examples.

Offer to throw in some fixtures and fittings. If they are not mentioned as included in the sales particulars, you can offer to include the white goods in the kitchen, or the curtains or carpets. This probably won't cost you any money in reality, because you may not be planning to take them with you to your new property anyway. Fixtures and fittings always give some margin for negotiations.

You can offer to take the property off the market. A sensible buyer should insist that you take the property off the market as soon as the offer is accepted, but you can make it seem like a concession. It removes the anxiety from the buyer's mind that a better offer might come along. But in fact if your agents do receive another offer, they are duty bound to pass it on to you.

Strategies after a deal is agreed

Taking the property off the market
Once you find a buyer, the natural next step is to take the property off the market. This means the estate agents stop sending out the property particulars to prospective buyers and they tell anyone who asks that the property is under offer. They put an 'under offer' or 'sale agreed' sticker across the particulars in their window and across any 'for sale' board at the property. This is certainly a step which the buyers will want, because it removes the anxiety that someone else will come along with a higher offer. But does it work in your favour? These are some alternatives.

Taking the property off the market for a fixed period

Instead of agreeing to take the property off the market for however long it takes to exchange contracts, go for a particular period, such as four weeks, after which it is agreed that you can start marketing again. This puts pressure on the buyers to perform. If the buyers assure you during the negotiation stage that they can definitely exchange contracts within a month because they are cash buyers, or they already have their mortgage arranged, then they can't very well counter this suggestion. Then you don't have to make hard decisions if the deal becomes protracted, because putting the property back on the market has already been agreed. Buyers will often scramble to exchange contracts before marketing recommences.

We quite like this strategy. Buyers often make promises about how fast they will exchange contracts, which sellers naturally rely on, and some buyers seem to feel this imposes absolutely no commitment on them at all. They take their time organising their mortgage, and they fall back on blaming their solicitors or their lenders when the promised date passes. If the sellers then talk about putting the property back on the market, they are outraged, protest that the sellers are acting unreasonably, and threaten to pull out. Agree it at the outset, and not only can they not complain when it happens, but they will realise from the start they can't just mess around. As a result, you are much more likely to get the deal done by the agreed date, because you are relying on buyers' self-interest, which is usually a reliable motivator.

Giving the buyers a lock-out agreement

A lock-out agreement is an agreement with your proposed buyer that you won't sell the property to anyone else or market it for a fixed period. A lock-out agreement is not an agreement to sell to the buyers; it's an agreement not to sell to anyone else during the specified period. A lock-out agreement is better from a buyer's point of view than you simply taking the property off the market because it's contractual – it prohibits you from selling as well as marketing during that period.

Taking a non-refundable deposit

You could attempt to persuade the buyers to pay a non-refundable deposit which they lose if they don't proceed with the purchase. We don't recommend this. It sounds straightforward, but when you get down to trying to word the situations in which it is reasonable for the buyers to back out, it all becomes so time-consuming and complicated – and costly in extra legal fees – that you would have been better off just concentrating on getting the sale through in the first place.

Leaving the property on the market.

You can't do this in a buyer's market, or the buyers will simply walk away, but in a fairly active seller's market, you can tell buyers that you accept their offer and will start all the selling procedures, but you will still leave the property on the market and continue sending sales particulars out in the normal way. This protects you by allowing you to have other potential buyers in the wings if the people you are dealing with don't perform. It puts pressure on your buyers to perform quickly and exchange contracts.

How to sell well

How to extend your flat's lease term

Why Extend?

A short lease loses value
The most straightforward reason for extending your lease is that having a short lease can seriously reduce the value of your property. As each year passes, the value falls; and the fall becomes ever more precipitous as the term gets closer to zero.

Cost
The second reason is cost. It becomes much more costly to buy a lease extension once the existing lease term has fallen below 80 years. And then it becomes ever more costly as more time passes. It may reach a point where you simply can't afford to raise the cash to purchase the lease extension.

To make the property saleable
Mortgage lenders are reluctant to lend on 'short' leases. Some lenders regard 50 years as too short, and others 60 years. This means that you seriously reduce the pool of potential buyers by having a short lease.

Sell with the extension rights
If you are about to sell your flat which has a short lease, and you want to maximise its value, you may not need to extend your lease term in advance. If your buyers agree, you can start the procedure between exchange of contracts and completion and then the buyers can take over the procedure once they own the flat, saving you the cost and the effort.

Checking if you can extend your lease

Extending the lease
You may have the legal right to extend your lease term. This means you can buy an extra 90 years. The remaining 60 year lease term in our example becomes a 150 year lease term.

Critical dates

80 years is a critical date. The price you have to pay for the lease extension goes up if your lease term is less than 80 years when you exercise your right to extend. Once your lease has less than 3 years to go you lose all your rights.

Checking for the lease term

To discover how many years you have left, you need to look at your lease. If you own a flat, you have a lease. It's the document which sets out the rules for living in the flat. Your solicitor probably sent the original or a copy to you when you bought the flat. Or you can download your flat's title from the Land Registry website. The 'Property Register' on the first page will tell you the length and start date of your lease term.

A lease is granted for a period of time which is called the 'term'. The term is how long you can live in the flat before the landlord gets it back. The clock started ticking when the lease was first granted to the original flat owner.

Do you have the right to extend your lease?

You don't actually have to live in the flat to have the right to extend the lease. Companies and absentee landlords have the same rights as an owner-occupier. The principal criteria for being able to extend your lease are:

Flat. The property must be a flat. House owners can also extend their leases or even buy the freehold in many cases, but different rules apply to houses which we are not covering in this book.

Long lease. You must own a 'long lease' on the flat. A lease is a 'long lease' if it was originally granted for at least 21 years. If there is more than one long lease on a property because there is an intermediate lease – someone with a lease on the flat to whom you pay rent – there are rules to decide which leaseholder has the right to buy. Only one of you has the right.

Minimum lease term. There must be at least three years of the term remaining when you exercise your right to extend. Once the lease term has dipped below that level, you have lost the right to extend the lease.

2 years' ownership. You must have owned the lease for at least two years before you can exercise your right. But if you are buying, there is a way around that. You get your sellers to start the process (assuming they have owned it for two years) and you can take it over.

How much it costs to buy an extension

Four items make up the price you will have to pay for your lease extension. The following are the elements which make up the price.

We can recommend surveyors

Working out the cost of a lease extension is difficult. If it helps, we can recommend helpful surveyors to advise you.

---

1. Diminution in value of the landlord's interest in the flat.
When you get an extension lease, 90 years is added to what remains of your existing lease term. For example, if your lease has 60 years left to run, 90 years is added, giving you a new lease for a term of 150 years in total. Rent is cancelled altogether in the new lease, so if you currently pay, for example, £100 a year rent, that is reduced to zero immediately, even for the remaining 60 years of your existing lease term.

The landlord has now lost out in two ways. First, he has lost £100 a year for 60 years. Second, his opportunity to sell the flat for its full market value in 60 years time, when your current lease was due to run out, has been deferred to 150 years time. The value of these two losses is the landlord's 'diminution in value'.

Rent loss. The rent the landlord has lost is £100 a year for 60 years, but the capital value today of the lost rent is not as simple as £100 x 60. Instead, the annual rent is multiplied by the 'Years' Purchase'. Valuers have to work this out on a case by case basis. But, as an example, if the

Years' Purchase was 20 then the capital value of the lost annual rent would be £100 x 20 = £2,000. That would be the landlord's 'diminution in value' in respect of the lost rent.

In basic terms, if the landlord were to put into an auction a property where his only interest is to receive £100 a year rent, a potential investor-purchaser would be saying to himself 'what sort of return would I want on my money, taking account of what I could get by just leaving it in a bank and the hassle of collecting the rent?' Auction results might show that investors generally work on the basis that they need, for example, a 5% return to make it worthwhile. To achieve that return on £100 a year, the investor would have to pay no more than £2,000 (£2,000 x 5% = £100.) That means that the investor will pay 20 times the yearly rent to buy the right to receive the rent – or 20 Years' Purchase, for short. The landlord's surveyor and your surveyor will argue about how many years purchase it should actually be.

Reversion loss. The second loss to the landlord is the loss of the right to get the flat back in 60 years time – the reversion, as it is called. Let's assume the flat in question would sell for £800,000, if you put it on the market with a 60 year lease. It may be reasonable to assume that the value if the landlord were selling it would be £900,000, because he could sell it with a 999 year lease. That value is the starting point. The landlord could only expect to get his value in 60 years' time. So the reversion loss today is treated as the present value today of the right to receive £900,000 in 60 years' time. There are complicated calculations and actuarial tables to work out what the right to receive £900,000 in 60 years time is worth now. They involve assumptions about interest rates and tax. But the present value is often a surprisingly small figure. (To be entirely accurate, the calculation of loss also requires to be taken into account the value of the right to receive £900,000 in 150 years' time, which the landlord still has, but this is usually too small a figure to change the calculation of loss materially.)

2. Marriage value

There's one very important thing to flag. If you have more than 80 years left to go on your lease when you start the lease extension process, you don't pay marriage value. That can be a big saving. Slip below that period by a single day and you have to pay half the marriage value. So if your remaining term is close to 80 years, get extending quickly!

Pre-extension values. It may help if we illustrate this with an example – using arbitrary figures. As before, let's assume your current lease is worth £800,000 to you. Let's also assume the diminution of loss was calculated as £22,000. That means your current lease is worth £22,000 to the freeholder. The total value of yours and your landlord's interests in the flat is £822,000.

Post-extension values. Let's assume that with the extra 90 years you would get £900,000 from a buyer if you put your flat on the market immediately after the lease extension. That's the value of the new lease to you. After the extension, the value of the landlord's interest has fallen to zero because there's no rent to value anymore. The total value of the extended lease to you and to the landlord is therefore £900,000.

Marriage value. The 'marriage value' is the difference between the old and new totals – £900,000 – £822,000 = £78,000.

Landlord's share of marriage value. You have to pay half the marriage value to the landlord, which is £39,000.

3. Compensation for other losses

You also have to pay the landlord a reasonable sum for any other loss the landlord suffers. Suppose you have a top floor flat and granting you a new lease means that the landlord cannot redevelop the roof space when your existing lease term runs out. That future right has a value, discounted back to the present day. That is a loss he would claim for.

4. Costs

You have to pay some of the landlord's costs in going through the procedure. That will include the surveyor's costs in valuing the flat for the landlord, negotiating with your surveyor, preparing evidence for the hearing, and giving evidence at the hearing if there is one. It will also mean the cost of the landlord's solicitors in that process, and any barrister who is appointed for the hearing. This is all in addition to your own costs. However, although some cases do actually go to a hearing, most cases are negotiated and agreed before that point, which means that the costs are usually not unreasonable compared with the price being paid for the extension lease.

Procedure for extending your lease.

The tenant's notice

You claim the right to a new lease by giving a notice to your landlord. If you serve the notice, but then decide not to go ahead, that's fine, but you aren't allowed to serve another notice for at least 12 months. When you serve your notice, it is very important to get it right. You need a lawyer's help to do it. You also have to include a proposal for the price you wish to pay for the lease extension. This has to be a sensible proposal, because your entire application can be thrown out if the tribunal takes the view that the figure you proposed wasn't even realistic. So you also need to involve a surveyor at the initial stage, to advise you on the lowest reasonable figure you can put in.

The landlord's counter notice

The landlord must serve a counter notice. In it he must either admit your right – in which case you move on to discussing terms – or he must deny it. He might deny it if he thinks you have only owned the flat for one year, for example. In that case the court decides the issue at a hearing. In limited circumstances a landlord can oppose an application on the grounds that he intends to redevelop the property.

The landlord cannot avoid your right by doing a disappearing act or not responding. If the landlord cannot be found, the court will stand in for him so that your right can still be exercised. The court will even grant the new lease itself, if necessary.

Deposit

The landlord is entitled to require you to pay a deposit of 10% of the value you have put in your notice. If you eventually give up the claim, then you receive the deposit back, but it is evidence of your seriousness in issuing the original application.

Terms of new lease

If the landlord has admitted your right (or the court has confirmed it exists), you and the landlord are meant to agree the provisions of the new lease. They should be the same as in the old lease, except that the court has a limited power to bring them up to date or improve them.

Application to the tribunal

There is a time limit for negotiation. If you and the landlords have not agreed everything within a few months, you have to make an application to the Leasehold Valuation Tribunal for them to judge the case and say what the correct terms should be. If you don't make the application to the tribunal within the time limit, your application for a new lease fails and you have to wait at least another year before starting again.

More than one landlord

We have made an assumption in our description of the valuation process, which is that your landlord is the freeholder of the building. In some cases, there may be more than one landlord. For example, in the 1970s the freeholder might have granted a lease of the entire building to a tenant for a term on 120 years on the basis that the tenant would refurbish the building and then sell the flats individually. That tenant might then have sold the flats on 99 year leases, and you are now seeking to extend one of those leases. You have a landlord, the original tenant or someone who has bought his lease. Your landlord is the 'intermediate landlord'. Clearly, the intermediate landlord cannot grant you an extra 90 years, because his lease was only 21 years longer than yours in the first place. So you need to make your application to the freeholder, who can grant you an extra 90 years over the head of the intermediate landlord. In the valuation process, what you pay is still as set out above, but the freeholder and the intermediate landlord have to sort out between themselves how they split the money between them – another job for the surveyors.

Role of surveyors

Once you have served a notice and the landlord has served his counter notice confirming that he agrees you have the right to an extension, normally all that is outstanding is the question of the correct amount to pay. Your surveyor will be arguing for the lowest value for your flat, and the lowest year's purchase figure, in order to minimise the diminution and marriage value figures. The landlord's surveyor will be doing the exact opposite. They will both be producing reports justifying their arguments by reference to other sales of flats achieved in the building or nearby, and judgments from past cases.

Negotiation

The process requires that the surveyors get together to try to agree what they can and narrow the issues in dispute which ultimately have to be heard by the tribunal. But the real practical job is that they attempt to negotiate with each other to arrive at a price each side can live with. Sometimes one side or the other will play hardball and try to hold out for a figure which can't really be justified in the hope that the other side will cave in, but usually it makes commercial sense for everyone to try to agree a figure.

The figure usually gets agreed shortly before the hearing - the impetus behind the final concessions is usually the nuisance of having to prepare final reports and take time off to go to a hearing. Once agreement is reached in principle, the hearing is cancelled, and the solicitors agree the new form of lease to reflect the new terms.

New lease

The process of agreeing the new lease usually isn't contentious at all, because there are standard forms and precedents which solicitors use. Often, the new lease is quite a short document, recording the revised lease term and the cancellation of the rent, but otherwise stating that the terms and conditions set out in the original lease continue in force. So, after everything is completed, your Land Registry title will show the details of the new lease, but also the old lease, which is still relevant for most of the covenants and conditions.

Estate agents

These are the estate agents dealing with property in Notting Hill and Holland Park.

Anthony Sharp

118 Holland Park Avenue, London W11 4UA
Tel: 020 7243 8398 | www.anthony-sharp.com

Aylesford Residential

103 Kensington Church Street, London W8 7LN
Tel: 020 7727 6663 | www.aylesfordresidential.com

Bective Leslie Marsh

205 Westbourne Grove, London W11 2SB
Tel: 020 7221 4805 | www.bectivelesliemarsh.co.uk
10 Hornton Street, London W8 4NW
Tel: 020 7795 4288

Bruten and Company

4a Wellington Terrace, London W2 4LW
Tel: 020 7229 9262 | www.brutens.com

Carter Jonas

8 Addison Avenue, London W11 4QR
Tel: 020 7371 1111 | www.carterjonas.co.uk

Century 21

10 Clarendon Road, London W11 3AA
Tel: 020 7229 1414 | www.century21uk.com

Chard
123 Notting Hill Gate, London W11 3LB
Tel: 020 7243 4500 | www.chard.co.uk

Chesterton Humberts
116 Kensington High Street, London W8 7RW
Tel: 020 7937 7244 | www.chesterton.co.uk

Cluttons
5 Addison Avenue, London W11 4QS
Tel: 020 7371 3600 | www.cluttons.com

Crayson
10 Lambton Place, London W11 2SH
Tel: 020 7221 1117 | www.crayson.com

Domus Nova Limited
17 Kensington Park Road, London W11 2EU
Tel: 020 7727 1717 | www.domusnova.com

Douglas & Gordon
299 Westbourne Grove, London W11 2QA
Tel: 020 7727 7777 | www.dng.co.uk

Faron Sutaria
129/131 Notting Hill Gate, London W11 3LB
Tel: 020 7229 2404 | www.faronsutaria.co.uk

Foxtons
90 Notting Hill Gate, London W11 3HP
Tel: 020 7616 7000 | www.foxtons.co.uk

Hamptons

301 Westbourne Grove, London W11 2QA
Tel: 020 7034 0404 | www.hamptons.co.uk

8 Hornton Street, London W8 4NW
Tel: 020 7937 9371

Harpers & Harrison

53 Abingdon Road, London W8 6AN
Tel: 020 7938 2311 | www.harpersandharrison.co.uk

Jackson-Stops & Staff

14 Portland Road, London W11 4LA
Tel: 020 7727 5111 | www.jackson-stops.com

John D Wood & Co

162 Kensington Church Street, London W8 4BN
Tel: 020 7908 1100 | www.johndwood.co.uk

John Wilcox & Co

13 Addison Avenue, London W11 4QS
Tel: 020 7602 2352 | www.johnwilcoxandco.com

Knight Frank

298 Westbourne Grove London W11 2PS
Tel: 020 7229 0229 | www.knightfrank.com

54 Kensington Church Street, London, W8 4DB
Tel: 020 7938 4311

Marsh & Parsons

57 Norland Square, London W11 4QJ
Tel: 020 7605 6890 | www.marshandparsons.co.uk

2-6 Kensington Park Road, London W11 3BU
Tel. 020 7313 2890

McMahon King
The Studio, 57 Princedale Road, London W11 4NP
Tel: 020 7792 2031

Mountgrange Heritage
153 Notting Hill Gate, London W11 3LF
Tel: 020 7221 2277 | www.mountgrangeheritage.co.uk

Nick & Co
24 Notting Hill Gate, London W11 3JE
Tel: 020 7221 1988 | www.nickandco.com

Savills
145 Kensington Church Street, London W8 7LP
Tel: 020 7535 3302 | www.savills.com

Strutt & Parker
104 Kensington Church Street, London W8 4BU
Tel: 020 7938 3666 | www.struttandparker.co.uk

Winkworth
178 Westbourne Grove, London W11 2RH
Tel: 020 7727 3227 | www.winkworth.co.uk

Index

A

Abbotsbury Close 15
Abbotsbury Road 15
Addison Avenue 41
Addison Avenue 43
Addison Crescent 29
Addison Place 41
Addison Road 23
Addison, Joseph 41
Alba Place 139
Aldridge Road Villas 135
Allason, Thomas 78
Allom, Thomas 96
Anti-money-laundering 203
Architectural styles 168
Areas 181
Artesian Road 129
Arundel Gardens 90
Aubrey Road 151
Aubrey Walk 152

B

Balconies 176
    Balconettes 177
    Balustrades 176
    Railings 177
Balcony
    Continuous balcony 176
Baths 182
Bay windows 172
Blake, Charles Henry 98
Blenheim Crescent 58
Boot scrapers 176
Boyne Terrace Mews 70
Bricks 177
    Laying bricks 177
    Types of brick 177
Bulmer Mews 89

C

Callcott Street 157
Campden Hill Gardens 155
Campden Hill Place 155
Campden Hill Road 164
Campden Hill Square 149
Campden Street 164
Canted bays 172
Cantwell, Robert 36
Chadwick, William 80
Chepstow Crescent 115
Chepstow Road 133
Chepstow Villas 112
Chimneys 180
Clanricarde Gardens 125
Clarendon Road 54
Classical style 168
Clutterbuck, Joseph 158
Codrington Mews 61
Columns 174
    Corinthian columns 175
    Doric columns 174
    Ionic columns 174
Colville Houses 142
Colville Road 143
Colville Square 141
Colville Terrace 140
Completion 207
    Post completion 209
    What happens 209
Conservation areas
    Holland Park Conservation Area 19
    Ladbroke Conservation Area 50
    Norland Conservation Area 46
    Pembridge Conservation Area . 116
Contracts 205
Copy books 170
Cornices 171
Cornwall Crescent 58
Courtnell Road 130
Cullingford, William 118

D

Denbeigh Close 111
Denbeigh Road 110
Denbeigh Terrace 111
Deposit 205

Detached houses 165
Domestic Revival style 170
Door cases 175
Door knockers 176
Door, main 173
Drain pipes 180
Drew, William John 101
Dunworth Mews 139

E

Edge Street 162
Elevations 170
    Front elevations 170
    Rear elevations 171
Elgin Crescent 62
Estate agents
    Choose from our list 212
    Deals
        A ready willing and able buyer
            215
        Joint sole agency 213
        Multiple agency 214
        Sole agency 213
        Sole selling rights 215
    How to select a firm 212
    Why you need them 211
Extending your lease term
    80 years as a critical date 234
    Check if you have the right 233
    Negotiation 240
    Price
        Compensation 237
        Costs 237
        Diminution in value 235
        Marriage value 236
    Procedure 238
        Deposit 238
        Landlord's counter notice ... 238
        New lease 239
        Tenant's notice 238
        The tribunal 239
    Reasons to extend 233
    Selling with extension rights ... 233
    Surveyors 239

F

Facades .... See
    Stuccoed facades 170
Fanlights 175

Farm Place 157
Farmer Street 159
Fireplaces 182
Flats 186
    Alterations 189
    Converted flats 166
    Freehold purchase 190
    Insurance 189
    Landlord's obligations 188
    Lease extension 190
    Management 186
    Rights and obligations 188
    Service charges 187
    What you own 188
Floors 183
Floors of a house .... See Storeys
Fox, Charles Richard 26
Freehold 185

G

Gables 179
Gardens 180
    Communal gardens 180
        Addison Gardens 28
        Arundel and Elgin Garden 63
        Arundel and Ladbroke Gardens
            90
        Blenheim and Elgin Crescents
            Garden 59
        Clarendon Road and
            Lansdowne Road Garden . 55
        Hanover Gardens 77
        Holland Road and Russell Road
            Gardens 22
        Ladbroke Grove Garden 82
        Ladbroke Square Garden 87
        Lansdowne and Elgin Crescent
            Gardens 70
        Lansdowne Crescent Garden 73
        Lansdowne Road and
            Lansdowne Crescent Garden
            68
        Montpelier Garden 75
        Norland Square Garden 45
        Notting Hill Garden 67
        Royal Crescent Gardens 35
        St James's Gardens 37
        Stanley Crescent Garden 95
        Stanley Gardens North 92
        Stanley Gardens South 97

Front gardens 181
Garden squares 180
Lawns 181
Paving 181
Pembridge Square Garden 122
Railings 181
Garrets .... See Storeys:Attic floor
Gothic style 169

H

Hall, James 29
Hanson, Joshua Flesher 150
Hayden's Place 139
Hillgate Place 160
Hillgate Street 158
Hillsleigh Road 154
Hippodrome 54
Hippodrome Mews 53
Holland Park 11
Holland Park Gardens 28
Holland Park Mews 14
Holland Park Road 20
Holland Villas Road 30
Holland, The Fourth Baron 14
Holland, The Third Baron 12
Hoods 175
Horbury Crescent 106
Horbury Mews 105

I

Ilchester Place 16
Ilchester scheme of management 17
Ilchester, The Fifth Earl 16
Insurance, buildings 206
Italianate style 169

J

Jameson Street 159
Jenkins, William Henry 114

K

Kensington Park Gardens 99
Kensington Park Road 86
Kensington Place 161
Kitchens 183

L

Ladbroke Association 50
Ladbroke Crescent 58
Ladbroke Estate, The 61
Ladbroke Gardens 91
Ladbroke Grove 81
Ladbroke Mews 81
Ladbroke Road 78
Ladbroke Square 101
Ladbroke Terrace 104
Ladbroke Walk 104
Lancaster Road 138
Lansdowne Crescent 72
Lansdowne Mews 71
Lansdowne Rise 74
Lansdowne Road 65
Lansdowne Walk 76
Lavatory 182
Leamington Road Villas 136
Leasehold 185
   Is it ok? 186
   Leasehold houses 186
Leases 185
Ledbury Road 147
Linden Gardens 126
Lloyd family estate 152
Local authority searches 205
Lock out agreements 230
Lower Addison Gardens 28

M

Mansion blocks 166
McGregor Road 138
Melbury Road 18
Mews 165
Moorhouse Road 131
Mortgages 203
   Mortgage offer 206

N

Napier Close 22
Napier Place 23
Napier Road 22
Negotiating
   For buyers 198
   For sellers 225
      Compromises 229
      Responding to buyers 227

Strategies for competing offers 228
Neoclassical style 169
Norland Conservation Society 46
Norland Estate, The 34
Norland Place 44
Norland Square 44
Northumberland Place 133
Notting Hill Gate 103

O

Oakwood Court 17

P

Paint colour .... *See*
Palladianism .... *See* Classical style
Pediments .... *See* Windows
Peel Street 162
Pembridge Association 116
Pembridge Crescent 116
Pembridge Gardens 122
Pembridge Mews 119
Pembridge Place 120
Pembridge Square 121
Pembridge Villas 118
Penzance Place 38
Phillips, Stephen 74
Pocock, Thomas 85
Porches 173
   Architraves 175
   Columns .... *See* Columns
   Paired porches 174
Portland Road 50
Portobello Road 107
Pottery Lane 49
Powis Gardens 144
Powis Square 144
Powis Terrace 146
Princedale Road 46
Punter, John 163

Q

Queen Anne style 169
Queensdale Place 40
Queensdale Road 39
Queensdale Walk 43
Quoins 171

R

Radford, William and Francis 13
Ramsay, David Allan 65, 73
Reynolds, William 57
Richardson, Charles 40
Roofs 178
   Hip roofs 179
   Mansard roofs 179
   Pitched roofs 178
   Slates 179
Rosmead Road 70
Roy, Richard 53
Royal Crescent 34
Royal Crescent Mews 35

S

Semi detached houses 165
Service charges 187
Solicitors 203
St Ann's Villas 33
St James's Gardens 36
St John's Gardens 76
St Luke's Mews 138
St Luke's Road 137
St Mark's Place 60
St Mary Abbots Terrace 21
St Stephen's Crescent 135
St Stephen's Gardens 135
Stables .... *See* Mews
Stamp duty land tax 208
Stanley Crescent 94
Stanley Gardens 97
Storeys 166
   Attic floor 168
   Basement 167
   First floor 167
   Ground floor 167
   Second floor 168
   Third floor 168
Strangways Terrace 20
Stucco 178
Surveys 204
   Full structural survey 204
   Homebuyer's report 205
Sutherland Place 132

T

Talbot Estate, The 141

Talbot Road 134
Terrace houses 165
Tippett, George 142

U

Upper Addison Gardens 27

V

Vermiculation 171
Victoria Gardens 105
viewings
    let the agents do it 221
Viewings 192
    For buyers
        First viewings 192
        Handling the sellers 198
        Questions to ask 195
        Second viewings 194
        Things to note down 193
    For sellers
        Answering questions 224
        Feedback 224
        How to handle them 221
        Preparing the property 220

Second viewings 225

W

Walker, Dr Samuel 71
Walls 177
Ward, William 163
Water supply 182
Westbourne Grove 109
Westbourne Park Road 85
Westbourne, The 110
Wilby Mews 103
Windows 171
    Architraves 173
    Blocked windows 173
    Casement windows 172
    Dormer windows 172
    French windows 172
    Glass 173
    Paint colour 173
    Proportions 172
    Sash windows 171
    Window surrounds 173
Woodsford Square 26
Wycombe Square 153

Index